1997 PRACTICAL GUIDE

HYDRAULICS

AND

HYDROLOGY

HAESTAD PRESS

1997 Practical Guide to Hydraulics and Hydrology

HAESTAD PRESS

Contributing Editors

Donald V. Chase, PE Darrow Kirkpatrick

Jack Cook Robert Mankowski, PE

Maureen Farmer, PE John Powell, PE

David T. Ford, PE Houjung Rhee, PE

Michael K. Glazner Erik Symonds

Other Contributions

Construction Metrication Council
of the National Institute of Building Sciences

GarverPlus Engineers

Editor In Chief

Gregg A. Herrin

Peer Review

Donald V. Chase, Ph.D., PE

University of Dayton

Michael Meadows, Ph.D., PE

University of South Carolina

Thomas Walski, Ph.D., PE

Wilkes University

*To the civil engineers and modelers who
enable us to live our daily lives free from the worries
of flooded neighborhoods, backed-up sewers,
or contaminated drinking water.*

CONTENTS

Contents (Continued)

PREFACE

Filling the Gap

There are hundreds of engineering textbooks available on the market today, providing a wealth of equations, mathematical theory, and basic engineering history.

There are also thousands of engineers in the world today, offering their expertise to less experienced engineers who are just learning the ropes. They provide much-needed guidance with issues like permitting, client relations, business, and of course, engineering judgments.

But this leaves a noticeable void in the engineer's toolbox – what links the theories to the practices? It's an awfully big step from the pages of a textbook to the projects of the real world. And how is a busy engineer supposed to learn about modeling techniques and methodologies, let alone keep up to date on current computer technology?

There hasn't been a publication to truly fill this gap in your engineering library -- until now.

You'll find that this book isn't weighted down by dozens of intense mathematical equations and matrix manipulation, and it also doesn't get bogged down in building codes and permitting issues. Simply put, it covers engineering and modeling in a comprehensive, practical way.

No, this isn't meant to replace your textbooks, or to devalue the importance of an engineering apprenticeship. It is meant to be an important resource – to fill a gap – helping you stay informed and competitive in the world of engineering. Now get back to work.

STORMWATER MODELING TECHNIQUES

Section Contents

POND ROUTING TECHNIQUES: STANDARD VS. INTERCONNECTED

When are interconnected pond modeling techniques required instead of standard pond routing methods?

This article explains the difference between standard pond routing and interconnected pond routing techniques. Through the use of examples, it demonstrates how these two approaches differ and why. The conclusion includes tips on determining which pond routing techniques may apply to your next project.

Pond Routing Overview

Detention ponds are typically used to attenuate and control increased stormwater runoff due to development. Pond routing is a mathematical procedure that models a detention pond's response to a given storm event. By routing a stormwater hydrograph through a pond, engineers can determine how the water surface elevation, outflow and storage values vary during (and after) the storm.

The computed results may vary depending on which mathematical routing technique is used, so it is important for engineers to readily identify which routing techniques apply to the given conditions.

History

Pond routing techniques were originally established as a means to hand-compute the operation of large reservoirs (lakes) and spillways. Although repetitious, these hand methods were a practical way of assessing the response of large facilities before the advent of computers.

We apply these same techniques when analyzing detention ponds. The difference is that detention models use a much smaller scale in terms of volume, inflow and outflow, and sometimes in terms of time step.

The Working Relationship

Various names have been used to describe "standard" pond routing techniques. Routing methods such as Storage Indication, Modified Puls and Level Pool Routing are all based on the same fundamental relationship:

$$\Delta \forall = \Delta t \cdot [\text{Avg. Inflow} - \text{Avg. Outflow}]$$

where $\Delta \forall$ is the change in pond volume during one time step
Δt is the time step length

For each time step on the inflow hydrograph, this equation is solved to compute the change in storage for that time single step. If the average inflow is greater than the outflow, change in storage is positive and the water surface is rising. If the average inflow is less than the outflow, change in storage is negative, and the water surface is receding.

Standard Pond Routing

The Basic Concept

Figure 1 demonstrates the fundamental assumption used in standard pond routing. Notice that the downstream pond does not affect the hydraulics of the upstream pond. In addition, the downstream pond is unaffected by the free outfall conditions. Standard pond routing techniques could be used to analyze both ponds shown in this figure.

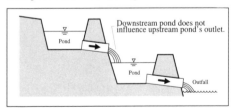

Figure 1: Standard Pond Routing

The Key to Standard Routing: Tailwater (TW) is Fixed or Flow Dependent

Standard routing techniques apply if the *tailwater is fixed* or if the downstream water surface is a *function of flow* rate only (not time or downstream volume).

Examples of Fixed TW or Flow Variant TW Elevation:

* Free outfall

* Fixed (constant) outfall elevation

* Outlet outfall water surface elevation based on downstream channel normal depth (solved using equations such as Manning's)

* Outlet outfall water surface elevation solved using backwater rating table of downstream elevation vs. flow (from programs such as HEC-2 or HEC-RAS).

When these assumptions apply, the total outflow for all elevations in the pond can be modeled with a single performance curve like the one shown in Figure 2. During the routing process, outflow can be solved as a direct function of pond headwater depth using this curve.

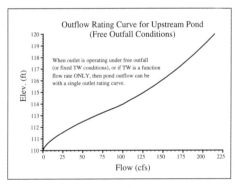

Figure 2: Outlet Performance Curve

Software That Performs Standard Routing

Since standard routing techniques are repetitive, they are ideal for computers. Mainframe programs such as the Army Corps of Engineers' HEC-1 and the Soil Conservation Services' TR-20 were used for reservoir routing more than 25 years ago.

In the mid-1980s, these programs were ported to run on PCs, and private sector software such as the Pond Pack (released in 1987) was written specifically for use in detention pond design. Each of these programs can model standard reservoir routing techniques.

Example 1: Standard Pond Routing

This example demonstrates a case where standard pond routing techniques apply. The results from this example will be compared with Example 2 for an interconnected pond scenario.

Given: The two ponds in Figure 3 are directly connected with a box culvert. The downstream pond discharges through a box culvert with a free outfall into the receiving river.

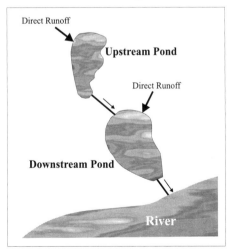

Figure 3: Standard Pond Routing Example

The Analyses:

The runoff hydrographs draining into each pond are shown in Figure 4. Standard routing techniques were performed to model the pond elevation, storage and outflow during an entire storm event.

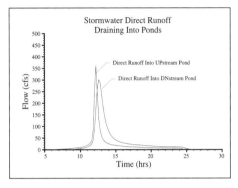

Figure 4: Drainage Runoff to Ponds

Standard routing results for this scenario will be appropriate only if the maximum water surface elevation of the downstream pond does not rise high enough to affect the discharge rate of the upstream pond.

Figure 5 shows the water surface elevations in both ponds during the course of the storm. The maximum elevation in the downstream pond stays below the upstream pond's outlet, so standard routing results are valid.

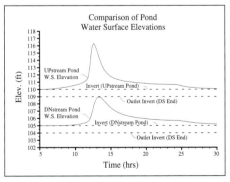

Figure 5: Elevations for Standard Routing

Figure 6 and Figure 7 display the inflow and outflow hydrographs for the upstream and downstream ponds. These routing results are applicable since the outfall water surface does not affect the downstream pond and the downstream pond water surface does not affect the upstream pond.

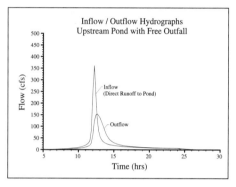

Figure 6: Upstream Pond Results

Conclusions for Example 1:

Figure 5 demonstrates that the downstream pond's maximum water surface stays below the outfall invert of the upstream pond's outlet invert. So for the given storm, the downstream pond does not affect the outflow rate of the upstream pond, thus verifying the assumption of standard routing conditions and results shown in Figure 6 and Figure 7.

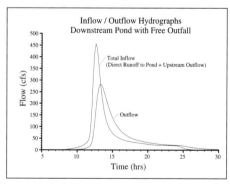

Figure 7: Downstream Pond Results

Therefore, standard routing techniques are applicable to this scenario (with free outfall to the river).

Interconnected Pond Routing

The Basic Concept

Figure 8 shows the fundamental relationship involved with interconnected pond routing. Notice how the downstream pond rises to a level high enough to influence the hydraulics of the upstream pond's outlet.

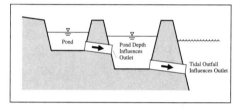

Figure 8: Interconnected Ponds

Tidal outfall conditions (water surface elevation that varies with time) may also require interconnected routing analyses. Figure 8 shows a tidal outfall that rises high enough to influence the downstream pond's outlet hydraulics.

The Key to Interconnected Analyses: Time Variant Tailwater Conditions

When two or more ponds are directly connected and have inverts at or near the same elevations, the water surface elevation in the downstream pond(s) might affect the outflow rate from the upstream pond. This situation produces time variant tailwater conditions since the water surface in each pond is a function of inflow, outflow, pond shape, pond size and pond outlet structures – all operating over time.

Examples of
Time Variant
Tailwater Elevation:

- Two (or more) ponds connected, with little or no vertical relief between pond inverts

- Tidal outfall into the ocean

- Outfall into time variant stream stage elevations

New Algorithms

In time variant tailwater situations, standard routing techniques will no longer apply if the downstream water surface elevation rises high enough to affect the outflow from the upstream pond. Interconnected pond routing techniques involve complex convergent algorithms that take into account the changing water surface elevation in each pond over the course of time.

The basic mass balance for pond routing still applies to interconnected pond routing, with one major exception: time variant tailwater conditions. For each time step, the outflow is a function of the water surface elevation in the downstream pond, which is a function of the volume, inflow and outflow of that pond.

For standard routing techniques, tailwater is assumed to be a function of flow rate only and can be solved directly based on the water surface in the pond. This technique cannot be applied to interconnected analyses since the tailwater is not simply a direct function of flow.

Software for Interconnected Pond Routing

The new version of Pond Pack handles time variant tailwater conditions for interconnected ponds and tidal outfalls. It handles reverse flow and can simulate flap gates (restricts flow to one direction).

This new software can model multiple interconnected pond outfalls (diversions) in a single watershed. It also models conditions where multiple ponds discharge into a single common pond, as well as conditions where a single pond discharges (diverts) into multiple downstream ponds.

Example 2: Interconnected Ponds

This example demonstrates a case where interconnected pond routing techniques apply. Results from this example will be compared with Example 1 for standard pond routing.

Given: Figure 9 models the identical pond system and storm event described in Example 1. The only exception is time variant tailwater at the river outfall. Figure 10 shows the flood stage information used for the outfall in this example.

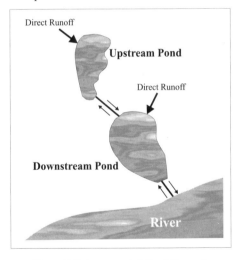

Figure 9: Interconnected Pond Example

If the river elevation rises high enough, it can impact the performance of the downstream pond, which, in turn, could impact the performance of the upstream pond. If the river rises high enough, it can potentially cause reverse flow conditions into the ponds (since there are no flap gates on the outlets).

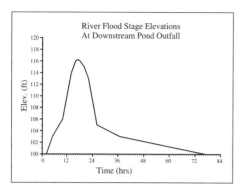

Figure 10: Flood Elevations at River Outfall

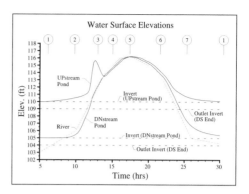

Figure 11: Routing Results: Elevations

The Analyses:

The runoff hydrographs into the ponds are the same ones used in Example 1 (see Figure 4). Interconnected routing techniques were performed to model pond elevations, storage and outflow during the storm.

Figure 11 displays the computed water surface elevations for each pond, based on interconnected routing. Seven different relationships are designated with circled numbers. These circled numbers also correspond to Figure 12.

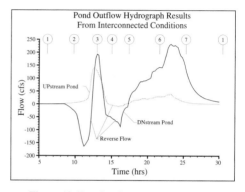

Figure 12: Routing Results: Hydrographs

The schematic profiles on the following page demonstrate conditions for the seven cases circled in Figure 11 and Figure 12.

Special Note:

Interconnected conditions do not require a tidal outfall as shown in these examples.

Two ponds will have interconnected effects as long as the water surface elevation in one pond affects the outflow of the other pond.

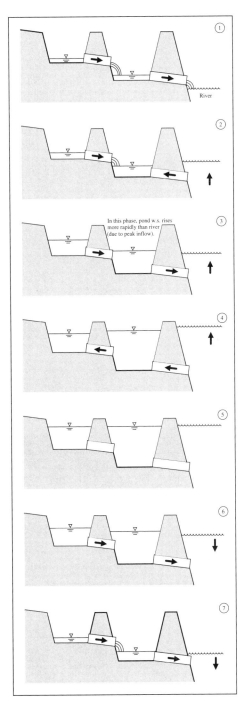

Conclusions for Example 2:

We see from Figure 11 and Figure 12 that interconnected pond routing was necessary since the river flood stage rose high enough to affect the downstream pond. In turn, the water surface elevation in the downstream pond rose high enough to affect the discharge of the upstream pond. Standard routing techniques are not applicable for this situation.

The schematic profiles shown on this page demonstrate how several different flow conditions (including reverse flow) can occur within a single routing event. Interconnected routing techniques can simulate each of these cases and when they occur.

On the rising leg of the river flood stage (profile case 2), reverse flow into the downstream pond is occurring, causing the downstream pond elevation to rise and "keep pace" with the rising river. Then between hours 12 and 14 (profile case 3), the downstream pond switches to forward flow because the combined flow from the upstream pond outlet and the direct runoff "outpaces" the rise in the river flood stage.

Comparing Results

This comparison between two examples will demonstrate the potential differences between standard routing and interconnected routing techniques. Example 1 modeled a free outfall scenario using standard routing techniques, whereas Example 2 modeled a flood stage table at the outfall point.

By comparing the water surface elevations and outflow hydrographs from these two examples, we can show how the downstream water surface assumptions can dramatically impact the routing results. In this comparison, standard routing results would be inappropriate for the scenario in Example 2, where a high flood stage coincides with the pond outflow.

Comparison for Upstream Pond

Figure 13 compares water surface elevations in the upstream pond. Notice the dramatic difference between the two examples. The backwater effects from the river flood stage prolonged the time that the water remained at a high level in the pond.

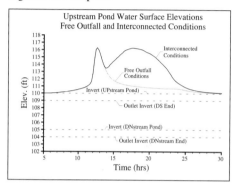

Figure 13: Elevations for Upstream Pond

Figure 14 compares the outflow from the upstream pond. The peak outflow rate was virtually unaffected since the peak elevation of the downstream pond did not coincide with the peak outflow of the upstream pond. For the interconnected scenario, there is a short period of reverse flow, and the total detention time is prolonged because of backwater effects.

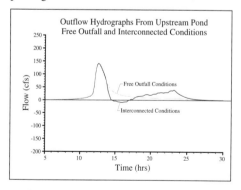

Figure 14: Outflow from Upstream Pond

Comparison for Downstream Pond

Figure 15 compares water surface elevations in the downstream pond. Notice the increased water surface elevation for the interconnected example. Both the maximum water surface and total detention time are greatly increased because of backwater effects from the river.

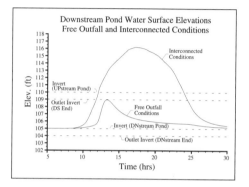

Figure 15: Elevations for Downstream Pond

Figure 16 compares outflow from the downstream pond. The interconnected backwater effects actually *reduce* the maximum outflow rate because of increased tailwater effects. Interconnected reverse flow also adds water to the downstream pond, thereby increasing the total storage volume and detention time in the downstream pond.

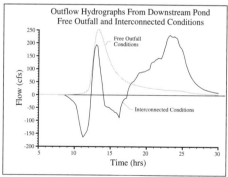

Figure 16: Outflow from Downstream Pond

Haestad Methods, Inc. www.haestad.com

Example 3: Flap Gates

This example is identical to Example 2, except that flap gates are modeled for both pond outlets in order to prevent reverse flow. The resulting water surface elevations and outflow rates are shown in Figure 17 and Figure 18.

Notice how the flap gates prevent reverse flow conditions and completely eliminate the outflow "spike" between hours 12 and 14 for the downstream pond (Figure 18). Since there is no reverse flow keeping the downstream pond's water surface near that of the river, the pond doesn't "catch up" to the river flood elevation during peak inflow (about 12 to 14 hours), thus preventing outflow until hour 20.

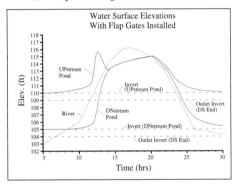

Figure 17: Elevations with Flap Gates

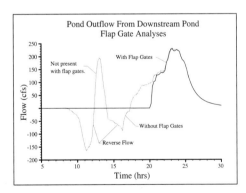

Figure 18: Outflow with Flap Gates

Flap gates in this case delay the outflow from the downstream pond, allowing them to occur only during the receding leg of the river flood stage.

Author: Michael K. Glazner
PondPack 6.0 software used for example computations and miscellaneous graphs

Key Concepts

Here are a few rules of thumb to help you determine which routing technique is appropriate:

• **Use standard routing techniques to calculate the maximum water surface elevation for each pond assuming they are not interconnected. If the maximum water surface elevation immediately downstream of each pond stays below the outfall invert, standard routing techniques apply. If the maximum water surface downstream of any pond rises above the outfall invert of the upstream connecting pond, interconnected analyses may be more appropriate.**

• **Time variant outfall elevations (such as ocean and river tides) require interconnected analyses if the TW elevation rises high enough to affect the pond outlet hydraulics. If the outfall TW is time variant but never rises high enough to affect the outflow rate of the connecting pond, standard routing techniques can be used.**

• **When in doubt, check the analyses using interconnected routing techniques. If standard routing techniques apply, the interconnected results should compare closely to the standard routing results.**

I-D-F CURVES VS. RAINFALL CURVES

Confusion often surrounds the differences between I-D-F data and rainfall curves. Know what type of rainfall data applies to your project.

This article explains the differences between I-D-F curves and rainfall curves, and the type of hydrologic methods to which they apply.

What is an I-D-F Curve?

Intensity-Duration-Frequency (I-D-F) curves are statistical descriptions of the expected rainfall intensity for a given duration and storm frequency. Figure 19 displays I-D-F curves that span several return events.

How do you read an I-D-F curve?

Figure 19 shows an example of using an I-D-F curve. For a 5-year frequency, the resulting average intensity is 5 inches an hour for 12 minutes. In other words, if an average intensity of 5 inches/hour falls for a period lasting 12 minutes, it would be considered a 5-year event.

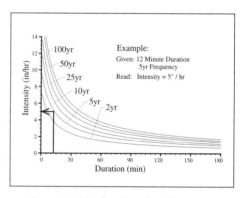

Figure 19: Intensity-Duration -Frequency

Intensity

Intensity is a measure of the *rate* of rainfall and is defined on the Y-axis. Intensity represents how "hard" it is raining. An intensity of 0.1 inch an hour would be a light sprinkle, whereas 5 inches an hour would be a downpour.

Duration

Duration is the time over which an expected average intensity is maintained. For example, Figure 19 shows the intensity corresponding to a duration of 12 minutes.

This event does not literally mean that the storm instantaneously goes from 0 inches an hour to 5 inches an hour, maintains a constant intensity for exactly 12 minutes, then ends instantaneously. Even if 1 inch of rainfall is expected to fall over a 12-minute period, the actual intensity might vary within the 12 minutes. But, since 1-inch total depth is accumulated, the *average* is 5 inches an hour.

Duration does not necessarily mean the entire length of a storm; it can also apply to the duration of average intensity found *within* a longer storm. Figure 20 shows an example of this concept for a 12-minute (0.20 hour) segment within a 2.5-hour storm.

Frequency

Each curve in Figure 19 represents one return frequency, which represents the magnitude of the storm. For a given duration, a larger return frequency yields a higher intensity. Frequency is defined as the inverse probability of occurrence. For example, if a storm has a 20% probability of occurring this year, the return frequency is $(1 \div 0.20 = 5)$, or a 5-year event.

What is a Rainfall Curve?

A rainfall curve is the measure of rainfall depth as it varies throughout the storm. Figure 20 demonstrates this principle by using a rain gauge as the Y-axis.

Total depth (the highest point) and total storm duration (time at which the highest point is reached) can be read directly from the graph. Intensity can be computed for a given time slice within the graph.

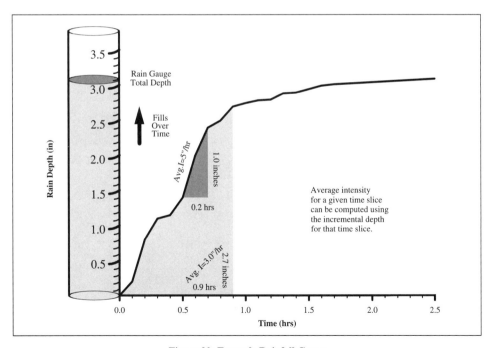

Figure 20: Example Rainfall Curve

For a real storm event, intensity may vary throughout the duration of the storm. Steep portions on the rainfall curve represent periods of higher intensity. Conversely, flatter portions on the curve represent periods of lower intensity.

Figure 20 shows that the computed average intensity depends on which part of the rainfall curve is selected for the computation. (For an in-depth discussion of rainfall curves and distributions, see the article titled "Interpreting SCS 24 Hour Storms.")

What is the Difference?

Many engineers confuse I-D-F curves with rainfall distributions, thinking they are one and the same. But actually, these graphs represent two different types of rainfall information that are applied to different runoff methods.

An I-D-F curve is a measure of rate, or "*how hard*" it is raining during a given *portion* of a storm. A rainfall curve, on the other hand, is a "diary" or "history" of a storm, showing how the *depth* in a rainfall gauge varies throughout the *entire* storm.

What Runoff Methods Use I-D-F Data?

Typically, peak discharge methods such as the Rational Method use I-D-F data. Because the data for a given duration represent the most intense portion of a storm, these curves are ideal for estimating the resulting peak rate of runoff. In cases where only flow capacity is of interest (such as inlet design), this approach is quite useful.

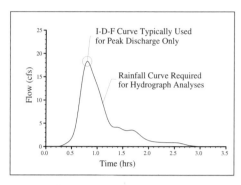

Figure 21: Runoff Hydrograph

What Runoff Methods Use Rainfall Curves?

Since rainfall curves represent a history of the entire storm, they are ideal for use in computing hydrographs. Unit hydrograph methods such as the SCS Unit Hydrograph Method require rainfall data that are representative of the entire storm. This information is modeled using dimensionless rainfall distributions or actual gauged events (see the article titled "Interpreting SCS 24-Hour Storms" for more discussion on rainfall curves and distributions).

Can I-D-F Data Substitute for Rainfall Curves?

Rule of Thumb: No.

Here's a question many engineers ask the first time they try to compute a runoff hydrograph: "How do I use my I-D-F data to compute the hydrograph?" For most hydrograph methods, the answer is: "You don't."

Haestad Methods, Inc. www.haestad.com

As previously noted, most hydrograph methods require rainfall distributions (curves) that describe how the gauged depth of rainfall varies with time; these curves are not the same thing as I-D-F curves.

Exception to the Rule

Only a few hydrograph methods use I-D-F data directly as the source of rainfall data. These methods are typically spin-offs from the Rational Method, such as various Modified Rational Methods and Rational Method Hydrograph Templates.

Creating Rainfall Curves from I-D-F Data

You cannot use I-D-F curves *directly* for most complex hydrograph computations (such as the SCS Unit Hydrograph Method), but you can use I-D-F data *indirectly*. That is, you can create rainfall distribution curves from I-D-F data and then use those curves for the hydrograph computations.

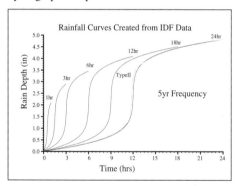

Figure 22: Rainfall Curves Created from I-D-F

Figure 22 displays rainfall curves for various durations that were created from the 5-year frequency curve from Figure 19. These rainfall

curves are "center peaking," with the most intense portion of the storm placed in the center of the curve. (Various types of rainfall curves are discussed and compared in the article "Rainfall Distributions: Center Peaking vs. Statistical.")

Note: Only the first 3 (of 24) hours are shown for the I-D-F curves in Figure 19.

Author: Michael K. Glazner

PondPack 6.0 software used for example computations and miscellaneous graphs

Key Concepts

This article addresses the confusion that often surrounds the differences between I-D-F data and rainfall curves. Here is a quick review:

- **Definition of an I-D-F curve and discussion of its various components**

- **Definition of gauged rainfall data and rainfall curves**

- **Comparison of I-D-F data and rainfall curves**

- **Methods that require I-D-F data**

- **Methods that require rainfall curves**

- **Interchangeability between I-D-F data and rainfall curves**

INTERPRETING SCS 24-HOUR STORMS

Understand how rainfall distributions impact your stormwater designs.

The U.S. Soil Conservation Service (SCS) 24-hour rainfall distributions (Types I, IA, II, and III) are some of the most widely used rainfall curves in the United States. This article explains the basic concept of a rainfall curve and discusses four SCS 24-hour distributions and how they impact hydrograph shape and peak flow rate.

The Basics

What is a rainfall curve?

A rainfall curve is the measure of total rainfall depth as it varies throughout a storm. A good way to understand a rainfall curve is to visualize the Y-axis as a rainfall gauge (see Figure 23). As the storm progresses, the gauge begins to fill. The curve describes the gauged rainfall depth at each point during the storm.

The steeper the curve's slope, the faster the gauge is filling. Hence, the rate of rainfall is more intense. In Figure 23, the most intense portion of the storm occurs between 0.1 and 0.2 hours and again between 0.5 and 0.6 hours (about 0.6" over 0.1 hour = 6"/hour intensity).

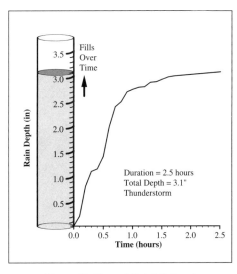

Figure 23: Gauged Rainfall Event

Rainfall curves are a mathematical means for simulating different storms. Figure 24 shows conditions for two types of storms. Figure 25 and Figure 26 display dramatic differences between these two rainfall events, even though *the total depth and volume are the same* for each storm.

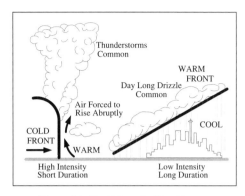

Figure 24: Conditions for Two Storms

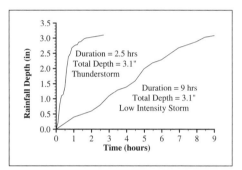

Figure 25: Comparison of Two Storms

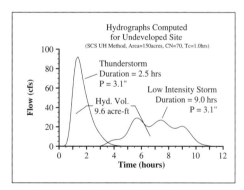

Figure 26: Hydrographs for Two Storms

The Diary of a Storm

A rainfall curve is a history, or "diary," of the recorded storm. Several pieces of information can be derived from rainfall curves:

- **Storm Duration** – Duration is the time between a storm's first and last raindrops. In Figure 23, the duration is 2.5 hours.

- **Total Depth** – Because the curve represents cumulative depth, the total depth (highest point) will be at the end of the storm. In Figure 23, the total depth is 3.1 inches.

- **Storm Intensity** – The slope of the line indicates the rainfall intensity as it varies throughout the storm. The steeper the line, the more intense (or "harder") the rainfall rate. In Figure 23, the most intense portions (about 6 inches per hour) of the storm are between 0.1 and 0.2 hours and between 0.5 and 0.6 hours.

- **Hydrograph Time to Peak** – When using the SCS unit hydrograph method, a *rough* rule of thumb for time to peak is:

$T_P = T_{EI} + $ Lag, where:
T_P = Time to peak on hydrograph
T_{EI} = End of long, intense segment
Lag = Drainage lag (about $0.6 \cdot T_C$ for SCS methods)

In Figure 23, the end of the longest, most intense portion of the curve ends at about 0.7 hour. Therefore, the expected time to peak (for T_C =1.0 hrs) would be about:

$T_P = 0.7 + $ Lag $ = 0.7 + 0.6 T_C$
$= 0.7 + (0.6)(1.0)$
Expected T_P is about: 1.3 hours.
From Figure 26, the actual T_P = 1.35 hrs.

For natural rainfall curves there may be multiple inflection points that result in multiple "humps" on the hydrograph. (See 9-hour storm in Figure 25 and Figure 26).

- **Hydrograph Shape** – A steeper rainfall curve results in a higher peak discharge with a more "spiked" shape. A flatter rainfall curve yields a lower peak discharge with a more "rounded" shape.

- **Hydrograph Volume** – For runoff methods such as the SCS CN method, the *shape* of the rainfall curve does not affect total hydrograph *volume*. The total *depth* of rainfall impacts the total runoff volume. In Figure 26, the two hydrograph volumes are equal since each storm had the same total depth (applied to SCS methods).

Note: Some infiltration/runoff methods might result in runoff volumes that are a function of rainfall intensity (and therefore a function of the rain curve *shape*).

What are SCS 24-Hour Rainfall Curves?

Figure 27 displays four SCS distributions used in the United States (Types I, IA, II, and III). Figure 28 shows the approximate geographic boundaries for these rainfall distributions.

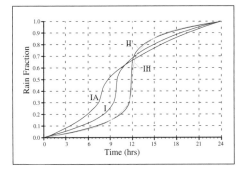

Figure 27: SCS 24-hour Rainfall Distributions

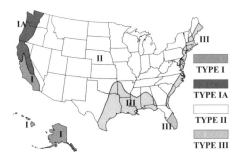

Figure 28: Approximate Boundaries

Why Do We Need SCS Distributions?

Rainfall curves (not I-D-F curves) are needed for site designs that require hydrograph analyses (such as detention ponds, watershed studies, etc). Because local rainfall distribution curves have not been established for many areas in the United States, engineers often opt to use SCS distributions to compute hydrographs.

How Do SCS Distributions Model Storms?

The SCS distributions are dimensionless in their raw form (see Figure 27). To create a design rainfall curve, multiply the Y-axis by the 24-hour total rainfall depth. Figure 29 shows what each distribution looks like when applied to a 24-hour total depth of 3.1 inches. Figure 30 displays hydrographs resulting from these distributions (applied to same site as Figure 26).

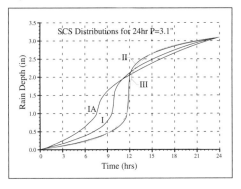

Figure 29: SCS Distributions, 24-hour P=3.1"

Comparison of Results

Figure 30 compares hydrographs computed using identical conditions for each scenario, changing only the shape and duration of the rainfall curve. The same total *depth* of 3.1 inches was used in each case and applied to the same site used for Figure 26 (Area=150 acres,

CN=70 and Tc=1.0 hours). The SCS unit hydrograph procedure was used to compute the runoff hydrographs for each storm.

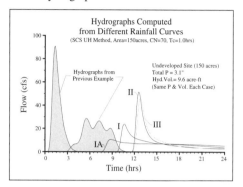

Figure 30: SCS Hydrographs, 24-hour P=3.1"

This comparison shows that even for a given identical rainfall depth, the computed runoff hydrographs vary dramatically depending on the *shape and duration* of the rainfall curve. So before using any rainfall distribution, an engineer should understand the implied storm it represents.

Diary of the SCS 24-Hour Storm

An SCS dimensionless 24-hour rainfall distribution shares many of the same basic characteristics of a gauged storm event. Each SCS distribution provides a variety of information that will help you visualize the kind of storm it is modeling.

Here's a summary of important characteristics:

- **Storm Duration** – The SCS distributions in Figure 27 model only a 24-hour duration.

- **Total Depth** – Since the storm duration is 24 hours, the total depth applied to these distributions *must be for a 24-hour period*.

- **Why is the Y-axis dimensionless?** – The Y-axis is defined as fraction of total depth, ranging from 0 to 1.0 (0% to 100%). Multiply the Y-axis by total rainfall depth to "convert" the distribution to a rainfall depth curve.

  Defining the Y-axis as a *fraction* of total depth enables us to apply *different depths* to the same curve. The 24-hour rainfall depth varies with respect to storm *frequency* (2-year, 5-year, 25-year, etc), and *geographical region*.

- **Storm Intensity** – The steepest slope on a rainfall distribution represents the most intense portion of the storm. For the distributions in Figure 27, an intense period of rainfall is preceded and followed by several hours of lower-intensity rainfall.

  A range of average intensities can be computed for a rainfall curve, depending on the time "slice". Therefore, good judgment should be used in selecting the time step and location on the curve from which to compute the average intensity.

  Figure 31 shows three examples for computing the average intensity for a portion of a rainfall curve. In these examples, the average intensities were computed for sections of the curve that had a relatively uniform slope.

  Depth = 0.25" from <u>0 to 6 hrs</u>
  Avg. Intensity = 0.25"/ 6 hrs = **0.04"/hr**

  Depth = 0.96" from <u>11.7 to 12.0 hrs</u>
  Avg. Intensity = 0.96"/0.3 hrs = **3.2"/hr**

  Depth = 0.25" from <u>18 to 24 hrs</u>
  Avg. Intensity = 0.25"/ 6hrs = **0.04"/hr**

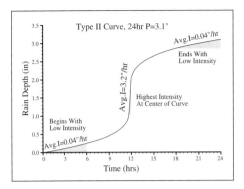

Figure 31: Average Intensity Examples

- **Hydrograph Time to Peak** – The time to peak on a hydrograph will usually occur after the longest, steepest (most intense) portion of the curve. In Figure 27, the most intense portion for each SCS distribution ends at about:

Type IA – 8.2 hours
Type I – 10.0 hours
Type II – 12.0 hours
Type III – 12.2 hours

From previous discussion, $T_p = T_{EI}$ +Lag. For the Type II example in Figure 29, the expected time to peak is about:
$T_p = 12.0 + (0.6)(1.0) = 12.6$ hours. Actual $T_p = 12.55$ hours (Figure 30).

Figure 30 includes the hydrographs computed for each of the SCS 24-hour rainfall curves. Note how each hydrograph peak time occurs after the long, steep (most intense) segment within the curve. Because there is only one inflection point on each SCS distribution, each resulting hydrograph has only one "hump."

- **Hydrograph Shape** – Figure 29 and Figure 30 show that as the slope of the rainfall distribution increases, the resulting hydrograph peak also increases. When comparing these SCS distributions, Type

IA yields the least intense storms and Type II yields the most intense storms.

- **Hydrograph Volume** – For runoff methods such as the SCS CN method, the *shape* of the rainfall curve does not affect the total hydrograph *volume*. Only the total rainfall depth impacts runoff volume. So for the examples in Figure 30, the total hydrograph *volume* is identical in each case, even though the shapes are different.

Note: Some infiltration/runoff methods can result in runoff volumes that are a function of rainfall intensity (and therefore a function of the rain curve *shape*).

What Kinds of Storms Do They Simulate?
Center Peaking Storms

The SCS distributions (particularly Types II and III) can be described as center peaking storms. That is, the beginning and ends of the storms have a relatively low intensity compared to the middle portion's higher intensity.

A Closer Look

By "walking" along the rainfall distribution, we can better understand what kinds of storms these distributions model. Let's take a detailed look at the Type II distribution and visualize what kind of storm it models.

For the Type II storm in Figure 27, only 15% of total depth accumulates during the first 9 hours. About 70% of total depth falls in 6 hours (between 9 and 15 hours). The remaining 15% of total depth falls in about 9 hours. In other words, most of the rainfall accumulates in the center of the storm. In particular, *about 40% falls in a 40-minute period* (from 11.6 to 12.3 hours).

So the 24-hour Type II storm doesn't really model an intense storm that lasts for 24 hours. It models an intense storm of a few hours that is sandwiched between several hours of "drizzle" on each side.

Limitations

Although the SCS 24-hour rainfall distributions are readily available and easy to apply in the United States, they do have some limitations:

- **Regional Variation** – Figure 28 shows how each SCS distribution covers a large region of the United States. More studies are needed to provide rainfall distributions for site-specific locations.

- **Only 24-hour Duration** – These SCS distributions are only for a 24-hour storm. More studies are needed to provide engineers with rainfall distributions for a wider variety of storm durations.

The Need

Only a handful of different SCS 24-hour rainfall distributions are applied across the entire United States. Studies are needed to provide engineers with more site-specific rainfall data for a wider range of durations (not just 24-hour).

Check with local and state drainage authorities to see if additional or newer rainfall curve data are available for your area.

Newer Rainfall Studies

Efforts are being made to better approximate rainfall curves for specific locations. Some areas in the United States now provide engineers with rainfall depths and distributions that replace or supplement the standard SCS 24-hour storms.

One example of updated rainfall information is found in the Illinois State Water Survey's Bulletin 70, "Frequency Distributions and Hydroclimatic Characteristics of Heavy Rainstorms in Illinois." This document provides rainfall *depths* for a variety of return events and durations (not limited to 24 hours only). Bulletin 70 also provides rainfall distribution curves for a variety of durations. Additional discussion on the development of these dimensionless rainfall distributions is included in Circular 173, "Time Distributions of Heavy Rainstorms in Illinois," also by the Illinois State Water Survey.

Author: Michael K. Glazner
PondPack 6.0 software used for example computations and miscellaneous graphs

Key Concepts

This article is designed to help engineers better understand SCS rainfall distributions. Here is a quick review of the topics discussed:

- How to read a gauged rainfall curve

- How to visualize an SCS rainfall distribution

- Comparing the differences between SCS distributions and gauged data

- How rainfall curves dramatically affect the shape of a hydrograph, even for the same total depth of rainfall

- Limitations of the 24-hour distributions

- The need for more research and rainfall information to be made available to practicing engineers

RAINFALL DISTRIBUTIONS: CENTER-PEAKING VS. STATISTICAL

*Identify various types of rainfall curves and
their underlying assumptions. They might
not be modeling quite what you think...*

Various types of rainfall distribution
curves have been developed for use in
hydrograph calculations. This article
uses examples to demonstrate the differences
between two major categories of rainfall
curves: center peaking and statistically derived
distributions.

Center Peaking Distribution

These types of rainfall curves are symmetrical
in appearance and model storms in which the
most intense (steepest slope on curve) portion
of the storm is located near the center of the
curve. Figure 32 is a classic example of a
center peaking distribution. It shows the SCS
24-hour Type II rainfall distribution with a
total depth of 3.1 inches applied.

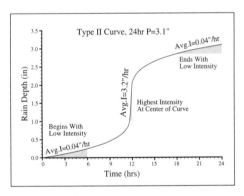

Figure 32: Type II 24-hour Rainfall Curve

This Type II rainfall distribution models an
intense "thunderstorm" preceded and followed
by periods of much lesser intensity. The article
titled "Interpreting SCS 24-Hour Storms"
provides detailed discussion on visualizing and
understanding rainfall curves.

Other examples of center peaking distributions are those created from I-D-F curves. Different duration storms can be created using a single I-D-F curve (for one frequency).

The table in Figure 33 shows depth vs. duration data established in a recent rainfall study for a certain area in the United States. The I-D-F curve for the 10-year frequency was fit through the intensity points derived in the table.

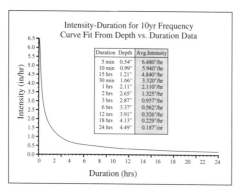

Figure 33: Intensity-Duration-Frequency

Figure 34 represents the rainfall distributions for various durations. These rainfall curves were created from the I-D-F curve in Figure 33. (For more discussion on creating rainfall distributions from I-D-F curves, see the article titled "I-D-F Curves vs. Rainfall Curves.")

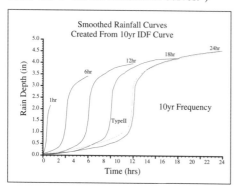

Figure 34: Rainfall Curves Created from I-D-F

Note that the *intensity* (slope) of the center portion of each curve created from I-D-F data is *identical* (for the same frequency). That is, the beginning and end "tails" of the same curve were lengthened to attain the desired duration and corresponding total depth.

These types of curves indicate that the most intense portions of the storms are the same, regardless of storm duration. This concept differs from the statistical distributions described below.

Statistical Distribution

These rainfall curve distributions are developed based on statistical analyses of storm events for different durations. When developed properly for a specific location, these types of rainfall distributions provide the flexibility of modeling a variety of storms other than the standard 24-hour event.

Statistical distributions are not necessarily center peaking and might have different maximum intensities compared to center peaking distributions.

The basic philosophy of this approach is that longer-duration storms are expected to "behave" differently than shorter-duration storms. For example, the most intense portion of a 24-hour storm is expected to differ from the most intense portion of a 1-hour storm.

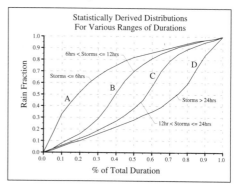

Figure 35: Statistical Distributions

Typically, these types of curves are dimensionless, so they can be applied to a wide range of durations and rainfall depths.

Figure 35 displays dimensionless rainfall curves established for different ranges of durations. To create a rainfall depth curve, select the curve for the desired duration. Then, multiply the X-axis by total storm duration and multiply the Y-axis by the total rainfall depth for that given duration.

Example

Statistical analyses were performed using updated rainfall information for a certain geographic location in the United States. This study yielded the table shown in Figure 33 and the statistical distributions shown in Figure 35.

Given: Rainfall depths from Figure 33.

Find: Rainfall curves for the 1-, 6-, 12-, 18- and 24-hour durations, using the statistically derived distributions in Figure 35.

Solution: First, select the distribution from Figure 35 that corresponds to each desired duration. Then multiply the Y-axis by the total rainfall depth for that duration and the X-axis by that duration.

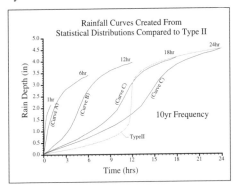

Figure 36: Solution to Example

Figure 36 displays the results of this example. Different curve types (A, B and C from Figure 35) were used to model different duration storms. Note how the total depth increases, but overall intensity (slope of the curve) decreases as the duration is lengthened.

Implementation

One example of the statistical approach is found in the Illinois State Water Survey's Bulletin 70, "Frequency Distributions and Hydroclimatic Characteristics of Heavy Rainstorms in Illinois." This document provides rainfall depths for a variety of return events and durations (not just 24 hours).

Bulletin 70 also provides rainfall distribution curves for a variety of durations. Additional discussion on the development of these dimensionless rainfall distributions is included in Circular 173, "Time Distributions of Heavy Rainstorms in Illinois," also issued by the Illinois State Water Survey.

By coupling the total depth for different durations and return events, these reports provide engineers with a wide range of design storms (for Illinois). And because the dimensionless rainfall curves cover a wide range of durations, engineers can develop a complete rainfall vs. depth curve for any of the included durations and return events.

Comparisons

24-Hour Duration Storms

Figure 37 compares 24-hour rainfall curves for a geographical area where the Type II rainfall curve is applicable. Three types of distributions are compared: a center peaking rainfall distribution; SCS Type II 24 hour; and a statistically derived rainfall curve.

The Type II and center peaking distribution are similar in shape. Conversely, the statistically derived distribution has an overall more uniform and lower intensity (milder slope) than the two center peaking storms.

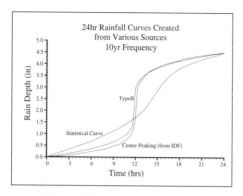

Figure 37: 24-hour Rainfall Curves

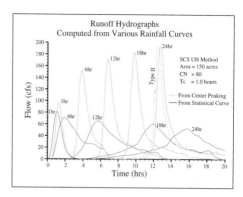

Figure 39: Hydrograph Comparisons

Various Durations

Figure 38 directly compares the rainfall curves from Figure 34 and Figure 36. Note how center peaking distributions have the same maximum intensity in the center of the storm for each duration, compared to the statistically derived distributions where maximum intensity tends to decrease with an increase in storm duration.

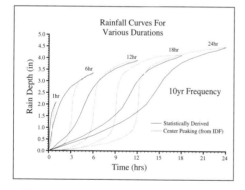

Figure 38: Comparison of Distribution Types

Figure 39 compares the hydrographs computed with these rainfall curves, using the same watershed data for each calculation. The center peaking distributions yield hydrographs that increase in peak discharge with an increase in duration. The statistically derived distributions, on the other hand, yield hydrographs that decrease in peak discharge with an increase in duration.

In each case, an increase in duration yields a higher total hydrograph volume since the total depth of rainfall increases with duration.

Total Volume

Runoff volume is only a function of total rainfall *depth* and runoff coefficient when using procedures such as the SCS Runoff CN method. As duration increases, the total volume increases because there is an increase in total depth of rainfall.

However, the hydrograph volume for each *duration* (same rainfall depth) is identical for both center peaking and statistically derived distributions, even though the hydrograph *shapes* are dramatically different.

Case Studies

Which is better?

As we have seen, there can be huge variations between center peaking and statistically derived distributions. Which one best models or predicts "real world" events?

Some people might argue that statistically derived rainfall distributions for a specific area would better represent the overall "average" shape of rainfall curves for different duration storm events. However, even if this assumption could be proved to be true,

---

eventually rainfall events will still occur that significantly differ from the statistically calculated rainfall curves.

Maybe the question should be reworded to ask: "What type of storm is most appropriate for your design?" In other words, would a storm with a more uniform intensity or one with center peaking high intensity have the most significant impact on your design?

In the field, drainage facilities will encounter hundreds of variations of duration and intensity. Rarely will a site encounter two storms with identical duration, depth and rainfall curve shape.

By understanding the kinds of storms various rainfall distributions model, engineers can better judge their applicability for design situations. Engineers might want to model a system using more than one duration and/or type of rainfall distribution. By doing so, a design's response can be checked for greatly varying rainfall conditions.

Case Study: The Need for More Curves

A large event (7.76 inches over 19 hours) was recorded at a particular gauging station in the Eastern United States. The Type III 24-hour distribution is normally applied to this geographic location.

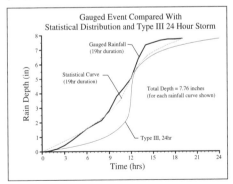

Figure 40: Gauged vs. Synthetic Data

Figure 40 compares the actual gauged storm with a statistically derived distribution for the same duration and total rainfall depth. The 24-hour Type III storm is also compared using the same total rainfall depth.

For this particular event, the gauged data show an overall more uniform and lower intensity than the Type III 24-hour event. The statistically derived 19-hour distribution appears to better approximate the actual event than does the center peaking 24-hour Type III distribution.

This storm represents only a single historic event at this geographic location. Even though the engineer may consider the statistically derived distribution relevant for this case study, an actual event of this same magnitude will someday impact the design site, but cannot be expected to match this same rainfall distribution assumption.

Figure 41 compares a hydrograph computed using the real gauged data to hydrographs computed from two different synthetic rainfall distributions (using the same total depth of 7.76 inches).

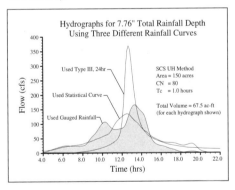

Figure 41: Hydrograph Results from Gauged and Synthetic Data

Another way to review the comparison would be to say the hydrograph from the Type III storm is the one the engineer used for design, while the gauged rainfall event is the one that actually occurred.

In this case study, is the Type III hydrograph conservative compared to the gauged event? The answer depends on the design situation.

If only one uniform subarea is being analyzed, and the outfall structure is designed *only* for *peak* discharge rate, the Type III storm would be conservative.

However, for more complex systems, such as detention ponds or watershed networks, the comparisons become more difficult. In order to assess the effectiveness of rainfall design assumptions, the entire system should be analyzed for *both* pre- and post-developed conditions using both gauged rainfall data and synthetic design distributions.

In this particular case, a statistically derived rainfall curve produces a closer (but not perfect) approximation of the actual gauged event. This case study shows why more research is needed to provide practicing drainage engineers with a much wider range of design rainfall distributions.

Author: Michael K. Glazner
PondPack 6.0 software used for example computations and miscellaneous graphs

Key Concepts

This article discusses two distinctly different approaches to modeling rainfall curves: center peaking, and statistically derived distributions. Here is a review of the topics covered:

• **Definition and examples of center peaking distributions**

• **Definition and examples of statistically derived distributions**

• **Comparisons of these two types of rainfall distributions and their significant differences in storm intensity**

• **Discussion of the dramatic differences between the hydrographs resulting from each type of rainfall distribution**

• **Case studies comparing real gauged data with center peaking and statistically based rainfall distributions**

• **Discussion of the need for more research and better rainfall models**

Gauged Rainfall Source

Rainfall and other meteorological data from across the United States and around the world are compiled and archived at the National Climatic Data Center. This agency has daily precipitation depths and in some cases hourly precipitation data.

National Climatic Data Center
151 Patton Ave., Room 120
Federal Building
Asheville, NC 28801-5001

Phone: (704) 271-4800
Internet: www.ncdc.noaa.gov

PREDEVELOPED VS. POSTDEVELOPED ANALYSES

Are you really restoring a developed site to predeveloped conditions by using peak outflow criteria?

Many areas in the United States have a stormwater detention pond ordinance that requires the postdeveloped outflow from a site to discharge at a rate equal to or less than the predeveloped peak flow rate. This might sound like restoring the site to its predeveloped runoff state, but is that really the case?

This article discusses the impacts of increased stormwater volume because of development and reviews how this might impact developed areas. An example progresses throughout the different sections of this article to demonstrate these ideas. For simplicity, only one return event (5-year) is reviewed.

Example

Figure 42 shows the 5-year pre- and postdeveloped hydrographs for a proposed site. To conform to a peak outflow criteria, the engineer must design a detention pond that restricts the maximum postdeveloped outflow

to the predeveloped peak rate. The SCS unit hydrograph method was used for this design.

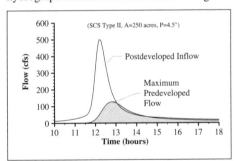

Figure 42: 5-year Pre- and Postdeveloped

Figure 43 compares the predeveloped hydrograph with the final pond design's postdeveloped pond inflow and outflow. Based on the given criteria, this pond would pass review for this 5-year event.

                    Haestad Methods, Inc. www.haestad.com

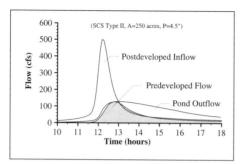

Figure 43: Review of Final Design

The Difference: Pre vs. Post

Even if the peak outflow is attenuated to match the predeveloped peak, at least two differences typically occur:

1) Time to peak is shifted (earlier or later)

2) Total *volume* of outflow is increased

Volumes for this example:
Predeveloped Runoff = 29.4 acre-ft
Postdeveloped Inflow = 60.6 acre-ft
Pond Outflow   = 60.6 acre-ft

Figure 43 shows that the engineer successfully attenuated the peak outflow rate. But what about the shape and volume of the outflow hydrograph? Note that the overall shape and volume of the predeveloped and pond outflow hydrographs are *different*. In this example, the runoff volume more than doubled for the postdeveloped conditions.

Because the hydrograph is shifted in time and has an overall greater volume compared to the predeveloped hydrograph, the pond outflow hydrograph adds differently to downstream confluences, impacting drainage systems farther downstream. These types of downstream impacts are better approximated by including the pond design site as a *subset* of an overall larger model of the watershed.

The Impacts

Perhaps the most crucial difference in postdeveloped hydrographs is the increase in total runoff volume due to development. Figure 44 shows graphically that the pond's outflow volume is significantly more than the predeveloped runoff hydrograph.

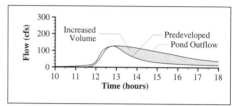

Figure 44: Increased Runoff Volume

For most detention ponds (ones that completely drain after a storm), this means that most or all of the increased volume is eventually passed downstream. So the pond mitigates the peak discharge effect, but not the increase in volume.

From Figure 44, we can see the level of outflow is above predeveloped rates for almost the entire storm. Therefore, the downstream channels are encountering higher depths of flow for longer periods of time, even if technically not "flooding."

Some effects of increased runoff volume are:

• Prolonged rise in water surface downstream, which might affect the slope stability of channels.

• The increased volume affects the way the hydrograph will add up downstream, changing the downstream flow rates.

• The increase in volume represents the amount of groundwater recharge that is no longer being absorbed for that size event (this runoff is now being discharged into the downstream conveyance system).

• Increased volume feeding into existing downstream detention ponds.

The Solution

The ultimate solution (outside of zero development) in terms of mitigating the increased runoff volume downstream would be to design a pond that yields an outflow hydrograph of the exact *shape* and volume of the hydrograph for predeveloped conditions. That would ensure that the water flowing from the site is impacting downstream reaches in a fashion identical to predeveloped conditions.

A variation of this idea would be to use on-site detention to mitigate the initial peak discharge rates and capture the initial runoff pollutants. Then, use regional detention to hold back the increased volume in water for the overall watershed, while also reshaping the outflow hydrograph to closely match the predeveloped state for the overall watershed. Perhaps these regional ponds could be incorporated in parks and golf courses and even be used for irrigation if the water quality is good enough.

A Tall Order

Think carefully before you rush to vote-in a new drainage ordinance that requires the postdeveloped outflow hydrograph to exactly match the predeveloped hydrograph in shape and volume. Here are just a few of the difficult challenges that are involved with accomplishing this concept:

- It will be very time-intensive to design grading plans and channel slopes to decrease or increase time of concentration and reach routing times so that the time to peak on the routed pond outflow matches the predeveloped time to peak.

- The *shape* of the outflow hydrograph (as well as the peak) will have to be considered when designing outlets for the pond.

- The most common way to keep the additional volume from releasing downstream is to hold it on-site. This might mean a significant increase in required storage, with the ability to evaporate or infiltrate the additional volume back into the groundwater.

- If the increased volume is handled on a per-lot basis, underground infiltration may cause "wet spots," or localized drainage problems in adverse soils.

- Extra safety precautions might be necessary because of permanent pools if the increased volume is held on-site via a wet pond or separate evaporation and infiltration pond.

- If this additional volume is infiltrated back into the groundwater, care must be taken not to introduce stormwater pollutants into the groundwater.

- Even if the predeveloped hydrograph shape is matched, the conditions might change from predeveloped nonpoint (sheet flow) outflow to a single discharge point (pond outlet structure).

The Impossible Dream?

In practical terms of today's design and construction practices, it would be very difficult, if not impossible, to achieve a perfect match to the predeveloped state. There are many complex issues, including water quality (surface and groundwater), that interplay with this idea and must be considered before establishing drainage criteria. Until we collect much more research data, this hydrograph matching concept is more like a "compass" that points in the direction we may hopefully one day achieve.

Research Needed

Here are just a few research areas that could help provide engineers with the necessary tools for better detention design:

- Establish much more "life-like" rainfall distributions that better model the real world for both pre- and postdeveloped conditions. For more information about the impacts of rainfall assumptions, read the rainfall articles in this Practical Guide.

- Understand the effects of stormwater recharge on groundwater quality infiltration (through drainage surfaces, ponds, infiltration chambers, etc.).

- Study the environmental impacts of using detention water for irrigation purposes.

- Develop new ideas for detaining water on a lot-by-lot basis to better emulate predeveloped groundwater recharge throughout the site.

- Find new methods for removing storm water pollution from detention so water quality matches the predeveloped state.

- Study impacts of stormwater pollution on clogging soil pore space, which affects the infiltration rates through a pond bottom.

- Analyze groundwater mounding effects on detention.

- Develop better outlet rating curve data for typical outlet structures.

- Design new outlet devices that can help shape the outflow hydrograph for different types of storms.

- Find new ways of shaping sites to better emulate the runoff response times of the predeveloped conditions.

- Establish tolerance limits for determining if the predeveloped and postdeveloped hydrograph shapes match "closely

enough." In other words, do some kind of statistical check, ordinate by ordinate, to see if the overall hydrographs match within an acceptable range.

Author: Michael K. Glazner
PondPack 6.0 software used for example computations and miscellaneous graphs

Key Concepts

- **Detention ponds are typically designed to attenuate the postdeveloped runoff *rate* to be less than or equal to the predeveloped peak flow rate.**

- **Unless postdeveloped stormwater is held on-site, there will usually be an increase in the total runoff volume that is passed downstream.**

- **A duplication of the predeveloped state can only be accomplished if the outflow hydrograph matches both the size and shape of the predeveloped conditions.**

- **Without significant research, the concept of truly matching predeveloped and postdeveloped conditions might not be possible in the near future.**

DESIGNING DETENTION PONDS WITH VISUAL HEC-1

While specialized programs like Pond Pack automate all aspects of detention, Visual HEC-1 can model fundamental pond routing within a complex watershed analysis.

What's the Impact of Development on Runoff?

Development in a catchment usually increases both the volume of runoff and the peak discharge rate for significant rainstorms. The reasons for this are simple:

- Development is commonly accompanied by an increase in impervious area. This increased impervious area decreases the open space, and hence decreases the volume of infiltration. As the volume of infiltration decreases, the volume of runoff increases.

- Development also "improves" the hydraulic characteristics of the ground surfaces and the channels in the catchment. Water then runs off with less energy loss and with little storage. This reduces the time to peak and increases the magnitude of the peak.

The magnitude of the increase in volume and peak discharge depends, of course, on the magnitude and timing of the rainfall. For small rainfall events, development might have little significant impact. For larger events with more intense rainfall, however, we would expect greatly increased flow because of development, and unless we take action to mitigate, we might see flood damage downstream.

We could use a rainfall-runoff-routing model to get an idea of the magnitude of the increases in discharge and volume. The proper method of runoff computation is the subject of some differences of opinion. A popular combination for comparing pre- and postdevelopment runoff is the SCS curve number (CN) infiltration model and the SCS single-parameter UH model. Both are described in the SCS Technical Report 55, commonly known as TR-55 (USDA, 1986). The CN model estimates the volume of runoff and the UH model estimates the time distribution of that runoff. To use these models for comparison of pre- and postdevelopment runoff, we estimate the model parameters for existing catchment conditions and compute runoff from the storm. Then we alter the appropriate model parameters to reflect changes in impervious area, ground surfaces and channels, and re-run the model with the same rainfall data. By comparing the computed peaks and volumes, we can quantify the impacts of urbanization.

We could use the rainfall-runoff model with historical rainfall data, but analysis with historical storms doesn't quantify the risk of flooding because of the development unless we know something about the likelihood of occurrence of similar storms in the future. To quantify the risk, we could instead evaluate the impact of changes using design storms: storms of known probability. In using design storms, we commonly assume that "... if median or average values of all other parameters [of a rainfall-runoff-routing model] are used, the frequency of the derived flood should be approximately equal to the frequency of the design rainfall (Pilgrim and Cordery, 1975)."

In the United States, a commonly-considered design storm is the 100-year storm. This storm is one that has annual probability of exceedence of 0.01, or 1 chance in 100. According to the assumption, this storm will yield the 100-year runoff peak. Local, state and federal agencies have conflicting ideas about how such storms should be defined, but the Soil Conservation Service (SCS) design-storm method is typical. This method first defines the 24-hour 100-year total storm depth using the results of rainfall depth-duration-frequency studies. Then it distributes this total storm depth temporally with a pattern that represents common rainfall events in the geographic region.

How Can We Evaluate the Impact with Visual HEC-1?

To answer this question, we include here an illustration of the procedure. In this example, consider the runoff changes because of development in a 144-acre catchment in northern California. The catchment is undeveloped and is covered with brush, weeds and natural grasses. The soil is a sandy loam that falls in the SCS hydrologic soil group B. Proposed development includes converting the land to 1/4-acre residential lots, with paved streets with curbs and gutters. Tables in TR-55 provide the CN estimates for these conditions, as shown in Column 2 of Table 45. We used the method suggested in TR-55 to estimate the lag, the only parameter of the SCS UH model. The SCS suggests using lag equal to 60% of the time of concentration. We estimated the time of concentration for both pre- and postdevelopment as the sum of sheet-flow time, shallow-flow time and channel-flow time. For the existing condition, the time of concentration is 40 minutes, and for the postdevelopment condition, it is 30 minutes.

Condition	CN	UH lag (hours)
Predevelopment	60	0.40
Postdevelopment	75	0.30

Table 45: Estimated Model Parameters

The reduction is a consequence of reduction in the sheet-flow distances and of "smoothing" of the overland-flow surfaces. The latter is represented by a reduction in the overland-flow roughness parameter in the SCS procedure. The estimated UH lag values are shown in Column 3 of Table 45.

For the catchment in this example, we referred to NOAA Atlas 2 (U.S. Department of Commerce, 1973). There we found that the 100-year, 24-hour depth was estimated to be 5.83 inches. We then referred to TR-55 and discovered that for this site in northern California the appropriate storm pattern was the SCS Type I storm. With this information, we were able to define a 24-hour storm that we could use to evaluate the impact of the development.

To prepare the input and run HEC-1, we started Visual HEC-1 and dragged a runoff object onto the workspace, as shown in Figure 46. Then we double-clicked the runoff object to open the dialog boxes into which we entered the runoff model parameters and the design storm rainfall. Then we selected "Simulate" from the menu, ran HEC-1 and reviewed the output on-screen with the output browser.

Figure 46: Visual HEC-1 Workspace with a Single Runoff Object

We did this twice: first for the existing conditions and then for the proposed condition. Table 47 shows the results. The changes in land use increased the runoff peak by 104 cfs and the runoff volume by 16 acre-feet.

Condition	Peak (cfs)	Time of Peak from Beginning of Event (hours)	Runoff Volume (acre·ft)
Predeveloped	74	10.30	22
Postdeveloped	178	10.13	38

Table 47: Runoff from 100-year Design Storm

What Can We Do to Mitigate the Impacts?

The adverse impacts of increased runoff because of development can be mitigated by storing all or a portion of that increased runoff. That is, the water in excess of the predevelopment runoff can be impounded and then released in a manner that will prevent flood damage downstream of the development.

According to the WEF/ASCE Manual of Practice No. 77 (1992, pg. 439), the major types of stormwater impoundments are:

Retention

Storage provided in a facility without a positive outlet or with a specially regulated outlet, where all or a portion of the inflow is stored for a prolonged period. Infiltration basins are a common type of retention facility. Ponds that maintain water permanently, with freeboard provided for flood storage, are probably the most common type of retention facility.

Detention

The temporary storage of flood water that is usually released by a measured but uncontrolled outlet. Detention facilities typically flatten and spread the inflow hydrograph, lowering the peak. Structures that release storage over a period of 12 to 36 (or more) hours can also serve water quality purposes.

Here, we considered only detention ponds, as these tend to be more efficient and less of a maintenance problem. In particular, we considered the simple pond design shown in Figure 48. In this, water is impounded behind the embankment and is discharged through an outlet pipe. The flow is not controlled by gates or valves. If the water surface rises sufficiently high in the pond, water may flow over the emergency spillway. This spillway flow, like the outlet flow, is not controlled by gates or valves.

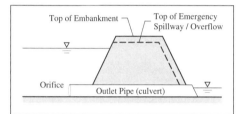

Figure 48: Simple Detention Pond Configuration

We can evaluate the impact of such a pond with a numerical model of the hydraulic performance of the pond. The modified Puls routing model is a common choice. This model discretizes time into equal intervals of duration Δt. It then solves recursively the following one-dimensional approximation of the continuity equation:

$$I_{AVG} - O_{AVG} = \frac{\Delta S}{\Delta t}$$

where I_{AVG} is the average inflow during the time interval
O_{AVG} is the average outflow during a time interval
ΔS is the rate of change of storage.

For convenience, this equation can be rewritten as:

$$\frac{I_{t-1} + I_t}{2} - \frac{O_{t-1} + O_t}{2} = \frac{S_t - S_{t-1}}{\Delta t}$$

(for t = 1, 2, 3, ...)

where I_{t-1} and I_t are the instantaneous inflow values at times t-1 and t, respectively
O_{t-1} and O_t are the instantaneous outflow values at times t-1 and t, respectively
S_{t-1} and S_t are the corresponding storage values

The inflow values I_{t-1} and I_t in this equation are known for all times t; these are the computed design-storm runoff hydrograph ordinates. The outflows and storages are to be determined.

Rearranging the equation to isolate the unknown values at time t yields:

$$\left(\frac{2S_t}{\Delta t} + O_t\right) = \left(I_{t-1} + I_t\right) + \left(\frac{2S_{t-1}}{\Delta t} - O_{t-1}\right)$$

The values of O_{t-1} and S_{t-1} are known. At time t = 0, they are the initial conditions, and for each subsequent time interval, they are the result of the solution of the equation for the previous interval. Thus, all terms on the right-hand side of the equation are known. But the left-hand side of the equation includes two unknowns: O_t and S_t. How can we solve this single equation with two unknowns? The answer is to develop a relationship of these unknowns.

The form of the storage-outflow relationship depends on the characteristics of the pond and its outlets. Given the characteristics, we can apply simple geometric and hydraulics concepts to develop the relationship. Figure 49 illustrates this. Figure 49(a) is the outlet-rating function. An uncontrolled outlet and a culvert perform identically, so this function can be derived from culvert-rating nomographs, equations or a computer program such as CulvertMaster. Figure 49(b) is the spillway-rating function. In the simplest case, this function can be developed with the weir equation. For more complex spillways, we could refer to publications of the U.S. Army Corps of Engineers (1965), the Soil Conservation Service (1985), and the Bureau of Reclamation (1977) for appropriate procedures. Figure 49(a) and Figure 49(b) are combined to yield Figure 49(c), a function that defines total outflow, given the water-surface elevation in the pond. Figure 49(d) is the pond surface area-water-surface elevation relationship. This can be developed from topographic maps or grading plans. Figure 49(e) is developed from this using solid-geometry principles, such as average-end-area computations or the conic method. Finally, for an arbitrarily selected elevation, the storage volume can be found from Figure 49(e) and the corresponding total flow can be found from Figure 49(c). This manipulation yields the desired storage-outflow relationship, as shown in Figure 49(f). With this, we can solve the

routing equation and compute O_t and S_t in the routing model.

For additional details on storage-routing computations, we recommend that you refer to a hydrology text, such as "Applied Hydrology" by Chow, Maidment and Mays (1988) or Hoggan's "Computer-Assisted Floodplain Hydrology & Hydraulics" (1989).

What are the Requirements for Detention Ponds?

Requirements for detention ponds vary by jurisdiction. Here are the primary design constraints imposed by a regulatory agency in northern California:

- The 100-year postdevelopment peak must not exceed the existing-condition peak.

- The pond must have an emergency spillway, but that spillway must not be used for the 100-year event or smaller events. That is, the spillway crest must be at or above the pond's design 100-year high-water line.

- The pond can be assumed empty at the beginning of the design event.

- The pond's maximum water depth for the 100-year event must be 6 feet or less. This reduces the risk of embankment failure and the hazard to the public.

- The outlet pipe for all ponds must be at least 24 inches in diameter. This reduces the risk of debris blockage.

Other constraints require such things as the addition of freeboard and the installation of trash racks. We certainly must satisfy these secondary constraints in our final design. Here, we are seeking the basic pond configuration, so we will postpone consideration of these requirements.

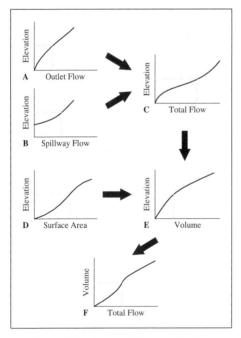

Figure 49: Derivation of Storage-Outflow Relationship

How Can We Find a Pond that Meets the Requirements?

The WEF/ASCE Manual of Practice No. 77 (1992, pp. 173-174) proposes the following steps for sizing a detention pond that will satisfy requirements such as those described:

A. Compute the predevelopment design-event hydrograph. This sets the "target" for sizing the pond.

B. Compute the postdevelopment design-event hydrograph. This represents the flow that is "controlled" to the target identified in Step A.

C. Select a pond site, and for that site, develop a relationship of water depth and storage. This is a function of basin geometry.

D. Select an outlet configuration and develop a relationship of depth and outflow for that configuration, recognizing that the relationship is a function of structure characteristics and flow conditions.

E. Select a routing interval (Δt) to ensure that 5 or 6 ordinates are described on the rising limb of the inflow hydrograph. One of the ordinates should be the inflow peak.

F. Construct the storage-outflow relationship by combining the relationship from Steps C and D.

G. Compute the outflow hydrograph.

H. Compare the maximum outflow rate with the target rate (determined in Step A).

I. Adjust the pond and/or outlet-structure configuration if the maximum outflow rate exceeds the target rate.

J. Repeat the procedure for alternative designs.

For our example, the predevelopment 100-year peak is 74 cfs, so this becomes the target flow for our detention design. The postdevelopment peak is 178 cfs, so our pond must reduce the peak by about 100 cfs.

For our example, we will use a pond of approximately constant surface area. The bottom of the pond will be at elevation 1214.00, but the pond area is to be determined. We will design a pond with the simple configuration shown in Figure 48, so we need to determine the number, size and characteristics of the outlet pipe, as well as the spillway elevation, width and hydraulic characteristics. Because of the complexity of this problem and the interaction of these design variables, we will seek these via a nominate-simulate-evaluate cycle.

How Do We Use Visual HEC-1 for the Nominate-Simulate-Evaluate Cycle?

Visual HEC-1 includes the modified Puls routing model, so we can use the program for the computations required for evaluation of alternative detention-pond designs. To do so, we can either:

• Develop the storage-outflow relationship by using the procedure illustrated in Figure 49 and specify this as input to HEC-1; or

• Provide the dimensions of the pond components, and HEC-1 will develop and manipulate the functions to derive the storage-outflow relationship.

The latter is particularly useful as we try different designs in our nominate-simulate-evaluate cycle.

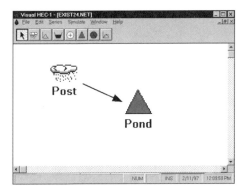

**Figure 50: Visual HEC-1 Workspace
with Detention Object**

Figure 50 shows the Visual HEC-1 workspace with a detention-pond object that we added by dragging it onto the workplace and connecting it to the runoff object.

Figure 51 shows the dialog box that appears when we double-click the detention object; it is here that we specify the dimensions of our pond. The grid on the left of the dialog in Figure 51 is where we will specify the area-elevation relationship for the pond. In our case, the area is approximately constant.

For our first iteration, we tried a pond with capacity equal to the difference in the

predevelopment and postdevelopment runoff volumes, or 16 acre-feet. If the maximum depth is to be 6 feet, that means that the pond should be 3 acres, more or less. Thus, if we want to try a 3-acre constant-surface-area pond, we can enter an area of 3.00 for elevation 1214.00 (the bottom of the pond) and an area of 3.00 for an arbitrarily large elevation, as shown.

For the low-level outlet, HEC-1 uses the orifice equation to establish a relationship of elevation and flow. (Note that this application of the orifice equation will introduce some error in our analysis if the flow is not inflow-controlled, pressure flow, but for preliminary sizing this simplifying assumption is acceptable.) To use this, we need only specify in the dialog box the size and the hydraulic characteristics of the outlet. In the example shown, we specified one 24-inch circular pipe; recall that this was the minimum acceptable size. If our configuration includes multiple pipes at the same elevation, we will specify here the total area of all pipes; all must be at the same elevation if we use this option of HEC-1. We specified the orifice coefficient at 0.60 and fixed the downstream centerline elevation of the pipe at elevation 1214.00

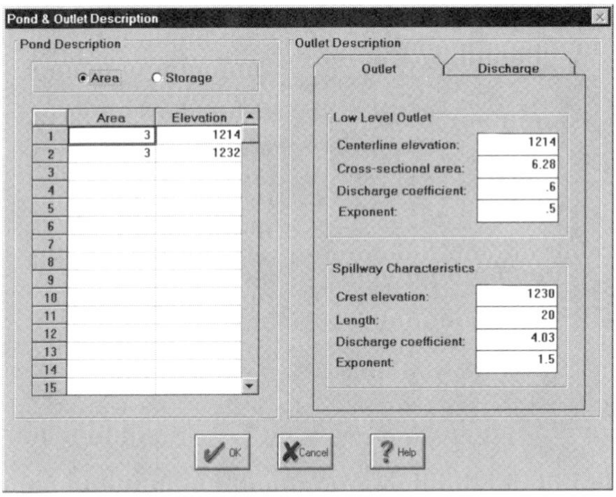

HEC-1 uses the weir equation to establish a relationship of spillway flow and depth. We must specify the crest elevation and the spillway characteristics. In the first iteration, we specified an arbitrarily large elevation to ensure that the spillway was not used. In subsequent iterations we lowered this crest elevation to a point just above the maximum stage reached during the 100-year event, checking to ensure that this stage was no greater than the maximum-allowable 6-foot depth.

Thus, to find an appropriate pond size with HEC-1 for our example,

Figure 51: Dialog Box for Describing Detention

Pond Area (acres)	Outlet Description	Computed Peak Outflow (cfs)	Computed Maximum Stage (ft)	Comments
3	1 @ 24"	31	1218.32	Meets all Criteria
3	2 @ 24"	54	1217.16	Meets all Criteria
3	3 @ 24"	73	1216.57	Meets all Criteria
2	1 @ 24"	36	1219.84	Meets all Criteria
2	2 @ 24"	62	1218.19	Meets all Criteria
2	3 @ 24"	82	1217.30	Peak Exceeds Target
1	1 @ 24"	47	1223.79	Stage Exceeds Allowable Maximum
1	2 @ 24"	77	1220.06	Close

Table 52: Summary of Our Iterations

we specify trial dimensions and characteristics in the appropriate dialog box, run HEC-1, and review the output to determine if the outflow target is met and if all design constraints are satisfied. If not, we alter one or more of these and reiterate.

Table 52 shows some of the iterations we made. We started with the values shown in Figure 51 and varied the design characteristics from there. Initially, we kept the pond area at 3 acres and used the minimum acceptable outlet: a 24-inch diameter pipe. This meets all requirements. We noted that if the outlet were larger, a greater outflow would still meet the criteria and the maximum stage would be less. A lower stage for the 100-year event would translate into a smaller embankment, and this, in turn, would save money. We tried two 24-inch outlets and found that this was acceptable, Then we tried three 24-inch outlets. This, too,

satisfied the outflow target. We noted in this case that the pond was filled to a depth of only 2.57 feet, so we next tried a pond with smaller area. We found that a 2-acre pond will satisfy the requirements if the outlet is configured properly. Finally, we tried a 1-acre pond. From the simulation with HEC-1, we learned that the peak target could be satisfied with this pond if the outlet is one 24-inch pipe. However, such an outlet restricts the flow so that the stage in the pond rises to 1223.79 feet. This corresponds to a depth of 9.79 feet, which exceeds the maximum allowable depth. To lower this peak stage, we increased the outlet size, using two 24-inch pipes. That design comes close to meeting all requirements: the peak discharge exceeds the target by only 3 cfs, and the maximum stage yields a depth of 6.06 feet. A little fine-tuning should yield an acceptable design.

Be Careful

We should note here that although drainage regulations commonly stipulate the event for which a structure is to be designed, you should review the performance of the structure with larger and smaller events. For example, suppose that you size a structure to reduce the postdevelopment peak because of a 100-year 24-hour event. As a component of the complete analysis, you should also determine downstream flows due to, for example, the 2-year and 10-year 24-hour events. Here's why:

- The runoff for even these frequent events will increase because of the development. Consequently, these postdevelopment peaks will be greater than the corresponding predevelopment peaks.

- A pond designed to "control" a rare, large event probably won't have much impact on smaller, frequent events. These frequent events might pass through the pond without any peak reduction.

- The frequent events, which are now larger because of development and uncontrolled by the pond, can now cause downstream damage. That is, the downstream flooding due to a smaller-than-design event may be greater, although detention is provided.

- In some cases, the detention may delay a flood peak so that it coincides with peak from another subcatchment downstream. In that case, the detention may actually increase downstream flooding for the design event.

You can use HEC-1 to evaluate these additional storms. With the Visual HEC-1 interface, you need only change the storm input. In fact, with the SCS design storm, you need only determine the total storm depth for the more-frequent event, change a single number and re-run the program.

Author: David Ford
Visual HEC-1 software used for example computations, screen captures, and miscellaneous charts and graphs

Key Concepts

- **Development typically increases peak runoff discharge from a catchment by covering surfaces that would otherwise allow infiltration and by decreasing the ground surface's natural ponding and resistance to flow.**

- **Ponds are typically designed with specific storm frequencies, such as a 100-year storm (a storm that only has a 1/100 chance of being exceeded in any given year.)**

- **Detention ponds store the water temporarily and slow the rate at which water leaves the site. Outlet structures are usually sized to "bottleneck" the water to control the rate at which it is discharged.**

- **Specific pond criteria should be obtained from the appropriate regulatory agency.**

- **Pond design can be accomplished through a Nominate-Simulate-Evaluate cycle, where a design is created, calculated with the Visual HEC-1 model, and then evaluated against the design criteria.**

- **Evaluate the pond behavior over a range of flow conditions. Just because the design is acceptable for a 100-year storm does not mean that it will work acceptably for a smaller or larger storm event.**

ESTIMATING DETENTION TIME

Achieve better stormwater runoff quality by utilizing detention time.

Deposition of sediments can be increased by detaining water in a pond for an extended period. Some reviewing agencies are starting to require engineers to consider detention time in an effort to increase stormwater quality.

This article reviews the general concept of detention time. Discussion is provided for some of the parameters that are vital to establishing effective criteria and computing detention time.

Using Detention for Stormwater Quality

High percentages of various pollutants are directly attached to particulates. Therefore, deposition of sediments within the pond will increase the quality of the pond outflow.

Note: Some pond sites might require an impervious liner to avoid groundwater contamination from polluted sediments. Sediments from these types of ponds might need to be cleaned out periodically and disposed of as hazardous waste.

Establishing the Criteria

Regardless of the complexity or precision of detention time calculations, the results will be meaningless if applied to ineffective criteria. It is important to establish detention time guidelines that are effective for the given pond shape and soil conditions.

Stokes Law

The basic premise of detention time is based on Stokes' law. In general, larger, denser particles settle to the bottom of a pond faster than smaller, less dense particles (given the same forward velocity and depth of the water). And conversely (for a given particle size and density), as the X velocity is decreased, a shorter distance in the X direction is required to drop the particle a given Y depth.

The detention time necessary to settle out a specified range of particle sizes is therefore a function of velocity, pond depth and the pond distance through which the water flows.

The "One-Size-Fits-All" Criteria

Given the same detention time, the actual trapping efficiency from pond to pond might vary widely, depending on such variables as pond shape, depth, length and the particle sizes deposited. It is therefore difficult to define a "blanket" rule of thumb or "critical" detention time that yields an adequate percentage of pollutant removal for all ponds.

Certain areas of the United States have various guidelines for detention times. Some of these criteria are based on such methods as minimum drain time or a single target detention time.

These types of criteria can be effective in significantly increasing stormwater quality, although the *actual* trapping efficiency can vary among different pond shapes and depths.

Spot Checking the Criteria

How can one check to see if a specific pond might require a *longer* detention time than that set by the local drainage criteria?

The following types of guidelines would need to be provided:

- The target range of particle sizes to remove
- The acceptable percentage of removal
- Settling velocities for given particle sizes

By using pond shape (width, length, maximum depth) and estimated settling velocities, an engineer can approximate the detention time required to remove the desired percentage of particulates. This detention time estimate can be compared against the standard criteria for that locale to see if a longer detention time might be appropriate for that pond.

Dead Storage Zones

An improperly designed pond may have zones of poor sediment trapping efficiency called "dead storage." These zones are typically due to short, wide ponds, or ponds where the main flow-current circumvents a significant portion of storage. Figure 53 demonstrates two different ponds with dead storage zones.

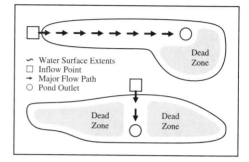

Figure 53: Pond Dead Storage Zones

Pond Shape

According to Stokes' law, the farther a settleable particle moves in the X direction (with constant X velocity), the farther it will drop in the Y direction. This relationship implies that ponds with large length-to-width ratios will settle out particles more efficiently than ponds with short length-to-width ratios.

As part of the water quality criteria, some areas in the United States require minimum standards with respect to length and width of the pond. Some of these are based on the ratio:

$$L:W = L / W_E$$

where: $L:W$ is the Effective Length-to-Width Ratio
L is the Length of the Pond
W_E is the Effective Width (which is the Surface Area / L)

Some agencies recommend minimum $L:W$ ratios *greater* than 2.0 to minimize dead storage zones and increase the sediment trap efficiency. If this criterion can't be met because of site constraints, baffles can be installed to "snake" the water through the pond, thereby increasing the effective flow length.

Haestad Methods, Inc. www.haestad.com

Estimating Detention Time

The required detention time only sets the criteria, or "goal." The engineer must still estimate the detention time for a given pond design to see if it meets the criteria.

This section discusses various ways to estimate the detention time for a pond. Because ponds exist in a wide variety of shapes, depths and sizes, most of these types of detention time methods are only approximations.

Minimum Drain Time

This method is a measure of the time it takes water to completely drain out, starting from a given water surface elevation in the pond. Because the pond's headwater depth and outflow vary over time, this calculation requires a time simulation (pond routing).

Water surface elevation is specified and an inflow hydrograph of zero flow is routed through the pond. The time it takes the pond to completely drain is the *minimum* drain time since zero inflow was used. For any inflows greater than zero, drain time would be longer.

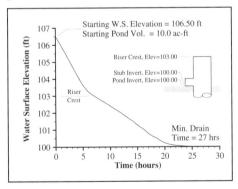

Figure 54: Min. Drain Time W.S. Elevation

Figure 54 displays the time vs. water surface elevation curve for a minimum drain time analysis. Note that the beginning water surface elevation is defined at time = 0 and that

detention time is defined where the water surface recedes to the invert of the pond.

The relationship of volume to drain time is very important when using minimum drain time for water quality criteria. Figure 54 shows the total drain time to be about 27 hours, but Figure 55 shows that 74% of the volume drains out in only six hours.

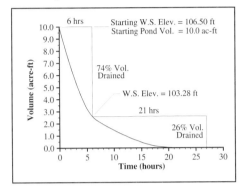

Figure 55: Time vs. Pond Volume

If the minimum drain time criteria are not specified based on percent-total volume vs. time, a pond could be designed to meet the minimum drain time for total volume but still not achieve the desired water quality effects.

For instance, the pond in Figure 55 would meet a total volume minimum drain time requirement of, say 24 hours, but detains only 26% of the total volume for longer than 6 hours. If, however, the minimum drain time criterion was that this pond detain 50% of the total volume for at least 24 hours, the pond would not meet the requirement.

First Flush Volume

The first flush is defined as the initial stage of a storm that "flushes" off pollutant particulates that have built up since the last storm. In the initial stages of a storm, pollutant quantity is high and stormwater volume is relatively low, resulting in higher pollutant concentrations than in later stages of the storm.

In order to increase water quality, some areas of the United States require *separate* "off-line" detention for treatment of the first flush volume. Water exits these types of ponds only through evaporation, infiltration or filtration drain systems.

Because the stormwater typically discharges through evaporation or filtration systems, the detention times may be long. It may be necessary to determine if enough volume has adequate time to drain or evaporate before the next significant event occurs. Minimum drain time (see previous page) can be used to estimate drain time for the first flush volume.

The first flush approximates the volume of concentrated pollutant water to detain until treated through evaporation or filtration. First flush volume can be approximated by:

$$V_{FF} = D_{FF} \cdot A_D$$

where: V_{FF} is the total volume of first flush water draining into the pond
D_{FF} is the depth of initial runoff containing a high percentage of pollutants
A_D is the runoff area contributing to the pond

First Flush Example:

Given:
A certain county requires a separate pond for treatment for a first flush runoff depth of half an inch. The total area draining to the pond is 24 acres.

Find:
The first flush volume draining to the pond.

Solution:
$V_{FF} = \frac{1}{2}" \cdot 24$ acres $= 12$ acre-in $= 1$ acre-ft

Peak to Peak

The time to peak for the pond outflow occurs some time after the inflow time to peak. As attenuation and storage in the pond increases, the peak inflow and outflow occur farther and

farther apart. Therefore, the longer the time between peak inflow and peak outflow, the more detention time.

Figure 56 shows how peak to peak time is measured. This method is probably the least used estimation of detention time since it doesn't take into account much about the overall relationship between inflow and outflow over time.

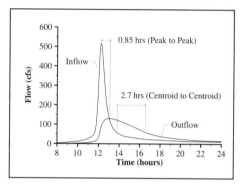

Figure 56: Various Detention Times

Centroid to Centroid

This estimate represents the average time it takes water coming into the pond to move through the pond and discharge. This method is more refined than the peak to peak method because it takes into account the way the volume is "spread" through the hydrographs.

This method measures the distance between the centroids of the inflow and outflow hydrographs. Figure 56 includes an example detention time between centroids. Note that the computed centroid is to the right of the time to peak because of long hydrograph receding limbs.

The centroid for each hydrograph is based on the volume slice within each hydrograph time step and the slice's distance from the origin. Basically, the centroid is calculated using moment arms about the Y-axis:

$$X_c = \frac{\sum\left[A_i \cdot X_i\right]}{\sum A_i}$$

where X_C is the centroid about the Y-axis,
               A_i are the individual areas, and
               X_i are the individual centroids

Approximating this for a hydrograph yields the following:

$$T_c = \frac{\sum\left[\left(q_i \cdot \Delta t_i\right) \cdot t_i\right]}{\sum\left[\left(q_i \cdot \Delta t_i\right)\right]}$$

where T_c is the centroid time on the
               hydrograph
               t_i are the ordinate times
               Δt_i are the time steps
               q_i are the flows at time t_i

And if the time step is uniform for the entire hydrograph, it drops out of the numerical relationship, yielding:

$$T_c = \frac{\sum\left[q_i \cdot t_i\right]}{\sum q_i}$$

Average Plug Flow

A plug flow model approximates the progression of water through a pond in terms of unmixed plugs of water. It is a first-in, first-out model over time.

Average plug flow approximates the time it takes the inflow volume *within each time step* to drain out of the pond. Figure 57 depicts the progression of a single volume plug. For each time step, the detention time is weighted by the inflow plug volume for that time step. The resulting weighted average approximates the time that a "typical" inflow volume plug is detained.

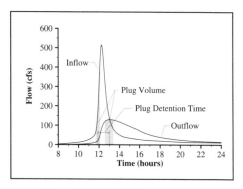

Figure 57: Plug Flow Detention Time

Author: Michael K. Glazner
PondPack 6.0 software used for example computations and miscellaneous graphs

Key Concepts

This article discussed the concept of increasing stormwater quality through detention time. Some of the highlights include:

• **General definition of detention time**

• **Establishing effective criteria**

• **Eliminating dead storage zone**

• **First flush volume**

• **Minimum drain time**

• **Estimating detention time using peak to peak, centroid to centroid, and plug flow**

COMMON HEC-2 & HEC-RAS WARNING MESSAGES: WHAT THEY REALLY MEAN

Legacy software programs like HEC-2 and HEC-RAS are often required for engineers and planners involved with site development. Without an understanding of the programs' idiosyncrasies, though, you just might be "up a creek."

Consider a community that participates in the Federal Emergency Management Association's National Flood Insurance Program. Chances are that FEMA maps have already been developed for all flood-prone areas within the community. Consequently, if one wishes to place a development adjacent to a stream that has been mapped, the engineer is responsible for ensuring that the development does not cause water surface elevations to increase. In fact, assurances should be made that a development situated next to a stream does not cause any adverse impact on the stream regardless of whether it has been mapped or not. The most common means of gauging the effect of development on water surface profiles is to use either the HEC-2 or HEC-RAS computer program.

HEC-2 is a venerable engineering model that has been in widespread use for over 30 years. HEC-RAS, on the other hand, is the new kid

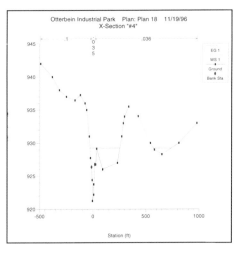

Figure 58: A Typical River cross-section

on the block, having been released during the summer of 1995. While HEC-2 is a DOS-based program, HEC-RAS operates in the Windows environment. However, HEC-RAS is more than just a Windows version of HEC-2. HEC-RAS has several hydraulic features that are not found in HEC-2, including improved bridge and culvert modeling, momentum-based junction analysis and multiple opening analysis. Be careful when using HEC-RAS to reproduce HEC-2 output, though. Unless told to do otherwise, the two models will compute cross-section conveyances differently.

Warnings and Errors

No matter if the HEC-2 or HEC-RAS application involves determining floodways, evaluating bridges or just finding the water surface elevation associated with a particular flood event, certain warning messages will almost certainly be present in your output files. In fact, experienced HEC-2 users will guarantee that the following messages almost always find their way into any water surface profiling project:

```
3685 20 TRIALS ATTEMPTED
WSEL,CWSEL

3693 PROBABLE MINIMUM
SPECIFIC ENERGY

3720 CRITICAL DEPTH ASSUMED

3302 WARNING: CONVEYANCE
CHANGE OUTSIDE OF ACCEPTABLE
RANGE,KRATIO = X.XX

3301 HV CHANGED MORE THAN
HVINS
```

Although the presence of these messages can be aggravating, they do not necessarily represent a numerical kiss of death. In fact, one may consider these messages to really be warnings and not errors since HEC-2 and HEC-RAS will successfully complete a simulation even though the messages are present. It is important, however, that the

modeler be aware of exactly what these messages mean. Armed with this knowledge, the modeler can then take appropriate steps to address these messages in proper fashion.

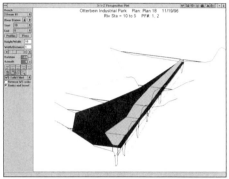

Figure 59: HEC-RAS X-Y-Z Perspective

20 Trials Attempted

HEC-2 and HEC-RAS compute water surface elevations by balancing the energy equation between two adjacent cross-sections. With the water surface elevation at one of the cross-sections known, the water surface elevation at the other cross-section is computed. Once the unknown water surface elevation has been found, the energy equation is balanced for another pair of cross-sections. However, this time the water level that was just found becomes the known water surface elevation. Computations proceed in this manner until the water surface elevation at all cross-sections has been computed.

The energy equation is solved in an iterative fashion until the computed water surface elevation agrees with an assumed water surface elevation within a given tolerance over a given number of iterations. In HEC-2, the tolerance is 0.01 feet (meters) and the maximum number of iterations is 20. HEC-RAS allows certain model tolerances to be changed, including the convergence tolerance criteria and the maximum number of iterations.

If the energy equation cannot balance within 20 iterations, HEC-2 will then set the computed water surface elevation equal to critical depth and water surface profile computations will proceed as before. But caution: What this means is that for the next pair of cross-sections, the known water surface elevation is equal to critical depth when the actual water level in the stream under the specified discharge may not be at critical depth. In other words, the model was simply unable to balance the energy equation.

HEC-RAS behaves a little differently. While the iterations are taking place for a given set of cross-sections, HEC-RAS stores the difference between the assumed and computed water surface elevations. If the energy equation cannot be balanced within the specified number of iterations (40 maximum for HEC-RAS), HEC-RAS checks the value of the smallest difference between assumed and computed water levels. If this value is less than a specified tolerance, HEC-RAS uses the computed water surface elevation associated with the smallest difference. If the smallest difference is larger than the specified tolerance, HEC-RAS sets the computed water surface elevation equal to critical depth just like HEC-2.

There are several reasons why the energy equation cannot be balanced within the maximum number of iterations. One reason is that the distance between cross-sections might be too large. More likely, however, the geometry of the cross-section where the water surface is being computed is very sensitive to changes in water level.

Conveyance Change Outside Acceptable Range

A very common warning message encountered in HEC-2 and HEC-RAS simulations is the message dealing with conveyance changes – more commonly known as the conveyance

ratio. Both programs compute friction losses in the reach between cross-sections by multiplying the reach length by an average friction slope. The friction slope at each cross-section is found using the conveyance of the section. Both programs offer four approaches to computing the average friction slope.

The conveyance is a measure of the carrying capacity of the stream. As the conveyance decreases, the friction slope increases. The friction slope can be thought of as the amount of energy needed to force a specified discharge through a cross-section having a given conveyance. Ideally, when computing the average friction slope the conveyance of each cross-section and hence the friction slope at each section should be roughly the same. If the conveyance of one cross-section is much lower than the conveyance of the adjacent section, the section with the lower conveyance (higher friction slope) can dominate the friction loss term. This may not accurately reflect the actual friction loss between cross-sections. HEC-2 and HEC-RAS will give the conveyance ratio warning when the ratio of conveyances between any two cross-sections is outside the range of 0.7 to 1.4.

The easiest, albeit most costly, way to address this message is to add cross-sections such that the hydraulic characteristics between any two adjacent cross-sections are fairly uniform. Recall that with surface profiling, a continuous water surface is being found using a series of discrete points, i.e. cross-sections. By increasing the number of cross-sections, one can more accurately model a true continuous profile. However, as the number of cross-sections is increased, the cost to obtain the cross-sectional geometry is also increased. Thus, the modeler must compromise by balancing the number of cross-sections with the cost of performing the analysis. Fortunately, the cross-section interpolation routine in HEC-RAS offers a low-cost means of gauging the effect of adding cross-sections.

Velocity Head Change More Than 0.5 Feet

As noted earlier, HEC-2 and HEC-RAS compute water surface elevations by balancing the energy equation between two adjacent cross-sections. As part of this process, the velocity head at each cross-section is computed. If the difference in velocity heads exceeds a specified value, a message to this effect is displayed. The allowable difference in velocity heads in HEC-2 and HEC-RAS is 0.5 feet.

There are several reasons why the difference in velocity heads is higher than allowed. Typically, this message will appear when there are rather significant changes in channel characteristics between two cross-sections – particularly the cross-sectional area. Again, recall that a continuous water surface profile is being modeled using a series of discrete points. The key in surface profiling is to select the location of cross-sections so that gradual changes in the hydraulic characteristics of a channel occur from cross-section to cross-section. It's also important that the channel characteristics associated with an individual cross-section be representative of the channel characteristics upstream and downstream of that cross-section.

Both models offer a means to test the effect of adding cross-sections by using interpolated cross-sections. HEC-2 inserts up to a maximum of three interpolated cross-sections between any two established sections based on the value of HVINS that is the variable in the 7th field of the J1 card. If the difference in velocity heads is greater than HVINS, an interpolated cross-section is inserted. A maximum of three interpolated cross-sections per violation of HVINS will be used by HEC-2. The geometry of the interpolated section is taken from the established cross-sections.

HEC-RAS, on the other hand, allows an unlimited number of interpolated cross-

sections to be included in the analysis. The number and location of the interpolated sections is based on a length that is specified by the modeler. By using interpolated cross-sections, the modeler can determine the number and location of any additional cross-sections that might need to be added. Interpolated cross-sections can also be used to help address problems with changes in conveyances and the inability of the energy equation to converge.

Author: Don Chase
HEC-2 and HEC-RAS software used for example computations, screen captures, and miscellaneous charts and graphs

Key Concepts

When using either the HEC-2 or HEC-RAS models, do not be surprised to see warning messages displayed in the program output. Common warning messages indicate:

• An inability to converge to a solution within the maximum number of iterations

• A conveyance ratio outside of the acceptable limits

• A change in velocity heads is greater than 0.5 feet

Usually, adding cross-sections to the analysis will help resolve the problems that produce these warning messages. However, simply adding cross-sections might not fix the problem. Therefore, it is important that the model user recognize why these messages are displayed so that appropriate corrective action can be taken.

REFERENCES

Brater, Ernest F. and Horace W. King, *Handbook of Hydraulics*
McGraw-Hill Book Company, New York. 1976

Bureau of Reclamation, *Design of Small Dams*
U.S. Department of the Interior, Washington, D.C. 1977

Chow, V.T, Maidment, D.R., and Mays, L.W.. *Applied Hydrology*
McGraw-Hill, New York, N.Y. 1988

Haan, Barfield, Hayes, "Design Hydrology and Sedimentology for Small Catchments"
Academic Press, Inc., 1994

Hoggan, Daniel, *Computer-Assisted Floodplain Hydrology & Hydraulics*
McGraw-Hill, New York, N.Y. 1989

Pilgrim, D.H., and Cordery, I., *"Rainfall Temporal Patterns for Design Floods"*
ASCE Journal of the Hydraulics Division, vol. 101, no. HY1, Jan. 1975, pp. 81-95.

U.S. Department of Agriculture, *"Earth Dams and Reservoirs."*
Technical Report 55, Soil Conservation Service, Springfield, VA. 1985

U.S. Department of Agriculture, *"Urban Hydrology for Small Watersheds."*
Technical Report 55, Soil Conservation Service, Springfield, VA. 1986

U.S. Army Corps of Engineers, *HEC-1: Flood Hydrograph Package User's Manual*,
Hydrologic Engineering Center, Davis, CA. 1990

U.S. Army Corps of Engineers, *"Hydraulic Design of Spillways."*
Engineering Manual 1110-2-1603. Office of Chief of Engineers, Washington, D.C. 1965

U.S. Department of Commerce,. *"Precipitation-Frequency Atlas of the Western United States,
Volume XI - California."*
NOAA Atlas 2. National Oceanic and Atmospheric Administration, Silver Spring, MD. 1973

U.S. Department of Transportation, Federal Highway Administration, "Hydrology"
Hydraulic Engineering Circular #19 (HEC-19), Washington, D.C., 1985

Water Environment Federation/American Society of Civil Engineers. *Design and Construction of
Urban Stormwater Management System.*
New York, N.Y. 1992

WATER DISTRIBUTION MODELING

Section Contents

Haestad Methods, Inc. www.haestad.com

WATER DISTRIBUTION MODELING FUNDAMENTALS

Hydraulic concepts are even more important for today's modeler than they were before anyone ever uttered the term "computer."

What exactly is a model? In the context of hydraulic analysis, a model is a mathematical representation of a system and is used to numerically describe the behavior of that system under various conditions. The model can be used to make predictions and recommendations about the system without the expense, difficulty and danger of manipulating the real-world system.

There are many models available in the fields of hydrology and hydraulics to predict such things as precipitation, stormwater runoff, pipe flow and flooding. For the remainder of this section, however, we will concentrate on models as they relate to a system that we all use every day when we take a shower, wash our laundry and rinse our dishes – a water distribution system.

Modeling Elements

There are many elements that are easily recognized in an actual water distribution system – various lengths of conduit, elbows, tees, service taps, elevated storage tanks, fire hydrants, and so forth. In order to make the

modeling process easier to learn and use, the elements in a distribution system can be separated into four basic categories:

- Boundary Node Elements

- Junction Node Elements

- Link Elements

- Composite Elements

Boundary Node Elements

A boundary node is a point in the system at which the hydraulic grade is defined. Boundaries represent the basic constraints that are used to determine the hydraulic condition of everything else in the system. Examples of boundary nodes include:

- **Reservoirs**. Reservoirs are "infinite" sources of water. For the purposes of analysis, reservoirs can accept or supply any inflow or outflow without changing the water surface elevation (such as a lake, river, etc.).

- **Tanks**. Tanks have a variable water

surface elevation, which may change over time because of water flowing into or out of the tank.

Junction Node Elements

A junction node is a specific point within the system where an event of interest occurs. The following are examples of points of interest that would be modeled as a junction node:

- **Pipe Intersections**. Wherever there is a change in pipe diameter, pipe roughness, or several pipes come together (such as at a tee, a wye, a cross, etc.) it should be modeled as a junction.

- **Points of Demand**. Large industrial consumers, clusters of residential buildings and fire hydrants can all be modeled as

junction nodes with specified water demands.

- **Critical Points in the System**. These are points of extreme high or low elevation or other locations where pressures are important for the analysis.

Link Elements

A link represents a consistent path that conveys water and controls the energy loss (or gain) from one node to another. In other words, a link is any length of pipe that has the same diameter, roughness characteristics and flowrate. Links include such items as the following:

- Miles of transmission piping with no active branches, tie-ins or services

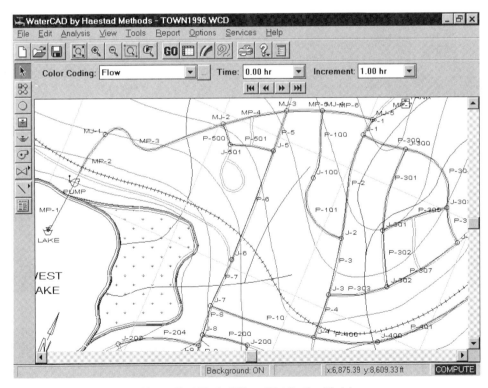

Figure 60: A Typical Water Distribution Model

- A stretch of piping between two intersections of a city-wide distribution grid (where the intersections are junction nodes)

- A "dead-end" pipe leading to a subdivision or a large industry

Composite Elements

Composite elements are not present in all models. Composites typically are thought of by the modeler as a node but may have numerical behavior that is more closely represented by a link or a combination of several elements. Examples of composite elements are:

- Pumps

- Regulating Valves

Pumps

A pump is usually thought of as having a distinct physical location, similar to a node. Mathematically, however, the behavior of a pump is more closely related to that of a link (both have characteristic curves that relate energy gain or loss exponentially to the flowrate).

As can be seen in Figure 61, both the head gain from a pump and the headloss through a pipe can be related exponentially to the flowrate:

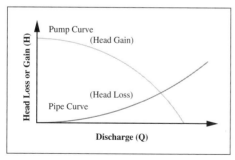

Figure 61: Pump Gains and Pipe Losses

$$H = A + B \cdot Q^C$$

where   H is the head gained or lost
Q is the flowrate
A, B and C are constants, dependent upon the characteristics of the specific pump or pipe

This shows the mathematical similarity between a pump and a pipe. But the concept of a pump as a link is a difficult one to grasp because a pump has physical characteristics more like those of a node – it has a specific location and has pipes connected to it.

So how can a user treat a pump as a node, while the internal model treats a pump like a link? Many programs rely on the user to model pumps as a link and accept the limitations that accompany that simplification.

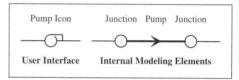

Figure 62: Composite Pump Element

In the WaterCAD computer model, a composite element is created in which the graphical pump symbol actually represents three elements: a junction node at the intake; a junction node at the discharge; and the connecting pump link. When the modeler double-clicks on the pump then, access is gained to not only the pump characteristics but also to the immediately upstream and downstream junctions.

Regulating Valves

A regulating valve, such as a pressure-regulating valve (PRV) or pressure-sustaining valve (PSV), also has a distinct physical location, similar to node elements. Because of the changing behavior of regulating valves (opening, closing and throttling to maintain the correct upstream or downstream conditions), a modeled valve also has changing characteristics.

When the PRV is wide open, it behaves as any pipe would, allowing fluid to pass through uninterrupted. When the PRV throttles, however, the behaviors of the upstream and downstream systems are different. The flow through the valve is based completely on the HGL setting of the valve and the downstream conditions. The flowrate must be the same just upstream from the valve, so the HGL of the upstream system can be determined – even though the HGL of the upstream system is independent of the valve setting.

This behavior is best explained as a composite of two separate nodes – a reservoir with a fixed hydraulic grade and a junction node with a fixed demand. The HGL of the reservoir is equal to the valve setting and is used to balance the flows in the downstream system. The demand at the junction node is then set equal to the flowrate leaving the reservoir and the upstream system can be balanced.

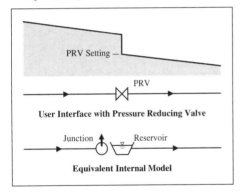

Figure 63: Throttled PRV Profile

Other valves operate similarly, but they might have slightly different configurations based on the upstream and downstream behavior of the valve. For example, a pressure-sustaining valve is intended to regulate the pressure upstream from the valve, not downstream like a PRV. When a PSV throttles, it can be modeled internally as a reservoir upstream and a junction downstream.

Solving a System

For any single pressure pipe, the calculations to determine headloss are straightforward and can quickly be calculated by hand, by spreadsheet or by using a software program such as FlowMaster. These problems are solved so easily because there is only one unknown (usually headloss or flowrate) and one equation.

For pipe networks, however, reaching a solution becomes more complicated. There might be multiple possible flow paths between any two points in the system, and the inclusion of pumps, regulating valves and other complications make a manual solution process impractical.

There are two basic concepts that govern the behavior of water distribution systems and are used to help determine a viable solution for the network: the conservation of mass and the conservation of energy.

Conservation of Mass (also known as Flow Continuity)

This principle is a simple one. All flows must be accounted for at every point in the system. This means that for any junction node (where there is no storage) the sum of flows coming in must be equal to the sum of the flows going out – including demands at the junction.

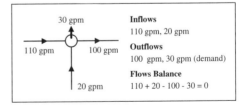

Figure 64: Conservation of Mass

The conservation of mass can also be applied to more than one element at a time. It can be applied to any subset of a system and could even be applied to the entire system. For example, look at the simple system shown in Figure 65:65.

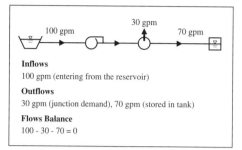

Inflows
100 gpm (entering from the reservoir)

Outflows
30 gpm (junction demand), 70 gpm (stored in tank)

Flows Balance
100 - 30 - 70 = 0

Figure 65: System-wide Conservation of Mass

The inclusion of a tank brings up an interesting point about the conservation of mass: The flow that goes into a tank actually remains in the system and is tracked as storage. For the intents and purposes of a flow balance at any given time, the tank could just as well be a reservoir. For analyses over time, however, the change in tank volume is also computed as

$$\Delta \forall = Q \cdot \Delta t$$

where $\Delta \forall$ is the change in storage
        Q is the flowrate into the tank
        Δt is the length of the time step

Conservation of Energy (also known as Headloss Continuity)

The conservation of energy is also simple conceptually – the head losses through the system must balance at each point. For pressure networks, this means that the head loss between any two points in the system must be the same regardless of what path is taken between the two points (and these head losses must be consistent with the appropriate friction loss method).

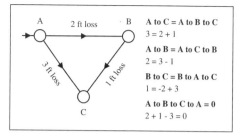

A to C = A to B to C
3 = 2 + 1

A to B = A to C to B
2 = 3 - 1

B to C = B to A to C
1 = -2 + 3

A to B to C to A = 0
2 + 1 - 3 = 0

Figure 66: Conservation of Energy

Although the equality can become more complicated with minor losses and controlling valves, the same basic principle can be applied to any path between two points. The sum of the headlosses around a loop (as shown above in path A-B-C-A) must equal zero – otherwise the hydraulic grade line would have an impossible discontinuity.

Calculating Hydraulic Grades

Every system must have at least one boundary node. Without a boundary node, there are no constraints on the hydraulic grade line (and there may not be a source of water for the system). Without any hydraulic grade constraint, headlosses can still be balanced but no values can be computed for the hydraulic grade at any location within the system, because there are an infinite number of possible solutions.

As an example, the system in Figure 67 shows a simple loop with a pump in it. There is no flow into or out of the system, so the only flow is around the loop in the direction the pump is pointing.

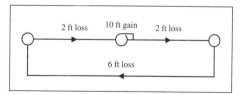

Figure 67: Loop and Pump System

Based on the pump and piping characteristics, the operating point of the pump and the losses for each pipe can be found. As we can see, the pump adds 10 feet of head, and then there are 2, 6, and 2 feet of loss through the piping back to the pump intake. So we know the relative grade at each location, but we have no way of telling if the hydraulic grade at the pump intake is 10 feet, 1,000 feet, or any other value. We need a boundary to help us "anchor" our hydraulic grade line.

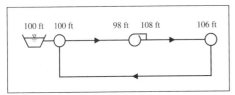

Figure 68: Loop & Pump System with Boundary

With the inclusion of the reservoir, as shown in Figure 68, we can now finish the computations and find the actual hydraulic grades throughout the system. If the reservoir grade is 100 feet, for example, then the grade at the pump intake will be 98 feet, the grade at the pump discharge is 108 feet, and so on.

Also note that the reservoir does not alter the flow characteristics of this network in any way. There are no demands in the system, so there is no flow through the pipe connecting to the boundary.

Hydraulic Analysis Type

There are two basic types of hydraulic analyses that are performed by most water distribution models:

- Steady-State Analysis
- Extended Period Analysis

Steady-State Analysis

Steady-state analyses determine the operating behavior of the system at a specific point in time, under unchanging (steady-state)

conditions. This type of analysis can be useful for determining short-term effects on the system because of fixed demand rates.

For this type of analysis, all boundary conditions are assumed to have constant hydraulic grade lines, including tanks. The network equations are then determined and solved, resulting in instantaneous values for flowrate, pressure, etc. These results may or may not be representative of the values of the system a few hours or even a few minutes later in time.

Extended Period Analysis

When the effects on the system over time are of importance, an extended period analysis is more appropriate than a steady-state simulation. This type of analysis allows the user to model tanks filling and draining, regulating valves opening and closing, and pressures and flowrates changing throughout the system in response to varying demand conditions and automatic control strategies formulated by the modeler.

An extended period analysis is essentially a series of steady-state solutions, with the results from each time step being used to predict the boundary conditions at the next calculation time. The rate at which a tank fills is used to predict the water surface elevation of the tank at the next time step, and pressure switch settings are checked to determine if pumps, valves or pipes should adjust their current status.

Small time steps result in instantaneous flows and pressures that are more representative of the continuous nature of an actual water distribution system, but there are also some drawbacks to using small time steps. The smaller the time step is, the more computations there are for any given duration. Depending on the size of the network and the number of time steps, this can create enough data to overwhelm any modeler. Normally the time step should be small enough that the boundary conditions do not change more than a few feet (or less, depending on the purpose and desired accuracy of the analysis).

An Example: Working with Steady-State and Extended Period Analysis

A common application of pressurized network modeling is for pumping analysis, since pumps are often designed with specific flow patterns in mind. Steady-state analyses can provide enough data to observe the system under numerous conditions, selecting various pumps and running the model to see how well the conditions are met.

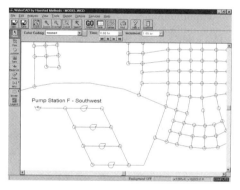

Figure 69: Pump Station

As an example, the pump station in Figure 69 is intended to provide flow to an urban area. Combined with storage (not pictured) the

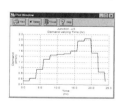

Figure 70: Daily Demand Graph

system should efficiently supply minimum daily demands, average daily demands and maximum daily demands – with emergency pumping for fire flow demands.

The pump station has several pumps, which may or may not be on depending on the

specific demand scenario. The modeler can easily create steady-state analyses, run the model and observe the pump operations for those specific conditions. With a steady-state model it is very easy to perform "cause-and-effect" analyses. Simply turn a pump on, close a pipe or adjust a demand, and then rerun the model.

This pump station can then be designed so that each pump has an appropriate flowrate and operating head. But how will the system actually behave? When will the pumps turn on and when will they turn off? How high or low does the storage get? And what if there is an emergency demand that lasts several hours? These questions can only be answered by working with extended period simulations.

In the real system, the pumps are intended to have pressure switches that turn the pumps on and off based on the level in the storage tank. The same thing is done in the model – controls are added to turn the pumps on and off based on levels in the tank.

Demands can also be added to represent emergency flows over a period of time. For example, a local fire department may have a regulation that an industrial site needs to provide 3,000 gpm for a four-hour duration to adequately battle a fire. This demand can be added easily and can even be shifted in time to simulate a fire at different times during the day.

Once the model has been appropriately set up and run for the extended period analysis, there is a lot of valuable information available in the results. These data can often be presented graphically, as shown below using features of the WaterCAD program.

Graphs can be created to display the total demand at any time, showing the combined effects of several different flow types at a single junction. This can be very helpful, especially when dealing with a junction node that has very different flow patterns, such as several industries with completely dissimilar usages.

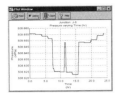

Figure 71: Nodal Pressure Graphed over a 24-Hour Period

Graphs can also be used to display results, such as showing the pressure or hydraulic grade line at a node over time, or showing tank levels or pump flowrates. By looking at these results, the modeler can almost instantly tell what is happening at any time during the analysis.

Choosing Between Steady-State and Extended Period Analysis

At first glance, it may appear that an extended period simulation is *always* more desirable than a steady-state analysis. Although an extended period analysis provides time variant results and shows pump operations and tank levels, there is a very significant drawback to extended period modeling: input data.

In addition to the information required for a steady-state analysis, an extended period model needs detailed information regarding water usage patterns, tank elevations and operational rules for pumps and regulating valves. If these data are not accurate, the model will become less and less realistic for each successive time step.

Author: Gregg Herrin
WaterCAD software used for example computations, screen captures, and miscellaneous charts and graphs

Key Concepts

• **A water distribution model is a mathematical representation of a physical system. A good model will be a fast, accurate tool for analyzing existing system behavior and predicting future behavior.**

• **As a hydraulic model, the network is defined using various types of nodes and links. The interface for the model may or may not reflect the internal mathematics.**

• **The Conservation of Mass states that for any node in the system, the sum of the inflows must equal the sum of the outflows.**

• **The Conservation of Energy states that a link's head loss or gain must agree with the hydraulic grade line of each end of the link.**

• **A steady-state analysis is a "snapshot" of the system at one point in time. It indicates only how the system behaves at that instant.**

• **An extended period analysis is used to model a system over a period of time. It can be used to predict tanks filling or draining, pumps turning on and off, and so forth.**

Skeletonizing a Water Distribution System Model

Achieve the desired level of precision
for an appropriate level of effort.

Attempting to include each individual service connection, gate valve and every other component of a large system in a model would be a huge undertaking. It would also result in tremendous amounts of data – enough data to make managing, using and trouble-shooting the model an overwhelming and error-prone task.

To produce reliable, accurate results without investing an astronomical amount of time and money requires the modeler to take a more practical approach to modeling the system. Skeletonization is this process of stripping a model down into a subset of the full system that only includes the most important components.

The process of skeletonization should not be confused with an omission of data. The portions of the system that are not modeled during the skeletonization process are not discarded – rather, their effects are simply added to the characteristics of a part of the system that is included in the model.

An Example of Skeletonization

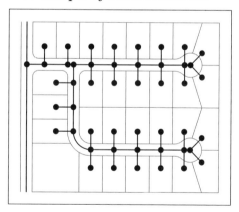

Figure 72: Almost No Skeletonization

A good example of skeletonization is shown in the following figures. The portion of the model shown is a subdivision, with water services at each building lot.

Figure 72 shows a model that has hardly been skeletonized at all. There are junctions at each service tap, with a pipe and junction at each household. There are also junctions at the main intersections, resulting in a total of almost fifty junctions (and there aren't even any fire hydrants shown in this hypothetical subdivision).

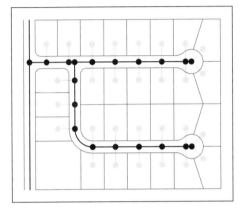

Figure 73: Some Skeletonization

Figure 73 shows the same subdivision but this time modeled with slightly more skeletonization. Instead of including each household, only the tie-ins and main intersections are included. This results in a junction count of less than twenty.

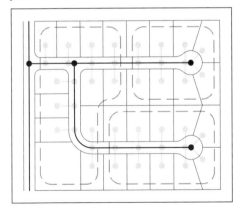

Figure 74: Even More Skeletonization

In Figure 74, the system has been skeletonized to just four junctions – modeling only the ends of the main piping and the major intersections. Attributing the demands to the junctions becomes a little trickier now because there isn't a junction modeled at each tap location. The demands for this model are attributed based on the nearest junction to the service (following the pipeline). The dashed boundary areas indicate the contributing services for each model junction. For example, the junction in the upper right will have a demand for eight houses, the lower right junction has demands for ten houses, etc.

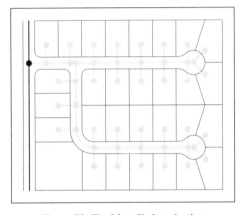

Figure 75: The Most Skeletonization

Figure 75 shows yet another extent of skeletonization – one single junction node. The piping within the entire subdivision has been removed, with all demands being attributed to the remaining junction.

There is even another level of skeletonization. It would be possible to not even include a junction node where the subdivision piping ties into the main line. The demands would simply be added to a nearby junction, where the effects of this subdivision may be combined with several other subdivisions that have not been included in detail. As this demonstrates, the extent of skeletonization is very much in the hands of the modeler.

Pipes of Unknown Importance

If the modeler is unsure what the effects may be of including or excluding specific pipes, there is a very simple method that can be used to find out exactly what the effects are on the system – run the model and see what happens.

A base skeleton can be created from the best judgment of the modeler, with pipes of questionable importance included. The model should be run over a range of conditions and the results noted. One or more questionable pipes can then be closed (preventing them from conveying water) and the model can be run again. If the modeler determines that the results from the two analyses are essentially the same, then the pipes apparently did not have a significant effect on the system and can be removed from the skeleton.

If it still cannot be determined whether or not the pipe has significance, it is usually better to leave the pipe in the model, especially considering the minimal costs of including and maintaining the additional data. With older, nongraphical interfaces it was often desirable to limit the number of pipes as much as possible in order to prevent becoming lost in the data. With the advanced computers and easy-to-use software tools of today, however, there are fewer reasons to exclude pipes from the model.

Skeletonization Guidelines

So what are the absolute criteria for determining whether a pipe should be included or not? There are none. Water distribution networks vary drastically from one system to another, and modeling judgment plays a large role in the creation of a solution. For a small-diameter system, such as household plumbing or a fire sprinkler system, small differences in estimated flowrate may have perceptible effects on the system headlosses. For a large city system, however, the effects of water demand from an entire subdivision may have

only as much impact as a night-light has on your electric bill.

The modeler must have a good understanding of what the model is intended for and what level of detail is appropriate for that intention. For small, looping systems there may be only a few pipes that are not included in the model. For much larger systems or dendritic systems, however, it may be desirable to include only pipes greater than a certain diameter (depending on the purpose of the model). Many modelers develop their own personal skeletonization guidelines.

Of course, any pipe sizing guidelines are only meant as general selection criteria, not as an absolute standards. If there are small-diameter pipes that complete loops or feed an important area within the system, these pipes should also be included in the model.

Author: Gregg Herrin
WaterCAD software used for example
computations, screen captures, and
miscellaneous charts and graphs

Key Concepts

• **For most models, the inclusion of each and every point of demand would require a ridiculous amount of time, for very little gain in accuracy.**

• **A skeleton can be created, ignoring inconsequential pipes and nodes, and focusing instead on major points of interest, such as large water demands and high points in the system.**

• **The amount of skeletonization depends on many factors, including the eventual purpose of the model and the effects that skeletonization has on the results.**

DETERMINING
JUNCTION DEMANDS

*Depending on available data, estimating junction
demands might be easy or might be difficult.
Either way, it has to be done – and done well.*

As a part of the skeletonization process, junction nodes are created in the model to represent points of interest. Once these junction nodes have been created, the modeler needs to determine the rate at which water is demanded from the system at these locations. If the demand estimates are not accurate, the flowrates in the pipes – and therefore the headlosses and hydraulic grades throughout the system – won't represent the system very well.

Demand Types

Land Use

Demands are often categorized according to land usage. This is typically done because land usage types are relatively simple to determine, especially when planning and zoning maps are available. A residential customer may use water at a rate that is similar to that of other residential customers but that differs dramatically from the usage for an industrial or commercial customer. By factoring the system

into common demand types, the model becomes more manageable. An added benefit is that the estimation and assignment of junction node demands can be done much faster.

Composite Demands

With composite demands, it's even easier and more reliable to keep track of demands in the system. A composite demand is one that is composed of more than one type of demand at a single junction.

For example, a particular junction node may have contributing demands from three land use types:

- Residential   180 gpm

- Industry ABC   120 gpm

- Industry XYZ   90 gpm

Without composite demands, the modeler would use a demand at this junction of 390 gallons per minute. Although the information could be tracked separately in spreadsheets or hand calculations, it is very difficult to keep the model in synch with external demand calculations, especially with no indication of where the information came from.

If the planning board doesn't approve the building of Industry ABC, the modeler must find and revise the demand calculation sheet and then update the model to reflect the changes. If the original calculations can't be found, the modeler has a serious problem. Even if the original calculations can be found, the process is still far more tedious than it needs to be.

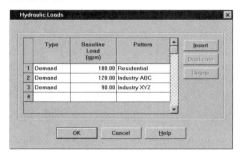

Figure 76: Composite Demand

With composites, it is much easier for the modeler to keep track of the demands and to view at a moment's notice exactly how the demand at any location is factored.

Figure 76 demonstrates how much clearer the demands can be managed by using composite demands. The modeler can immediately see how the demands are factored, so if Industry ABC is not approved, that portion of the demand can be deleted and the model can be reanalyzed in just a few seconds.

The modeler may also be able to spot errors more effectively by utilizing composite demands. For the demands shown above, for example, the digits may have inadvertently reversed as the demand was originally calculated, accidentally changing the 180 gpm demand into a demand of 810 gpm. It's a simple, fairly common typographical mistake, but it can have a substantial effect on the

calculations, bumping the total demand at this location from 390 gpm to 1020 gpm.

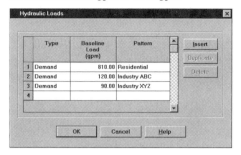

Figure 77: Typical Error

Without seeing the individual demands, the modeler may glance at the node and think that perhaps one of the industries has a high demand. A modeler who looks at the demand and sees that there are more than 800 gpm attributed to residential usage is more likely to notice, and the error can then be fixed.

Fire Flows

Another excellent use of composite demands is for analyzing the system under emergency conditions, such as fire flows. The fire flows may be demands that are placed on the system in addition to whatever demands would normally be there. By adding another demand to the composite from the example above, we obtain the following:

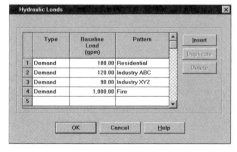

Figure 78: Fire Protection Demand

For this scenario, there is an additional 1,000 gpm demand at the junction to fight a fire. The

model can then be run under this scenario, and the results will show if the system maintains adequate pressures under these conditions. If the fire-fighting requirements change, the system can be promptly updated and reanalyzed – and the source of demand is perfectly clear.

Usage Patterns

The demands for every water distribution system change over time. From day to day, and even from minute to minute, the flows through the network may vary dramatically.

For the most part, these changes in flow are predictable. Resort areas may have increased flows during holidays and on weekends, as vacationers stream in. Industrial areas may have flow patterns that repeat precisely as manufacturing begins and ends each weekday. Residential areas may have increases in water usage during the summer months because of watering the lawn and recreational uses. All of these occurrences can be predicted by observing the system and generating patterns.

The key for a water distribution modeler is to find out what these patterns are and to predict what will happen when other demands are placed on the system – demands that are needed to provide for new development or for fire protection.

Daily (Diurnal) Patterns

Diurnal curves are patterns that relate to the changes in demand over the course of one day, reflecting times when people are using more or less water than average. Most patterns are based on a multiplication factor vs. time relationship, whereby a multiplication factor of 1 represents the base value (which is often the average demand value).

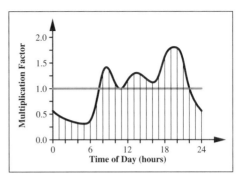

Figure 79: Example Diurnal Pattern

Looking at Figure 79 as an example diurnal pattern for a residential demand, we see that there is a peak in the diurnal curve in the morning as people take showers and prepare breakfast, another slight peak around noon, and a third peak in the evening as people arrive home from work and prepare dinner. Throughout the night, the pattern reflects the relative inactivity of the system, with very low flows compared to the average. (Note that this curve is conceptual and should not be misinterpreted as being representative of any specific network.)

There are two basic forms for representing a pattern: stepwise and continuous. A stepwise pattern is one that assumes a constant level of usage over a period of time and then jumps instantaneously to another level, where it remains steady again until the next jump. A continuous pattern is one for which several points in the pattern are known and sections in between are transitional, resulting in a smoother pattern.

Notice on the continuous pattern of Figure 79 that the value and slope at the start time and end times are the same – a continuity that should always occur for repetitious patterns. For stepwise patterns, a sharp drop or rise back to the initial value maintains the continuity at the beginning of the next cycle.

Haestad Methods, Inc. www.haestad.com

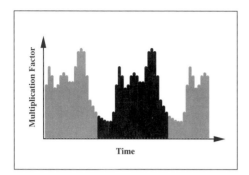

Figure 80: Repeating Pattern

Seasonal Variation

The changing seasons and weather conditions also have an effect on water usage. People are more likely to use water on hot summer days than during the winter months or when it rains.

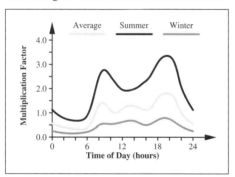

Figure 81: Seasonal Variation

Estimating Current Demands

As noted above, water usage rates and patterns vary greatly from system to system and are dependent on climate, culture and local industries. Every system is different, so the best source for estimating flow data comes directly from recorded data for the system. These are the only data that demonstrate exactly how and when consumers use water for the specific distribution network.

Obviously, having fingertip access to accurate, well-maintained records for any existing system is ideal, but that seldom (if ever) occurs. For this reason, the modeler must use judgment to estimate the demands based on less-than-complete data. These estimated demands can then be adjusted during the model calibration process.

Metered Information

System-wide average usage is often the easiest demand condition for which to obtain values. Most systems have metering equipment at tanks, pumps, wells and other key operational points. These data can be used to calculate the average, minimum and maximum daily consumption for the entire system. These data are often already being compiled into weekly, monthly, and/or annual reports by the water utility.

Although household meters are becoming more commonplace, residential usage is still often the biggest unknown when estimating consumption. Large industries are more likely to have metered usage and can therefore be accounted for more readily. The remaining usage can then be estimated, as the following example demonstrates.

Example Demand Calculation

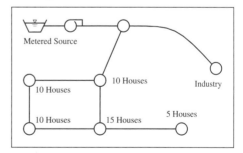

Figure 82: Example System

The simple system shown in Figure 82 supplies flow to one industry and fifty homes. The total demand for the system averages

---

24,000 gallons per day, with the industry accounting for 9,600 gallons per day (6.67 gpm average).

The remaining usage (14,400 gallons per day) is then divided evenly among the fifty residential customers, resulting in daily usage per home of 288 gallons (or 0.2 gallons per minute average for each house).

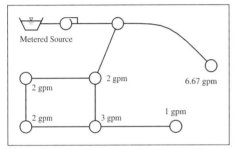

Figure 83: Applied Average Demands

Unaccounted-for Water

So far, all of the discussion has been based on all water being completely accounted for. In other words, every drop of water from the treatment plant can be followed through the system to an ultimate demand location. However, this is rarely the situation in a real-world distribution system.

If meters were placed on every connection to the system and then compared to a meter at the production source, as much as 20% of the water entering the system may be "lost." There are many places where water usage may not be metered within the system, including:

- Leakage at joints

- Breaks in the piping

- Hydrant and main flushing

- System cleaning and maintenance

- Unauthorized use

Note that some of the uses (such as flushing and other maintenance) are actually beneficial

to the system, while others (such as breaks and other leakage) are not beneficial and should be minimized or eliminated.

Unaccounted-for usage may not have a significant effect on a model. An unaccounted-for usage of 10% of the total average daily demand may only be 5% of the maximum daily demand, and perhaps only 2% of the peak hourly flow. At these higher demands, the relative effect of the "lost" flows is usually below the degree of accuracy in allocating the accountable demands.

Predicting Future Demands

Recorded data are fine for calibrating a system and observing the system under existing conditions, but what happens when you are interested in future demands, too? There are obviously no *recorded* data available for future demands, so the modeler has to predict the future demands based on judgment and extrapolation of existing data.

Population Growth

Population is usually a good indicator of water usage. Local and regional planning agencies are often an excellent source for obtaining population data, both for past population and expected future growth. There are some other factors, such as industrial growth and commercial development, that will also place burdens on a water distribution system and are not accounted for by population growth alone. Planning agencies may also have estimates for these types of future development, including areas that are specifically zoned for various land uses.

Usage Patterns

By comparing recorded population data with total system demand records, values for usage per capita can be computed. Any trends shown by these data can then be applied to estimates of future population, and the demands can be adjusted appropriately.

It is important to keep in mind that usage per capita is usually applied only to residential demands. The effects of large industrial users, for example, should be discounted when reviewing total demand records (as in the previous example demand calculation).

Conservation Efforts

People are becoming more and more conscious of how much waste is generated, including solid waste, electrical waste and even potable water waste. In an effort to reduce the amount of water wasted, many communities and public utilities offer incentives for people to conserve water by using such things as low-flow toilets and low-flow shower heads.

In areas where conservation efforts are established, the per capita usage of water may drop significantly. This means that there may actually be little or no increase in water usage even as the community continues to grow.

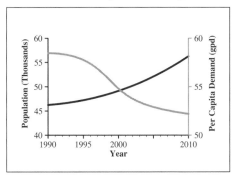

Figure 84: Example Population & Usage Trends

As a hydraulic modeler, these conservation efforts need to be evaluated realistically. The public will not always accept even the best-intended plans for conservation, and the overall trend still indicates a need for more potable water, not less.

Demand Scenarios

"Scenario" is a term that is widely used but a concept that is seldom implemented. For water distribution modeling, a scenario represents an alternative set of characteristics (usually system demands) under which the model is analyzed. The modeler may desire any number of different scenarios for a particular model, such as average day demands, maximum day demands, minimum day demands and emergency demand conditions.

Many models require that separate data files be created for each of these demand scenarios, with no continuity between the models. This is obviously an opportunity for error, since changes made to one file are not automatically reflected in the other files.

Figure 85: Demand Scenarios

With scenario management within a single model, it becomes much easier for the modeler to make changes to the system and observe the effects on any number of scenarios. This decreases the possibility of making errors, increases the productivity of the modeler, and eventually results in better data from which to draw conclusions and make recommendations.

Opportunities to Use Scenarios

There are an unlimited number of opportunities to use scenarios to become a more productive modeler. The primary usage is typically for modeling average daily demands, maximum daily demands, and so forth – often for several different planning years. The application of scenarios continues well past the basics, however, and includes such uses as the following:

- **Emergency Conditions**. Fire flows, pipe breaks, and so forth can all be modeled using scenarios, without any risk of losing data from a previous analysis.

- **Future Predictions**. As discussed previously, the future demands are often difficult to predict, especially trying to consider conservation efforts. By using scenarios to model several possible sets of future conditions, the modeler can check all of the most probable options. Scenarios allow more possibilities to be modeled in a short time, enabling the modeler to make better-educated decisions.

- **Uncertainty Analysis**. There may be relatively high unaccounted-for demands in the system, but the effects of these demands may not be known. With scenarios, the modeler can easily check the system with and without additional demands for the unaccounted flows. There may even be several scenarios dedicated to this to observe the effects of a wider range of unaccounted flows.

These are just a few examples of how demand scenarios can greatly enhance the usability of a model and the productivity of the modeler. After all, the entire purpose of a model is to adjust the model conditions and predict what the effect will be on the real system – and to do that quickly, accurately and as often as needed.

Author: Gregg Herrin
WaterCAD software used for example computations, screen captures, and miscellaneous charts and graphs

Key Concepts

- **Different water customers may use water in very different ways (an industrial site, for example, will have a completely different usage pattern than a private residence). An easy way to manage these differences is through the use of *demand types*.**

- **Demand types can be based on land use or other categorization. Demands may also be composites – several different types of demand at the same model node.**

- **Diurnal patterns represent the daily characteristics of a demand. Demands often have distinct weekly and yearly (seasonal) patterns, as well.**

- **Not all water that leaves the treatment plant can be accounted for at metered services. There may be leaks, unauthorized use or other unaccounted-for demands.**

- **Predicting future demands is a difficult but important part of determining the effectiveness of a distribution network. Just because a system functions well today does not mean that it will function well a year from now.**

- **Demand scenarios are a great way to manage all of the demand conditions that a system may encounter. Average daily demands, maximum daily demands, present demands, future demands, and an unlimited number of other conditions can all be modeled faster and more efficiently.**

Haestad Methods, Inc. www.haestad.com

ESTIMATING PIPE ROUGHNESSES

There are several popular methods of estimating pipe friction losses – but how accurate are your roughness coefficients?

There are many different methods of predicting friction losses in open channels and piping systems, including Manning's equation, Kutter's formula, Hazen-Williams method, and Darcy-Weisbach (Colebrook-White).

Of these, Manning's formula and Kutter's equation are most commonly used in free-surface gravity flow, such as a storm sewer, sanitary sewer or open channel. Hazen-Williams and Darcy-Weisbach, on the other hand, are by far the most popular for calculating losses in water distribution systems. For both of those, the pipe's resistance to flow is quantified through the use of a roughness coefficient that must be determined in order to compute a solution accurately.

Hazen-Williams

The Hazen-Williams formula is slightly different, depending on whether English units or S.I. (metric) units are being used.

$$H_f = \frac{3.02 \cdot L}{D^{1.16}} \left(\frac{V}{C} \right)^{1.85}$$

English Units

$$H_f = \frac{6.79 \cdot L}{D^{1.16}} \left(\frac{V}{C} \right)^{1.85}$$

System International (Metric) Units

where H_f is the headloss (ft, m)
         L is the pipe length (ft, m)
         D is the pipe diameter (ft, m)
         V is the velocity (ft/s, m/s)
         C is the roughness factor

Darcy-Weisbach

$$H_f = f \cdot \frac{L}{D} \frac{V^2}{2g}$$

where H_f is the headloss (ft, m)
         L is the pipe length (ft, m)
         D is the pipe diameter (ft, m)
        V is the velocity (ft/s, m/s)
        g is gravitational acceleration
        f is the roughness factor

There are two basic methods for predicting the value of a roughness coefficient:

- Field Measurement

- Estimation Based on Similar Piping

Field Measurement

Field-testing is the most accurate method of determining appropriate roughness coefficients for the piping within the distribution system. In order to obtain representative values of roughness, the section of piping selected for testing should meet the following criteria:

- A section of pipe should be chosen that has a known diameter, known length and a constant flowrate that is either known or controllable. To achieve a constant flowrate, it might be necessary to close valves to isolate the tested pipe.

- The pipe should be the same material and diameter throughout the length that is to be tested. Any change in the characteristics of the pipe would require the modeler to make assumptions about the relationship of the different types of piping, defeating the entire purpose of testing.

- The effect of test flowrates through the pipe should be sufficient to yield measurable headlosses. Typically, flowrates resulting in velocities of 4 to 8 feet per second are desired, across a pipe length of at least 1,000 feet.

- The ends of the pipe segment should be easily accessible to determine elevation and pressure values. Fire hydrants are often the most accessible point for testing and will be the assumed connection points for the remainder of this section.

Once the test locations have been selected, the field work can begin. The line to be tested should be isolated (leaving only a connection from the water source) and the equipment should be installed. Before flow is introduced into the pipeline, pressure readings should be taken at each hydrant to establish the static conditions.

There are two commonly used field measurement methods for determining the headlosses required to back-calculate the roughness coefficient for the tested pipe. Both of these methods require that the flowrate through the pipe be recorded, either from an in-line flow meter or by use of a pitot rod or other device. These two common methods are:

- Parallel Hose Test

- Pressure Gauge Test

Parallel Hose Test

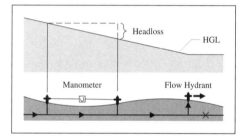

Figure 86: Parallel Hose Test Profile

A hose with a manometer in-line is connected to a hydrant at each end. Once the flowrate stabilizes, the manometer can be read to obtain the difference in hydraulic grade between the two hydrants. Pressures should also be measured directly at each hydrant, as a data check. This method is typically used for test lengths of one thousand to two thousand feet.

Pressure Gauge Test

This is a test where pressure gauges are used to record the pressure at each hydrant, rather than recording the pressure differential directly (as in the parallel hose test). These tests are typically performed on pipe lengths that are several thousand feet (too long for parallel hose testing).

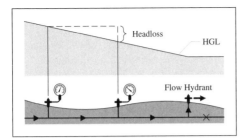

Figure 87: Pressure Gauge Test Profile

When using the pressure gauge test, elevation data are very important and should be determined to within about one-tenth of one foot (0.1 ft). For a parallel hose test, the elevation data are not as crucial because the differential head is recorded directly at a single location, so any elevation error would simply cancel out.

Example Determination of Roughness Coefficient

A section of piping is isolated and tubing is used to connect two static hydrants to a manometer. A third hydrant on the isolated line is opened and flows at a rate of 1,200 gpm. The manometer shows a hydraulic grade difference of 18 feet. If 1,460 feet of 10-inch diameter piping separate the two static hydrants, what is the Hazen-Williams roughness coefficient (C) for this piping?

First, we should rearrange the Hazen-Williams equation to solve for the roughness coefficient, C. The equation (in U.S. standard units) then becomes:

$$C = V \cdot \left(\frac{3.02 \cdot L}{D^{1.16} \cdot H_f} \right)^{0.54}$$

Our flow measurement needs to be converted into a velocity in order to use this equation. We can determine the velocity as follows:

$$V = \frac{Q}{A} = \frac{Q}{\pi \cdot D^2 / 4}$$

$$V = \frac{1200^{\text{gpm}} / 448.8^{\text{cfs}}/_{\text{gpm}}}{(\pi/4) \cdot (10^{\text{in}} / 12^{\text{in}}/_{\text{ft}})^2} = \frac{2.67^{\text{ft}^3}/_{\text{s}}}{0.55^{\text{ft}^2}} = 4.9^{\text{ft}}/_{\text{s}}$$

With the velocity in hand, we now have all of the input needed to determine the roughness coefficient. Solving the previous equation, we obtain:

$$C = 4.9 \cdot \left(\frac{3.02 \cdot 1460}{(10/12)^{1.16} \cdot 18} \right)^{0.54} = 107$$

The roughness of this section of piping can now be described by a Hazen-Williams C coefficient of 107, as long as the testing data are accurate. If the piping diameter isn't constant over the tested length, if the manometer is misread or if the flowrate is not correctly estimated, the results will not reflect the true condition of the piping.

Immediate, Accurate Results

A computer software program such as FlowMaster can have tremendous benefits for field-based roughness determination. As the previous computations show, there are several calculations involved in computing the roughness of a pipe based on field tests. These calculations include several unit conversions, and several nested exponents – both of which are easily overlooked during hand computations.

Figure 88: FlowMaster Determination of Hazen-Williams C-Coefficient of Roughness

Aside from the proven accuracy of FlowMaster, the program has several other advantages during field testing, such as:

- **Immediate Results**. Laptop computers have revolutionized the speed with which field data can be collected and analyzed. Data can be entered in the field as the test is being performed, and results are returned on the spot.

- **Error Spotting**. If there is a possible problem, such as a half-closed valve along the pipeline or poor elevation data, the results will instantly reflect the problem. The data can be re-checked and a solution can be found without delay.

- **Quick Recalculation**. If the data are in error, a recalculation is as simple as retyping one value. The program recalculates immediately, and the revised results are available at once.

- **Flexibility**. With mix-and-match units, there are no worries about incorrect conversion factors. FlowMaster also has the flexibility of working with several different friction methods, including both Hazen-Williams and Darcy-Weisbach. The ability to solve for any variable is also built in, so there is no danger of incorrectly rearranging an equation to solve for the needed characteristic.

- **Data Management**. Electronic worksheets allow the data to be stored in an intuitive, clutter-free manner. Rating tables and performance curves can also be generated easily, and worksheets can even have notes attached. Best of all – the information is legible.

Estimation Based on Similar Piping

Pipe roughnesses can also be estimated by comparing the material and age of the pipe with known characteristics from previous field research and laboratory experimentation. These empirical data reflect the conditions of similar pipes under similar conditions and should be used only as baseline estimations if no field data are available for the pipes being modeled.

Because these estimations are based on similar piping and not on the actual piping being modeled, the roughness coefficients determined by this method should be treated only as estimates and not as finalized values. The roughness coefficients will more than likely be adjusted somewhat during the calibration process.

Example Estimation of Roughness Coefficient

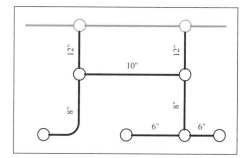

Figure 89: Untested Distribution Piping

The piping within a subdivision was installed approximately twenty years ago. It is located within a section of the distribution system that has not been tested for roughness (and is not scheduled to be tested in the near future).

Other areas of the same distribution system have been tested, though, with the age, diameter and roughness values as shown on the following chart. Notice that these data are all for the same pipe material – cast iron. It is *not* appropriate to estimate one material's roughness based on another material's field-tested values.

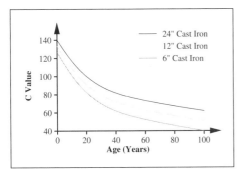

Figure 90: Recorded Cast Iron C-Coefficients

From this chart of recorded C-values, we can estimate the piping for this subdivision as follows:

- 6" diameter, 20 years old ≈ 83

- 12" diameter, 20 years old ≈ 91

- 24" diameter, 20 years old ≈ 100

Unfortunately, the recorded C-values do not include piping that is 8 inches or 10 inches in diameter. To obtain estimates for these diameters, we must interpolate between the data for 6-inch and 12-inch diameter piping. A linear interpolation will probably suffice (since this is only an approximation anyway), but for this example we will look at a curve fit to the three points we do know – for 6-inch, 12-inch and 24-inch diameters.

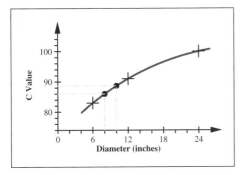

Figure 91: 25-Year-old Cast Iron Piping

From this chart, we can now pick off the two other coefficients we need. The 8-inch

diameter C-value can be estimated as 86 and the 10-inch C-value rounds to 89. This maps onto the subdivision as shown below.

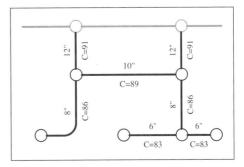

Figure 92: Estimated Roughnesses

Author: Gregg Herrin
WaterCAD and FlowMaster software used for example computations, screen captures, and miscellaneous charts and graphs

Key Concepts

- **Not all modelers take the time to ensure that their roughness estimates are accurate, but they should.**

- **Parallel hose tests use a manometer and hoses to directly read a head differential between two points along a pipeline. Pressure gauge tests allow the field technician to indirectly calculate the head differential – as long as the pressure gauges and elevation estimates are accurate.**

- **Roughness can also be estimated by comparing characteristics of the unknown pipe with previously tested pipes.**

- **Estimated pipe roughness values will probably be adjusted during calibration.**

CALIBRATING
THE MODEL

Gain confidence in your model by bringing it into agreement with recorded field conditions. Calibration is your best guarantee that the model represents the real system.

A pipe distribution network model is created from a combination of assumptions, modeling judgment and best guesses based on theoretical information. Obviously, this will not always generate results that agree perfectly with a non-theoretical, real-world system.

Calibration is the process of adjusting the characteristics of the water distribution model to better reflect the behavior of the real system. The process of calibration may include changing system demands, fine-tuning pipe roughnesses, altering pump operating characteristics, or any number of other things that affect the performance of the model.

The Significance of Calibration

The calibration process is a necessary and important operation for several reasons:

- **Confidence**. Calibration demonstrates the model's ability to reproduce existing conditions (thereby increasing the confidence in the model to predict future conditions).

- **Understanding**. Calibration also acts as an excellent introduction to the performance of the system, familiarizing the modeler with the changing behavior of the network caused by alterations to different components.

- **Trouble-shooting**. One area of calibration that is often overlooked is the ability to uncover missing information or misinformation about the system (such as incorrect pipe diameters or closed valves).

Collecting Field Data

Collecting field data is a large part of the calibration process, because without field data there is nothing to compare the model to. Data collection is usually separated into three categories:

- Physical Data

- Operational Data

- Reactive Data

Physical Data

This category includes verification of many system characteristics that are already known (or are thought to be known) and that are used to create the base model. Examples of these data are:

- Pipe roughness

- Pump head and discharge characteristics

- Regulating valve behavior

- Tank diameters, elevations, etc.

- Control switch settings

These are the data that set the physical guidelines for how the system will react to a variety of conditions. If these data are not represented accurately in the model, it will be impossible to achieve a high level of confidence.

Operational Data

Operational data are collected by continuously monitoring the system, usually for a week or two. Important areas to observe include:

- Flow and water surface elevation readings at the boundary locations (groundwater wells, treatment facilities, storage tanks, etc.)

- Flow and pressure readings at other key locations within the system (regulating valves, pump stations, etc.)

- Demands for high-consumption customers

The best locations to collect operational data can often be determined by observing the base model, even in a noncalibrated condition. The model can be used to predict which components of the system are the most sensitive to changes in the input data and are therefore the most crucial components to monitor.

Operational data, like physical data, are often collected during the development of the base model.

Reactive Data

Reactive data are gathered by stressing the system to simulate a fire flow, power outage or other extreme situation (provided this will not damage the system or adversely affect the system's customers). If a good base model has been developed from the physical and operational data, it can be used to predict the best field locations for performing reactive testing.

At the time of testing, boundary conditions, flowrates and pressures are recorded at various key locations throughout the system. These values may be recorded instantaneously for use in a steady-state calibration or they can be tracked over time for an extended-period calibration.

One of the most common places to monitor the system and control the testing process is through a fire hydrant. A hydrant is readily accessible, and flows and pressures can be measured with appropriate equipment. Fire flow testing requires at least two points of access to the distribution system:

- **Flow Hydrant**. This is the hydrant that is actually opened, discharging enough water to create measurable pressure drops in the system. If one open hydrant does not create a large enough drop, additional hydrants in the area can be opened to generate larger flows. Flow is typically measured using a pitot gauge – an instrument that is placed in the discharge stream.

- **Pressure Hydrant**. This hydrant is used to record static and residual pressures, since pressures at the flow hydrant fluctuate too much to obtain reliable readings. The pressure hydrant should be in the same vicinity as the flow hydrant to ensure that

the pressure drop is a direct result of the
opened hydrant.

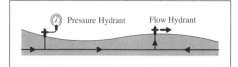

Figure 93: Hydrant Flow Test

The incentive behind reactive testing is to
observe the system under stressed conditions,
so a test time should be picked that is close to
the maximum demand that the system usually
sees. For most systems, this kind of testing
would be performed between 2 p.m. and 6 p.m.
during the hottest week of the summer.

Adjusting the Model

The most time consuming part of calibrating a
model is the process of making adjustments to
the model, in order to bring it into agreement
with the field results. If the base model has the
correct physical data, the adjustment process
consists primarily of making iterative changes
to pipe roughnesses and junction demands.

The guidelines for making adjustments are
fairly simple and relate directly to the
characteristics of a pipe. When the flow is
greater, or when there is more roughness, the
pipe will have more headloss. Based on this
relationship, actions can be taken to adjust the
model.

If the model hydraulic grades are *higher* than
field recorded values: This indicates that the
model is not predicting enough headloss. To
produce larger headlosses, roughen the pipes
or increase junction demands.

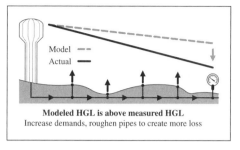

Modeled HGL is above measured HGL
Increase demands, roughen pipes to create more loss

Figure 94: Modeled HGL Too High

If the model hydraulic grades are *lower* than
field recorded values: This indicates that the
model is predicting too much headloss. To
produce smaller headlosses, smooth the pipes
or decrease junction demands.

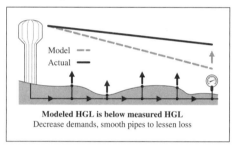

Modeled HGL is below measured HGL
Decrease demands, smooth pipes to lessen loss

Figure 95: Modeled HGL Too Low

Working with Data Comparisons

When comparisons are done between field
results and modeled results, there is no
mathematical reason to use pressures instead
of hydraulic grades, or vice versa. Because
pressure is just a converted representation of
the height of the hydraulic grade line above the
ground elevation, the two are essentially
equivalent for comparison purposes.

For model management, however, there are
several compelling arguments for working
with hydraulic grades rather than pressures:

- Hydraulic grades provide the modeler with
  a sense of the accuracy and reliability of
  the data. If one hydraulic grade value is
  drastically different from another, it should

immediately signal to the modeler that there might be erroneous data. Unless the ground is perfectly flat, pressure differences are not as easily noticed (because elevation changes alone can cause significant pressure changes).

- Hydraulic grades give an indication of the direction of flow (from higher grade to lower). This information can give the modeler further insight into the behavior of the network – insight that pressures do not provide.

- Working with hydraulic grades relaxes the modeler's need for precise elevations at the test locations. The elevation at which the test measurements are taken might not be the same as the elevations that is chosen for the modeled junction node. Dealing with pressures could result in a discrepancy, but hydraulic grade comparisons avoid this problem.

In essence, hydraulic grade or pressure comparisons will both lead to the same results, if all other factors are equal. Pressure comparisons make it much easier to overlook errors, however, and also make it much harder to track down inconsistencies between the field and the model. Working with hydraulic grades does not require any additional effort, but it can have large time-savings during calibration troubleshooting.

Troubleshooting

In an ideal world, measured field data and predicted model results would match perfectly every time. Unfortunately, the real world is far from perfect, and models can produce results that do not match field values. In fact, the model results may be so far away from the field measurements that simple errors in roughness and demand estimation cannot possibly account for the differences.

Differences between the field results and model results can obviously only come from two places: blunders in the input data (such as typographical errors or other mistakes in transcribing the data into the model); or incorrect field data (incorrect pipe diameters, closed valves or other inaccurate assumptions). Double-checking the input data for the model against the source of information is a straightforward way of ruling out typographical blunders, but tracking down incorrect field data can be much more difficult.

Using the Model to Locate Errors in the Field

Before rushing out in the field randomly searching for closed valves or other problems, try using the model to focus on where the uncertainty is originating. Try opening or closing a pipe, turning a pump on or off or adjusting a valve. This process only takes a few minutes and can save both time and money in the field by narrowing the scope of the troubleshooting effort.

Allowable Error?

Do not confuse the term "error" with the term "blunder." Blunders (human mistakes) are only one type of error and are not the *only* source of disagreement between field measurements and model results. Other errors can come from pressure gauge readings, estimated water demands and random variations in the system conditions.

Every model will have some level of error because of the imprecision in assumed conditions and available modeling techniques. It is unreasonable to expect a model to agree exactly with field data for every condition. The objective of creating a model is to generate a tool for predicting network behavior to a tolerable accuracy level, not to perfection.

Minimizing Errors
by Calibrating Extremes

Errors within the model will be exaggerated at higher flowrates. Differences at very low flowrates usually indicate errors in junction elevation or reservoir water surface levels. At higher flowrates, larger errors occur because pipe headloss is related exponentially to the flowrate (usually by a power of about 2).

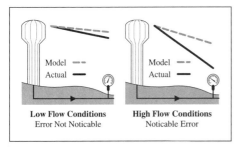

Model ---	Model ---
Actual —	Actual —
Low Flow Conditions	**High Flow Conditions**
Error Not Noticable	Noticable Error

Figure 96: Exaggerated Error at High Flowrate

These exaggerated headlosses demonstrate the importance of focusing on times when the network is under high demand stress, because these measurements provide larger headlosses for comparison against the model. A model that is calibrated for peak demand conditions can be used in confidence to model low demand conditions – a model that is calibrated for low demand conditions *cannot* be extended with as much confidence to model peak demand conditions.

Author: Gregg Herrin
WaterCAD software used for example
computations, screen captures, and
miscellaneous charts and graphs

Key Concepts

• Calibration is the process of adjusting the model until it agrees with the behavior of the real system.

• A model of an existing system should always be calibrated before it is used for any serious design or analysis purposes. An uncalibrated model may be able to give the modeler a "ballpark" feel for the behavior of the system, but the results should absolutely *not* be misinterpreted as being fully representative of the actual system.

• It is important to gather information regarding the system's physical data (pipe roughnesses, tank elevations, etc.), operational data (pressure switch settings, flow readings, etc.) and reactive data (fire flow tests).

• Many of the model characteristics can be adjusted during calibration, including pipe roughnesses and junction demands.

• The model can actually be used in some instances to track down problems, such as a closed pipe or throttled valve that the modeler did not originally know about.

• Calibrating to extreme conditions helps minimize errors in the model.

AN EXAMPLE CALIBRATION OF A WATER DISTRIBUTION SYSTEM MODEL

Sometimes the best way to learn is by example.
The modeling process is the same whether you're
working on a 25-pipe model or a 25,000-pipe model.

A base model has been developed for the water distribution system of the small, hillside community shown in Figure 96. The system collects water from a series of shallow wells in an elevated area northwest of the town center. These wells feed into the storage reservoir, where the water is chlorinated and fed by gravity through the pressurized distribution piping.

The majority of the water consumers are residential in nature – single-family homes and some condominiums. There are a few small shops and restaurants, a nursing facility and an elementary school. There is also one major industrial user in town.

The town would like a model developed to match field-observed hydraulic grades within ±10 feet (a pressure equivalent of about 4 psi) over a range of flow conditions.

Collecting Field Data

Physical Data

The physical data for this system are simple – there are no pumps because the entire system is gravity-fed from the hillside reservoir. There are also no regulating valves, and it has only the single reservoir as a water source. Pipe roughness tests were performed at several locations throughout the system during the creation of the base model, so no additional physical data are needed.

From the physical data gathered, the base model can be built by laying out the reservoir, junction nodes and the connecting pipes in accordance with some basic skeletonization guidelines:

- Include junctions at all major pipe intersections

- Include junctions at major dead-ends

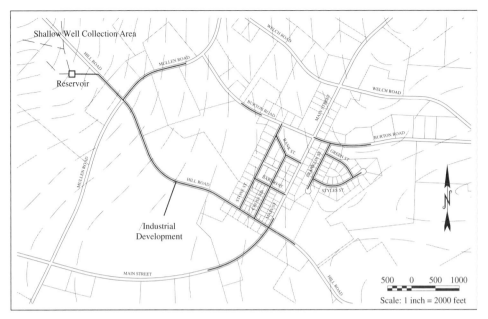

Figure 97: Basemap of an Example Water Distribution System

- Include junctions at the highest services

- Include a junction at the industry

Based on the collected data and the skeletonization criteria, the base model is created as shown in Figure 97 (using the WaterCAD software program).

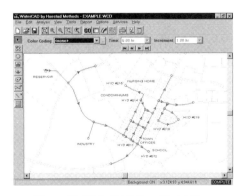

Figure 98: WaterCAD Base Model Plan

A DXF map of the town was imported from a popular drafting program into the background of WaterCAD's graphical editor for this system. This allows the modeler to lay the system out to scale, and the model nodes have the same coordinates as the background DXF.

In some cases, a CAD map may not be available, or there may be areas of the system that are disorderly and confusing when displayed to-scale (such as the complex piping of a pump station). For these occasions, the modeler can work with the entire system schematically (entering lengths for all pipes) or just override the scaled length of a few pipes and enter a user-defined value.

Operational Data

Operational records are also available, including metered water usage at the school, nursing home and industry. The town is in the process of installing meters at every service, so

---

Haestad Methods, Inc. www.haestad.com

there is also limited metered information available for residential usage.

Through analysis of this operational data, the usage rates and patterns are determined for each of the various customer types. Records for daily system water usage also provide enough information to determine the relationship between average daily conditions, minimum daily usage and maximum daily usage.

Reactive Data

FIRE FLOW TESTING SUMMARY REPORT			
Flow Hydrant(s)	# 212	# 215	# 218
Total Hydrant Flow (gpm)	860	620	410
Pressure Hydrant Location	# 211	# 214	# 219
Elevation (ft)	512	506	472
Static Pressure (psig)	80.0	81.9	95.5
Static HGL (ft)	696	695	693
Residual Pressure (psig)	52.9	57.8	28.3
Residual HGL (ft)	634	640	537
NOTES			
Total System Flow (gpm):	1030	804	563
Non-Hydrant Demand:	170	184	153

Figure 99: Flow Test Results

With the physical and operational data accounted for, the uncalibrated model is used to help select several field hydrants to test. Many hydrants are considered for testing and scenarios are created in the model to aid in the selection of test locations. Although isolated hydrants can be very useful for determining accuracy in a specific area, it is more desirable for a limited testing scope to choose test locations that demonstrate more widespread effects on the system. This results in head losses that are common to as many sub-systems as possible.

Based on the proximity of possible flow and static hydrants and preliminary analysis with the base model, three test locations are identified. During a hot afternoon in mid-August, the fire flow test measurements are recorded, as tabulated in Figure 99.

Throughout the testing, the reservoir's water level changed by only a few inches – well within the desired accuracy of the model.

Demand Scenarios

The total flowrate is different at the time of each test, meaning that there are actually six additional demand conditions that are needed for the accurate calibration of this model – scenarios for three tests, each with and without the additional hydrant flows.

These varying demand conditions (also called demand scenarios) can be difficult to maintain and track, and they are prone to errors if separate files are required for each scenario. To simplify the management and avoid duplicate files for the same basic system, WaterCAD's scenario manager is used.

Creating Scenarios

Figure 100: Static Scenario

For this example, we will focus on creating scenarios for the first fire-flow test. The process is identical for the other two tests.

The "Average Daily Demand" scenario has already been created, based on the operational data. This scenario is duplicated and given the name "Test #1 – Static".

The average daily residential customer uses a total of 290 gallons each day and the industry uses water at a constant rate of 15 gallons per minute. At the time of the first flow test, the total system demand breaks down as follows:

- 15 gpm Industrial Demand

- 155 gpm Residential Demand

- 860 gpm Fire Flow

The industrial demand is constant regardless of the daily conditions, and the fire flow is present only once the test had started. The only demands that need to be adjusted for "Test #1 – Static" are the residential demands (the total residential usage for the "Average Daily Demand" scenario is only 45 gpm).

A tabular view of the system is opened, displaying all of the network's junction nodes. The table is then filtered to display only the residential demands.

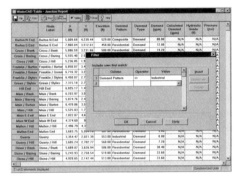

Figure 101: Junction Table

After filtering the table, a *global edit* can be performed. This applies a constant multiplicative, divisive, additive or subtractive value to all items in a table (excluding any elements that have been filtered out of the display). A global edit can also be used to change all items in a column to a specific value. In this case, a multiplier is applied to all the residential demands. The multiplier is equal to (155 gpm / 45 gpm), which is 3.5.

Figure 102: Global Edit

The "Test #1 – Static" scenario can now be run to check the values, which do indeed total 170 gallons per minute. This scenario can now be duplicated to create a "Test #1 – Flow" scenario to model the system with the additional flow from the hydrant test. By double clicking on the junction that represents hydrant #212, a fire flow demand of 860 gpm can be added (forming a composite demand at this junction).

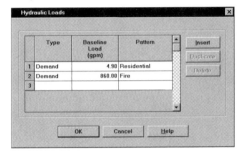

Figure 103: Composite Demand

By repeating this process for the other two test locations, all six calibration scenarios can be created in just a few minutes. Once created, the remarkable power of scenarios becomes evident. Scenarios allow the modeler to switch back and forth between system conditions effortlessly, recalculating the system and observing changes in a fraction of the time it would otherwise take to perform these iterations.

Beginning the Calibration Iterations

The first hydrant test (pressure hydrant #211, flow hydrant #212) is an excellent starting point for the calibration of this model. The path that the water will take to reach the hydrant location is direct from the reservoir, through the main distribution line that is common piping to almost all customers. If this major distribution piping is not calibrated well, the remainder of the network will not fall into agreement.

Haestad Methods, Inc. www.haestad.com

The calibration process typically involves adjusting junction demands, pipe roughnesses, pump curves, regulating valve settings, and so on, until the model results and field results agree within the desired accuracy. For this system, there are no pumps or regulating valves, and the flowrates have been metered. With these variables well accounted for, the calibration adjustments will focus on the pipe conditions.

Initial Test for Accuracy

The pipe roughnesses have been estimated during the collection of physical data. By running the model in its current form, we can tell how accurate our estimations are and whether the pipes need to have higher or lower roughness values to agree with field values. This iterative process of changing pipe roughnesses and recalculating continues until the system has been calibrated to match the field results.

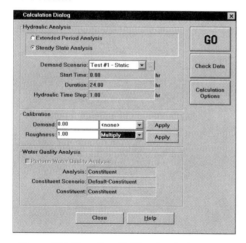

Figure 104: Run-time Calibration Adjustments

With the WaterCAD model, the iteration process is enhanced by the use of calculation-time demand and roughness factors. These enable the modeler to temporarily use a different roughness factor or demand factor, calculate the system, and observe the results –

without corrupting the original data. When it is time to accept the calibration factors, the modeler can simply click on the "Apply" button and the values are updated to a permanent status.

With no calibration factor applied to the pipe roughnesses, we can see how the modeled values compare with the observed values and how close the model is to being calibrated within the desired accuracy.

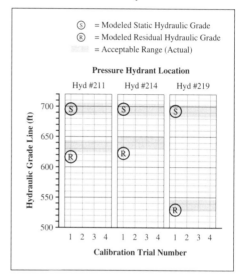

Figure 105: Uncalibrated Results

This first analysis shows that the modeled hydraulic grade lines are lower overall than the field data. This indicates too much headloss in the model, suggesting that the pipes have a slightly higher Hazen-Williams C-factor than originally estimated. The static hydraulic grade lines agree almost exactly with the field values, implying that the elevation data and flow estimates are reasonable.

Adjusting the Roughnesses

For the next trial, a multiplication factor of 1.2 is applied to the roughnesses. The model is recalculated, with the following results:

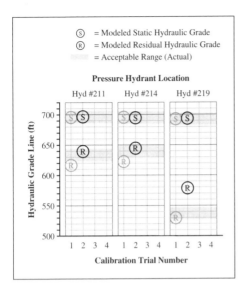

Figure 106: Calibration, 1.20 Roughness Factor

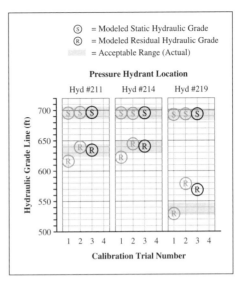

Figure 107: Calibration, 1.15 Roughness Factor

This calibration run seems to bring the results of the first two hydrant tests into alignment, but the third test seems to have skyrocketed away from the expected results. At this point, it is unclear if this is just a particularly sensitive part of the system or if there may be something amiss – such as a closed pipe or a partially closed valve. After another iteration it should be clearer.

The results after this second analysis show hydraulic grades above those measured in the field. A factor of 1.0 proved to be too low, and a factor of 1.2 is too high, so a calibration factor of 1.15 should be closer. The results are shown in Figure 107.

This calibration trial seems to have brought everything into almost exact agreement, except for the flow test at Hydrant #219. Another trial with a slightly different calibration factor might be able to bring the model within the desired accuracy in all cases, but the erratic behavior at this one location indicates that there may be a problem with the data that a roughness adjustment will not account for.

Troubleshooting

At this point, a crew could be sent into the field to search for closed valves or partially closed valves. This would be a rather random search, however, since the location of the problematic pipe could be almost anywhere in the majority of the central town.

In order to narrow the search, the model is used once again. The three flow tests are compared to see what the major paths of water flow are during each test. The second and third tests are discovered to have almost identical pipe flows along the major flow path for the third test. This indicates that the problem is most likely not in this section, since a problem in this area would have thrown off the results for the second test, also.

This leaves only a few pipes that may be the culprit. Because all of these pipes need to be at least partially open in order for *any* flow to get through, the problem is most likely a half-open valve somewhere along one of these three pipe sections.

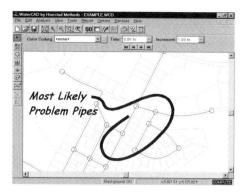

Figure 108: Trouble Spot

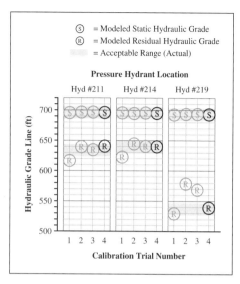

Figure 109: Final Calibration Check

The model is run with a large minor loss on the piping in this area, and the results begin to match more closely with field results. A crew can now be sent out to verify the problem and determine the exact location and a more detailed description of the problem.

Field verification indicates that there is a valve at the entrance to the subdivision that was only one-quarter to halfway open. This discovered change in field conditions now becomes a permanent change to the model. Although the valve is fully opened in the field, for calibration purposes the valve should be modeled as throttled (since that was the condition during testing). For later purposes, where other conditions are modeled, the minor loss can be removed.

Summary of Results

With the updated minor loss on the appropriate Franklin Street pipe segment, the results are checked once again for each of the flow test conditions.

With a roughness calibration factor of 1.15 and the minor loss in place on the correct pipe, the model agrees well with the field test results. This model could be adjusted even more to balance the negative and positive errors, but the intent of this calibration exercise was only to calibrate the system within ±10 feet.

The model has been brought to within the allowable tolerance, so any changes made at this point would simply be shifting the unknown errors. Although the numbers might agree more closely, this does not always indicate that the model is more accurate – if a pressure gauge was off by a few psi, the results might be shifted so that the results agree with erroneous data.

Author: Gregg Herrin
WaterCAD software used for example computations, screen captures, and miscellaneous charts and graphs

REFERENCES

Benedict, R. P., *Fundamentals of Pipe Flow*
John Wiley and Sons, Inc., New York. 1980

Brater, Ernest F. and Horace W. King, *Handbook of Hydraulics*
McGraw-Hill Book Company, New York. 1976

Cesario, A. Lee, *Modeling, Analysis, and Design of Water Distribution Systems*
American Water Works Association. 1985

Roberson, John A., Cassidy, John J. and Chaudhry, Hanif M., *Hydraulic Engineering*
Houghton Mifflin Company, Boston, 1988

Roberson, John A. and Crowe, Clayton T., *Engineering Fluid Mechanics (4th Edition)*
Houghton Mifflin Company, Boston. 1990

Rossman, Lewis A. et al., *"Numerical Methods for Modeling Water Quality in Distribution
    Systems: A Comparison"*
Journal of Water Resources Planning and Management, ASCE, New York. 1996

Rossman, Lewis A., *EPANet User's Manual (AWWA Workshop Edition)*,
Risk Reduction Engineering Laboratory, Office of Research and Development,USEPA,
    Cincinnati, Ohio. 1993

Sanks, Robert L., *Pumping Station Design*,
Butterworth-Heinemann, Inc, Stoneham, Massachusetts. 1989.

Walski, Thomas M., *Water System Modeling Using CYBERNET®*
Haestad Methods, Incorporated. 1993

ENGINEERING

BUSINESS

AND COMPUTERS

Section Contents

ITERATIVE DESIGN

Computer modeling software programs offer a faster, easier and less expensive way to handle projects.

How often have you been frustrated because you've had to redo tedious calculations that you spent hours, days or even weeks computing? A seemingly minor revision to a site plan often results in the need for many time-consuming recalculations. Unfortunately, it's happened to me a lot – and I'm sure it's happened to you, as well.

Let's face it: Hand calculations aren't cost-effective. Why not spend more time making engineering decisions and less time performing redundant calculations?

Thanks to computer modeling, you can focus on engineering decisions instead of redundant calculations.

Thanks to computer modeling, you can. After all, that *is* what your professional career is all about, isn't it? One of the great advantages of computer modeling is the speed with which changes and recalculations can be performed. All you need to do is spend a few minutes making revisions to your input data and within seconds the new results are recalculated for you. Never again will you have to spend late nights or weekends performing repetitive calculations.

"Measure Twice; Cut Once"

Under deadline pressures and time constraints, many civil engineers feel like they don't have the time to "measure twice," as the old adage says. The most obvious design may become final even though it might not be the best one. Who has time to try more than one or two options before performing the final computations?

The project design fees are based on the engineer's time to complete each task – time that runs out fast if design iterations are being done by hand. The most efficient and cost-effective solution may never be realized if the hourglass runs out too soon.

...Or Measure More than Twice

Computer models are the perfect solution for analyzing several design concepts or making revisions to an existing design. Various scenarios can be computed with just a few clicks of a mouse button – far fewer numbers than you'd have to push on a calculator or spreadsheet. And there's also less opportunity to make a mistake when all you have to change is one number (as opposed to reentering all the data for the entire site).

Advanced Methodology

Simplifying assumptions has always been a part of the engineering profession – and for good reason. Projects don't typically have the funding to support hours and hours of additional calculation time. Any savings in pipe costs or construction costs would be completely eaten by the engineer's computation costs.

Computer models make the most out of available calculation technology by implementing solutions that would be far too tedious (and error-prone) to perform by hand. As long as a computer is doing the calculations, what difference will a more accurate calculation make? Even with a few extra seconds here and there for complex solutions, it's still better than spending a few hours doing it by hand.

> *Computer models make the most out of available technology by implementing solutions that would be far too tedious (and error-prone) to perform by hand.*

Gradually Varied Flow

Gradually varied flow is an excellent example of how computers can save you time while improving the solution technique. Most engineers, if given a calculator and a pipe to design, would assume normal depth in the pipe (the water surface parallels the constructed slope). Of course, most pipes change in depth from one end to the other, so normal depth may not be an accurate assumption.

Both StormCAD and CulvertMaster use gradually varied flow methods to compute flow characteristics within a pipe (if the pipe has free-surface flow conditions; otherwise pressure calculations are performed). Starting from a given boundary control depth (usually the hydraulic grade at the downstream junction), the depth will gradually increase or decrease along the length of the pipe.

When the calculations are finished, the gradually varied flow model will give you a profile along each pipe and much more accurate values for the hydraulic grade line throughout the system.

Design Checking

Potential input errors are easy to locate with computer models because all of the input data and built-in validation is available at a moment's notice just by clicking with the mouse. There are no loose calculation sheets, no incomplete assumption statements, and the paper documentation can be easily reprinted if it's misplaced.

Perhaps best of all, though, is the amount of confidence that a good computer model can give you. Worries about misreading a nomograph or punching the wrong calculator button can be laid to rest.

> *Worries about misreading a nomograph or punching the wrong calculator button can be laid to rest.*

The Struggle: English Units vs. the Metric System

Associated Pennsylvania Constructors quoted a bridge engineer as saying, "If the good Lord wanted us to operate in metric, He would have had ten disciples rather than twelve." An alarming number of people agree with this philosophy, even though you could easily respond with: "If we were meant to use English units, we would all have twelve fingers and toes rather than ten."

In a time when calculators and computers were not as prevalent and mental tricks offered increased speed to performing calculations, the English unit system made a great deal of sense. After all, 12 is evenly divisible by 1, 2, 3, 6 and 12.

> *The only thing the U.S. and metric systems have in common are units of time – and times are changing.*

As Americans, we have all grown up understanding gallons, feet, miles and inches. The only thing we have in common with the metric system are units of time.

And times are changing.

More and more projects are requiring metric results, and even England doesn't use the English system anymore. The world has gone metric, and the United States is behind.

Even for metric projects, many engineers are wasting their time performing designs in English units and then converting everything to metric units later. With the back-and-forth unit switching, mistakes can easily go unnoticed – especially given the poor "feel" that most U.S. engineers have for metric units.

Computer software can help here, too. Software such as FlowMaster, StormCAD, WaterCAD and CulvertMaster all make use of a technology called FlexUnits, which was developed by Haestad Methods.

FlexUnits allows the engineer to work with almost any units, English or metric. You can even mix and match your units – displaying metric units alongside English units if you want to. In tabular forms, you can have side-by-side columns for the same variable in different units. It's the perfect way to gain that "feel" for the numbers you might not have yet.

Job Security?

Don't misinterpret computer models as being a ticket to Easy Street – or a replacement for civil engineers. There's still a lot of care that needs to be taken with any model, and anything that doesn't agree with your engineering judgment should be investigated and verified. But overall, you'll find that computer models are a great way to become more productive at the work you do.

Just imagine some of the example scenarios that follow – unless they've already come true for you.

STORM SEWER EXAMPLE

The Scenario

It's 3 p.m. and you're swamped with work. A client calls because the contractor's schedule has changed and they need the final plans for a parking lot by the end of the day.

You have some preliminary designs, and it is a small site – but a lot has changed since those pipes were sized – and you've got to put your stamp and signature on those plans. You can do the calculations by hand as you usually would or you can try out the computer model you recently purchased (but convinced yourself that you don't have time to learn).

Hand Calculations

Do some quick measuring and grab the contributing areas for the first catch basin. For the farthest catch basin upstream, the areas (A) and their associated rational coefficients (C) are found and then combined to obtain a total C·A value for the inlet.

With a quick calculation for the time of concentration, you can compute the total flow into this catch basin. The duration of the storm at this point is the same as the time of concentration to the inlet, so the intensity (I) of the storm is read from the I-D-F curves and the flow into the catch basin is computed as

Q = C·I·A

Now take a guess at the pipe slope based on the site layout. Use your judgment and try to

get it close because you don't have time to perform more iterations than you absolutely have to.

Dig out those old, blurry nomograph photocopies. Sure, they're based on normal depth calculations and probably a few other simplified (over-simplified?) assumptions, but you've got them in your hands and you know how to use them.

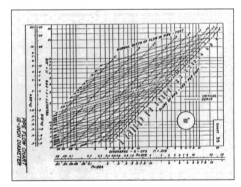

Figure 110: Sample Nomograph from HDS-3

- Choose a pipe size and flip to the corresponding nomograph.

- Find the appropriate graph axis for the Manning's n value you've selected.

- Draw a vertical line at the flowrate (which you calculated as the inlet discharge).

- Check to see where the vertical line intersects with the pipe-slope line. If it doesn't intersect, you'll have to choose a larger pipe or a different slope.

- If the flow line and slope line do intersect, the addition of a horizontal line across to the other axis allows you to pick off a value for the pipe velocity. Of course, if that's too high or too low, you'll still have to choose a different pipe or a different slope and then start over.

So you've got the flowrate for the first catch basin and the size of the first pipe. Now you just have to do the same thing for all the other pipes in the system – and hope you don't violate your cover constraints when you finally check your invert elevations.

And by the way, if something does change anywhere in the system, you'll have to recalculate from that point on. A change in discharge will obviously make a difference, but so will a change in pipe size (since that changes the depth of flow in the pipe – which changes the pipe velocity, which changes the pipe travel time, which changes the duration of the storm event, which changes the intensity of the storm, which changes the flowrate, and so on).

So, what are you left with after spending over 45 minutes working on a simple three-pipe system? A table of pipe sizes and inverts that you hope is correct.

LINE SEGMENT	TIME TO INLET (MIN)	TIME IN PIPE (MIN)	ACCUMULATED TIME (MIN)	At ENTERING INLET	SUM OF At IN SYSTEM	RAINFALL INTENSITY (IN/HR)	FLOW IN SYSTEM (CFS)	PIPE SIZE	LENGTH OF PIPE (FT)	SLOPE (FT/FT)	FULL CAPACITY (CFS)	VELOCITY (FT/S)	MANNINGS "N"
CB1-CB3	6	0.1	6.0	0.52	0.52	5.6	2.9	12"	30	0.01	3.2	4.5	0.015
CB2-CB3	5	0.3	5.0	0.77	0.77	6.2	4.8	15"	80	0.011	6.2	5.2	0.015
CB3-OUT	5	0.1	6.1	0.46	1.75	5.6	9.8	15"	56	0.0044	12	11	0.015

Figure 111: Hand Calculations

And you're not done yet. This information must still be checked and then drafted onto the construction plans for the client to review. Meanwhile, the clock is ticking.

Computer Model Solution (Using StormCAD)

Modeling a storm sewer system doesn't have to be so tedious. The following figures show how simple it is to model the same system using the StormCAD computer model.

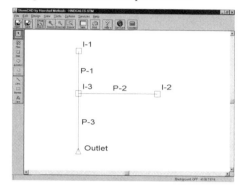

Figure 112: Storm-sewer Layout (Using the StormCAD Software Program)

The system is drawn on-screen by simply dragging and dropping the elements into place with the mouse. If you have an existing CAD drawing, chances are that you can even import a DXF site map into the background to use as a reference, so all your pipes will be to scale. If not, that's fine too – just enter the lengths of the pipes yourself.

It might not seem like much at first, but having just a schematic of the system makes a world of difference, even for this small three-pipe network. There's no need to worry about forgetting to account for upstream contributing flows because the model has the system connectivity built in. And if anything changes, just drag and drop the inlets to their new locations or connect the pipes differently – it's quick, it's effortless, and it's accurate.

Entering the rest of the data is easy, too:

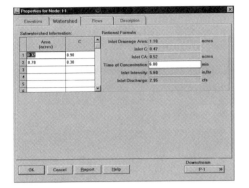

Figure 113: Watershed Input Data

- Double-click on an inlet to open the editor dialog.

- Type the area(s), runoff coefficient(s), time of concentration and inlet rim elevation in the appropriate spaces in the dialog box.

- Double-click on a pipe to open the editor dialog.

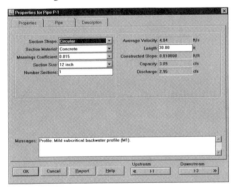

Figure 114: Pipe Input Data

- Select a pipe shape and material from the pull-down list on the dialog. An appropriate Manning's n value will be automatically selected for you or you can override the default value by simply typing in an alternate Manning's n if desired.

Repeat these steps for each inlet and pipe (or you can open a tabular view of the system and edit multiple elements at once).

Once all the data are ready, just select "Automatic Design" from the menus. You can also change your design constraints (velocity, slope and cover) to ensure that your design will meet all of your criteria. If this is your first time using StormCAD, you will also need to input an I-D-F equation or curve, which you can recall for any future projects.

A design will be automatically generated for you for the pipe sizes (and for the pipe inverts, if you desire). If there is anything that you don't like about the design, just change it and select "Calculate" from the menus. This will recompute the network hydraulics and let you know if your changes will meet your constraints or not.

For this example network, the whole process takes about 20 minutes – and that including all data entry, entering I-D-F curves, and checking several different storm frequencies.

In another few minutes, a profile can be automatically generated, annotation text can be moved and rescaled, and the whole thing can be printed out directly or output to a DXF file for import back into your favorite drafting program.

Even the tabular output can be fully customized to match whatever format you need. Rearrange the rows and columns by dragging and dropping them, sort the table in ascending or descending order for any variable, and even filter the list to provide a view of only a portion of the system.

Figure 115: Calculated Output

OPEN CHANNEL FLOW EXAMPLE

Some engineers develop spreadsheets to perform frequently requested calculations, such as simple open channel flow hydraulics. The equations in the spreadsheets are set up to solve for one unknown variable, such as the flow rate, which is great if you have a channel of a known size and slope and need to determine its capacity. But if you know the flow rate and want to determine the depth of flow for channels of various widths, side slopes or longitudinal slopes, the spreadsheet can become more of a burden than a helpful tool.

Once again, computer models can come to the rescue.

FlowMaster, for example, allows you the flexibility to solve for any variable in commonly used open channel and pressure flow discharge equations. This provides you, the design engineer, with the ability to quickly model several alternatives, regardless of how difficult or tedious the computations would be otherwise.

When your computations are done – or even during preliminary design stages – you can also make use of such output features as rating tables or performance curves to give you a better concept of the hydraulic behavior.

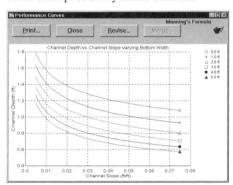

Figure 117: FlowMaster Performance Curves

Figure 116: FlowMaster Worksheet

CULVERT ANALYSIS EXAMPLE

A routine culvert calculation can take quite a while, especially when tailwater effects are considered and there's a possibility of roadway overtopping. A sensible engineer will steer clear of hand calculations for this type of analysis, but which software program should be used – HY-8 or CulvertMaster?

The Scenario

An experienced hydraulic engineer was given a set of common site characteristics, including multiple culvert barrels and a roadway profile. She was asked to perform the same analysis twice, once using the HY-8 program and once using the CulvertMaster program (the engineer had no previous experience with either model).

HY-8 Computer Model

After struggling for almost 25 minutes, the engineer finally came up with the results as shown in Figure 118.

```
      PERFORMANCE CURVE FOR CULVERT NO. 1 - 2( 3.00 ft by  3.00 ft) RCP

DIS-     HEAD-   INLET   OUTLET
CHARGE   WATER  CONTROL CONTROL FLOW  NORMAL CRIT. OUTLET  TW   OUTLET  TW
FLOW     ELEV.   DEPTH   DEPTH  TYPE   DEPTH  DEPTH DEPTH  DEPTH  VEL.   VEL.
(cfs)    (ft)    (ft)    (ft)   <F4>   (ft)   (ft)  (ft)   (ft)  (fps)  (fps)

   0    55.00    0.00   -0.80  0-NF   0.00   0.00  0.00   0.00   0.00   0.00
  15    56.16    1.10    1.16  1-S2n  0.57   0.86  0.60   0.84   7.42   1.84
  30    56.74    1.74    1.44  1-S2n  0.81   1.23  0.88   1.25   8.64   2.29
  45    57.24    2.24    1.75  1-S2n  1.01   1.52  1.10   1.56   9.51   2.59
  60    57.68    2.68    2.09  1-S2n  1.18   1.77  1.31   1.83  10.09   2.82
  75    58.12    3.12    2.48  1-S2n  1.33   1.99  1.51   2.06  10.56   3.01
  90    58.61    3.61    2.93  1-S2n  1.48   2.18  1.68   2.27  11.07   3.17
 105    59.17    4.17    3.42  5-S2n  1.63   2.35  1.84   2.46  11.54   3.31
 118    59.72    4.72    3.87  5-S2n  1.75   2.47  1.98   2.63  11.92   3.43
 121    59.89    4.89    4.07  5-S2n  1.78   2.50  2.02   2.80  12.02   3.55
 123    59.99    4.99    4.29  5-S2n  1.80   2.51  2.03   2.95  12.12   3.65

INVERT ELEVATIONS--> Inlet -   55.00 ft
FILE: SOURCEBK     Outlet -   54.20 ft     Crest -    0.00 ft
                                           Throat -   0.00 ft

        PRESS: <KEY> TO CONTINUE          <W> FOR PROFILE TABLE
               <P> TO PLOT                <I> FOR IMPROVED INLET TABLE
1-Help  2       3        4-Type 5-End  6     7      8      9-DOS   10
```

Figure 118: HY-8 Output Rating Table

CulvertMaster Computer Model

Although the engineer admitted that HY-8 was better than performing the calculations by hand, she was unimpressed by HY-8's lack of flexibility and she found it difficult to use.

She then installed the CulvertMaster program, and within ten minutes she had completed the on-line tutorials, entered all of the site data, completed the analysis, and even generated a full report. She also created and printed a rating table and a performance curve for the system (as shown in Figure 119).

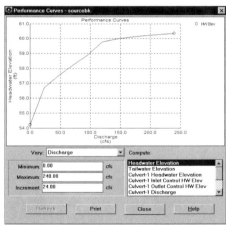

Figure 119: CulvertMaster Output Rating Curve

WHAT TO LOOK FOR
IN A MODEL

A computer model can be a great tool for use in modeling hydraulic systems. But how can you tell which models are going to suit your needs the best?

Here are a few general guidelines for selecting software – guidelines that can actually be applied to all types of software:

Ease of Learning, Ease of Using

Make sure it's easy to learn and easy to use. Frustration is a terrible thing, and if software isn't easy to learn the first time, imagine how frustrated you'll be if you have to relearn it every time you use it.

Software that is intuitive and easy to use immediately shows a great deal about the architecture of the software and the attitude of the developers. It shows an understanding of the way the user works, and it shows a commitment to making the user more productive (and happier). On the other hand, software that is difficult to learn and confusing to use indicates that the software developer may have had other priorities – like meeting a marketing deadline or making immediate profits.

Support

Look for quality technical support – and make sure that the support is either free of charge or reasonably priced. This shows a commitment to the product and to the user. If the company is reluctant to support their product, it's probably because they know about some problems with the software, and they don't really want to talk to you when you find those problems.

Look ahead

Perhaps most importantly, look to the future. What direction is the company taking and what is its attitude toward product development? If the software firm is too busy thinking about quarterly revenues to pay attention to long-term product architecture and a lifelong relationship with you, it might not be there for you in the future – and that leaves you to start over again from scratch.

Author: Maureen Farmer
StormCAD, FlowMaster, and CulvertMaster software used for example computations, screen captures, and miscellaneous charts and graphs

BOOT CAMP AT THE RITZ

For many engineers, the formal education process ends when they receive a diploma and walk out of the college gymnasium. The young graduate has a solid background in the fundamentals of engineering and is ready to take on the responsibilities of the most difficult design projects.

Well...almost.

There is, of course, a great deal of knowledge that comes from experience and from the teachings of mentors within the civil engineering community. Engineering is still an apprenticed profession in many respects, and the learning process continues throughout an engineer's career.

Why, then, are so many engineers hesitant to attend workshops, learn better approaches to solving problems and become more efficient at their job?

"I've had bad experiences."

We've had bad experiences, too.

We have all attended at least one of those "never-again" workshops. You know the type – the lights flicker and occasionally dim, the temperature varies randomly from 5°F to 105°F, and the lecturer might as well be a hypnotist, judging by the number of zombies in the audience. With all the distractions, it's no wonder there isn't a lot of listening, interacting or learning going on.

But we hope you won't allow a bad experience in the past to prejudice you against all workshops, any more than a bad experience with a car dealer should prevent you from buying a new car. (Of course, you might want to shop around for a better dealer.)

Building a Better Workshop

Our engineers and technicians regularly attend workshops on subjects ranging from computer network administration to object oriented programming to water quality analysis. Some of the workshops are better than others, and we pay close attention to what makes that difference. Our workshops are designed with our positive experiences in mind, and the result is a much more learning-oriented environment. Here's why our workshops make the difference:

- The locations are comfortable and safe. You shouldn't have distractions when you're trying to focus on difficult engineering concepts.

- Our instructors are experienced and personable. They are chosen not only for their knowledge but also for their friendly attitude and their ability to teach.

- We provide top-of-the-line computers, so every participant gets hands-on experience with the software.

- Interaction is encouraged. Although the workshop presentations have some structure (after all, you don't want chaos) questions and discussion are always encouraged. Even after hours, the instructors and Haestad Methods' engineers are available and willing to speak with participants.

It's no wonder the attendees consistently rate our workshops 9s and 10s.

"Money is tight."

It's a phrase that is heard quite frequently in any organization that deals with budgets, including engineering firms and municipalities. How are you going to scrape together money to attend an upcoming workshop?

Let's take a hard look at the financial side of attending a workshop. You'll see it's really not so tough.

Workshop Costs

Haestad Methods' workshops typically cost about $800 for two or three days, and the associated software is available at significantly reduced prices.

What does this entrance fee pay for? A top-notch instructor, state-of-the-art computers for every one or two attendees and access to a comfortable, quiet conference room, to name just a few things.

Travel Costs

If you are located within one hundred or two hundred miles of one of our workshops, you will probably end up driving to the location. For a round-trip journey, at a cost of 35 cents per mile, that's a cost of $70 to $140.

If you are farther away from the workshop, you might find it more reasonable to fly. For between $200 and $500 round-trip, you can go just about anywhere in the continental United States. With discounts – which we arrange – these costs might be even lower (see the table on the following page for recent airline fares).

No wonder the attendees consistently rate our workshops 9s and 10s.

Hotel Costs

Dreading those $180-per-night hotel bills? No need to worry. Yes, we select locations that are nice. But a part of our service for our guests is that we also negotiate lower hotel costs – usually well under $100 per night.

"I can't afford time away from productive work right now."

Time away from work is often the main reason engineers hesitate to attend a workshop. If they're going to be away from the office for two or three days, it had better be worth it.

It is.

One major reason why you'll come away from our workshops with a better knowledge and understanding of the subject matter is simple –

Workshop Location:	Atlanta	Austin	Cincinnati	Nashville	Orlando	Philadelphia	Salt Lake City	San Francisco	Toronto
Atlanta	-	80	140	80	40	60	190	170	200
Boston	140	150	130	100	90	90	170	170	80
Charlotte	60	130	130	90	170	160	210	230	200
Chicago	60	150	120	60	90	160	150	180	150
Cincinnati	130	120	-	160	100	140	190	130	190
Dallas	90	-	100	150	90	130	230	170	220
Denver	120	120	150	120	130	220	60	80	260
Detroit	130	150	120	80	180	150	160	120	160
Houston	110	-	110	90	120	260	180	210	230
Kansas City	70	100	90	40	70	100	120	90	90
Los Angeles	150	120	150	170	150	270	60	50	230
Memphis	-	150	120	80	200	90	180	230	210
Miami	70	200	140	70	80	120	150	150	180
Minneapolis	100	180	100	220	220	90	110	150	100
New York	100	220	140	140	90	100	240	160	140
Philadelphia	60	180	150	80	90	-	200	200	150
Phoenix	150	100	140	140	130	200	70	70	280
Pittsburgh	110	180	120	80	90	90	290	230	140
San Francisco	170	100	130	190	220	270	60	-	220
Seattle	160	140	150	190	170	260	80	60	330
Washington, D.C.	50	180	130	70	80	100	260	180	130

Note: All fares are subject to change and are one-way based on round-trip travel.
Fares are inventory controlled based on availability at the time of booking.

Table 120: Typical Airline Fares

you *are* away from your normal work environment. There's no ringing phone, no screeching fax machine, no noisy co-worker. The only interruptions you'll contend with at the workshops are lunch and coffee breaks.

Peer Interaction

And those coffee breaks and lunches are a surprisingly informative part of the workshop experience. They give the engineers a chance to mingle with colleagues from across North America, an opportunity that doesn't present itself every day on the job. Discussions of various regulations and practices, exposure to the engineering techniques of other firms and municipalities, and anecdotes – all are part of the personal interaction that occurs during the breaks and after the courses have finished for the day. All of these give the engineers a

Haestad Methods, Inc. www.haestad.com

slightly different view of their profession and a better understanding of their colleagues.

Educational Interaction

Of course, there is much more to a workshop than socializing with instructors and professional associates. The real benefit is that you learn everything you need to know to survive in a demanding and highly competitive industry in just a short period of time.

By learning techniques for quicker solutions and becoming more proficient at using software – and understanding the mathematics behind the models – you will become a more efficient modeler. How does that affect your projects? You'll be able to do the same work in less time – and probably achieve better results.

You can do the same work in less time – and probably achieve better results.

Okay, so maybe it isn't quite like having a drill sergeant running the workshops, but it will give you a fast, accurate and solid foundation in hydraulics and hydrology modeling.

"Why should I care about accreditation?"

You may have heard a lot about PDHs (Professional Development Hours) and CEUs (Continuing Education Units). A PDH is defined as one contact hour of instruction or presentation and a CEU is a unit of credit for 10 hours. So why should you care about continuing education credits? The three primary reasons are licensing requirements, project requirements and a guarantee of quality.

Licensing Requirements

As you might know, some state professional licensing boards already require engineers to earn a certain level of PDHs or CEUs in order to renew their license. Other states plan to institute CEU requirements within the next few years, and even more are discussing the possibilities.

Project Requirements

For many projects, a workshop is not only recommended as a way to learn more efficient modeling and gain better skills; it might be required. Oftentimes, a request for proposal will include a condition that the modeler "demonstrate attendance at a workshop."

Guarantee of Quality

You are guaranteed that the workshop meets the standards set by the accrediting associations. All of Haestad Methods' continuing education courses are accredited by both the International Association for Continuing Education and Training (IACET) and the Professional Development Registry for Engineers and Surveyors, a continuing education registry sponsored by the National Society of Professional Engineers and the National Society of Professional Surveyors.

So go ahead and take the time to further your education, get rejuvenated and earn credits from the best engineering drill sergeants in the world!

Author: Houjung Rhee

For more information about continuing education and the courses offered by Haestad Methods, please see Appendix B, Continuing Education.

EMBRACE THE INTERNET OR DIE!

Civil engineering organizations that are not on the Internet are running out of time.

Civil engineering businesses that want to stay competitive and communicate effectively with clients, vendors and other agencies must have an open door to the Internet. In fact, it could be argued that having an Internet presence is the 90s equivalent of having a business listing in the yellow pages. In a year's time, it will surely be as important as having telephone and fax service. More people are talking, communicating and doing business over the Internet every day, through electronic mail, discussion groups and Web pages.

If you have delayed your move to the Internet because of comments you've read or heard, you're probably pushing your luck. You must embrace the Internet now, before you lose your competitive advantage.

In this article, we provide an overview of the Internet. We'll give some practical advice on developing an Internet presence and exploiting the available technology. We'll also share some of our ideas and show you what other engineering organizations are doing. Let us help you learn from our own Internet experiences.

Many skeptics said that the World Wide Web was just a fad

The Web Explosion

Eighteen months ago, many industry analysts were cautioning against committing the resources necessary to join the fledgling Internet revolution. They said it was best to adopt a wait-and-see attitude and let the technology evolve.

The debate raged through 1995 and into 1996. Many skeptics said that the World Wide Web was just a fad destined to burn out and that people would come to believe that the Internet delivered no real value to the business world.

One widely published and respected industry pundit pronounced – with his characteristically acid-tipped pen – in early 1995:

> *Combine all the scenarios of time wasting, money wasting, information overload, Web hackers, and false promises and the Internet could take a serious tumble. We'll someday look back on the Internet sycophants and ask, "Gee, how did all those dinky companies think they could make money? ...The Internet probably should be completely shut down tomorrow for productivity reasons."*
>
> *-- John Dvorak, "Info Overload at Your Fingertips", PC Magazine, March 28, 1995*

But the Web was only beginning to emerge in the mainstream in 1995. And Dvorak's pronouncement then is in sharp contrast to his own statement made just over a year later:

> *Everyone should have a Web page. Why not? Unless you're living in a hole and want to stay there, Web pages are becoming so inexpensive that it's silly not to have one. With the upcoming Microsoft operating systems [Windows NT 4.0], it's actually going to be possible to put yourself on the Web with your own server, running on one of those $20-per-month AT&T connections.*
>
> *-- John Dvorak, "Isn't it About Time You Have Your Own URL", PC Magazine Online, July 9, 1996*

What turned skeptics like John Dvorak into believers?

For one thing, five months after Dvorak's initial pronouncement, Netscape sky-rocketed into Wall Street after hosting the most successful stock launch the market has ever seen. Netscape is the Internet software company that brought the World Wide Web

What turned skeptics like John Dvorak into believers?

into our lives with its popular Web browser, Netscape Navigator.

Shortly thereafter, Microsoft Corp. jumped squarely into the Internet fray. Microsoft's Internet Explorer 3.1 Web browser is available for free download from its corporate Web page.

We have also followed the adoption of Sun Microsystem's Java programming language, which allows clients to download actual program code from Web servers. Microsoft is licensing the Java technology now and extending it for Windows 95 and NT.

Internet technology has evolved and is standing up to all the tests it's being subjected to. The Internet is accepted and used by mainstream business. It's roaring along at high speed and sweeping all of us along with it.

Still, even today the ultimate future of the Internet remains uncertain. We have to wait to

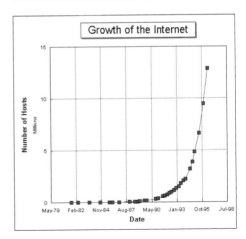

Figure 121: The Internet Explosion

Source - Network Wizards Internet Domain Survey at www.nw.com/zone/WWW/top.html

see whether it will adhere to the vision set down by many industry leaders.

For example, key players like Marc Andreesen, Netscape's vice president of technology; Larry Ellison, CEO of Oracle; and Scott McNeely, CEO of Sun; envision super-servers running Java based "thin-clients." But Haestad Methods is not completely convinced that this particular Internet future will come to pass, particularly as Microsoft and Intel work to reshape the technology around the PC.

One thing is certain, though: The Internet is evolving and progressing so rapidly that the pace very nearly outstrips the ability of analysts to publicize their guesswork in the media. Big companies that want to ride the Internet wave are making huge investments. It's the intellectual equivalent of the Oklahoma Land Rush of 1889: If you parked your wagon near the back of the pack for fear of being trampled, you ended up eating the dust of the aggressive homesteaders.

Internet surfing has become a mainstream business activity. A glance at Figure 121 shows that the number of Internet domain servers is growing exponentially, with no end in sight. A significant majority of the technical and political issues have now been answered and laid to rest. The Internet is here to stay, and the time for your organization to make the commitment is now.

Internet Web Primer

"The Web" is a shorthand term for the World Wide Web. A web is an appropriate metaphor

It's the intellectual equivalent of the Oklahoma Land Rush of 1889. And if you park your wagon near the back of the pack for fear of being trampled, you'll be eating the dust of the aggressive homesteaders.

for this network of hyper-linked information pages – pages that can contain images, sounds and video in addition to just text.

A Web page is accessed using something called a Web browser, such as Netscape Navigator or Internet Explorer, which is launched locally from your desktop computer.

A host server – your own network or an external Internet host – uploads contextual information to your client computer using the hypertext transfer protocol, or HTTP. Your Web browser software presents this information in an interactive, graphical fashion.

Within the browser window on your computer, you can jump to a hyper-linked information page by clicking your mouse on an image bitmap or phrase that is mapped to another location using a unique address called the uniform resource locator, or URL. A URL allows users located anywhere in the world to access a directory and file located on a Web host server – also located anywhere in the world – from their personal computer by running a Web browser. In fact, a URL can address a file on your own hard drive or a file on your own network. Files that a URL points to are typically blocks of ASCII text information that have been tagged using the hypertext markup language, known as HTML. This is the native format that is interpreted for display by Web browsers like Netscape Navigator or Internet Explorer. For example, the URL for the Haestad Methods Home Page is http://www.haestad.com.

Figure 122: Navigate the Web by Entering a URL into the Browser's Address Field

Employees who want to learn about their company's health insurance policy or 401(k) plan, for instance, could simply use their computer to find the information on the Intranet.

Because Intranet content is generally proprietary and is either protected by passwords or maintained on an isolated network, companies don't have to worry about unauthorized people accessing the information.

Putting A Web Browser to Work for Your Company

Now that you've seen how the Web is so accessible, easy to use and powerful, it's time to share some ways that you can put the Web to work for your company today. All you need is a Web browser, like Netscape Navigator or Microsoft Internet Explorer, and an Internet connection.

Figure 123: The Browser Software Finds the Site and Loads the Web Page Automatically

Locate Business and Product Information

While the *Internet* is the global network of inter-communicating servers that are linked together using a packet protocol – TCP/IP – there is also a private network equivalent called the *Intranet*. An Intranet, for instance, may be configured so that it's accessible only by the employees of a company.

The Intranet explosion arose when it became obvious that the same types of things you can do on the World Wide Web would be well-suited for managing internal corporate information, such as company policy, sales information and employee addresses.

The Intranet explosion arose when it became obvious that the same types of things you can do on the World Wide Web would be well-suited for managing internal corporate information

Every Web browser maintains built-in links to free Web search services. Using powerful services like AltaVista, you can search for something on the Web just by typing in some keywords. Or you can use a search service like Yahoo that provides category-based searches. These index services organize information in content or subject hierarchies – much like a library.

New Web sites for construction and engineering are being posted every day. One good example can be found at Sweets Group Online service Web page, where you can quickly locate suppliers of materials and services. While the Web service does not deliver the same amount of information that you will get from Sweet's extensive publications and CD-ROMs, it's a convenient starting place for your searches.

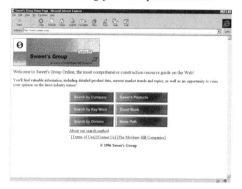

Figure 124: Sweets Group Online at http://www.sweets.com

Find Projects and Clients

Civil engineering consultants will want to visit Web sites maintained by state and federal agencies. Many agencies involved in high-volume procurement of engineering services are realizing that the Web is a good place to publicize projects and advertise the need for services. That's because it allows them to maximize exposure and streamline the procurement process. Going to the Web saves money, so those who routinely work with federal and state agencies will find themselves getting more job leads from the Internet.

NASA maintains a Web "jump station" for linking to an array of procurement postings for federal agencies. Visiting this site will open doorways into the federal procurement arena – procurement guidelines, procedures and project listings abound.

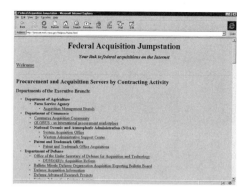

Figure 125: Federal Acquisition Jump Station at http://procure.msfc.nasa.gov/fedproc

You can now obtain detailed listings of federal requests for information, qualifications and proposals by accessing the Commerce Business Daily online via the federal CBDNet service.

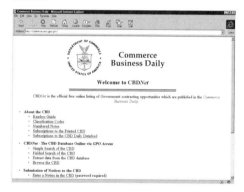

Figure 126: CBDNet to Find Government RFPs at http://cbdnet.access.gpo.gov

Using CBDNet, you can perform keyword searches to locate government contracting opportunities. Best of all, managers can get this information in a timely manner. You can also keep abreast of the federal procurement process.

If you want to locate potential customers or size up a developing market, you will find extremely useful Web pages that specialize in your exact area of interest. For example, you can link to "The Utility Connection" to find an array of links to water and sewer service providers and government agencies located throughout the country.

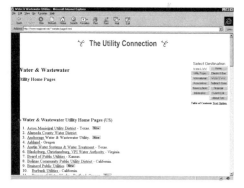

Figure 127: The Utility Connection Links Page at http://www.magicnet.net/~metzler/index.html

Perform Technical Research

There is no limit to the amount of technical information available on the Web. However, because of the sheer volume, culling information that is actually useful can be challenging. In general, your best strategy is to maintain in your Web browser an assortment of links – sometimes known as "bookmarks" – to proven, productive data sources maintained by providers you know and trust. That way, you can easily revisit the sites – much like picking up a book where you left off.

A Web surfer is actually a data prospector – sifting through the raw Web content and mapping the paths to the most relevant information mines using the Web browser "favorites" or bookmarks feature. Experienced Web surfers are skilled at grading the quality of the content

> *A Web surfer is actually a data prospector, sifting through raw Web content*

providers and can gauge a site's commitment to maintaining quality content over time.

Data mining is not random. It is a dynamic process that combines traditional use of search engines and diligent navigation of hypertext context jumps. In essence, the process requires a certain amount of mental focus because surfers will likely encounter an abundance of distractions along the way. It's easy for the neophyte – and even the skilled, for that matter – to be diverted by stumbling upon an interesting series of links and then drift completely out of the data hunt. If you have the time, randomly jumping around can be entertaining and even educational. But surfing is an acquired skill, and because of the relative newness of the breakaway Internet phenomenon, there are still few masters.

For those in the engineering profession, colleges and universities offer some real Web gems that you will probably return to regularly. One good example is the civil engineering virtual library site maintained by Georgia Tech.

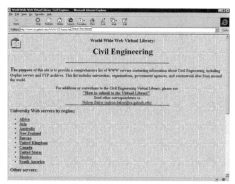

Figure 128: Civil Engineering Virtual Library at www.ce.gatech.edu/WWW-CE/home.html

It's difficult to locate noncommercial sites that maintain indexed lists of relevant technical literature for civil engineers. But a few excellent free literature search services do exist. For example, the American Society of Civil Engineers publications page offers a powerful literature search capability for all technical journals, symposia and publications.

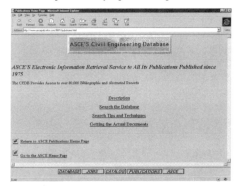

Figure 129: Electronic Index to ASCE Journals at www.ascepub.infor.com:8601/pubshome.html

Another useful literature database is maintained by the Water Resources Scientific Information Center, or WRSIC, of the USGS.

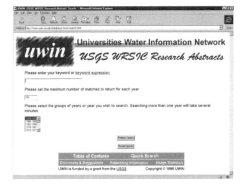

Figure 130: USGS WRSIC Technical Abstracts at www.uwin.siu.edu/databases/wrsic/index.html

Obtain Software Support

The technical support experts from Haestad Methods are on the Internet frequently, downloading the newest printer drivers, updating libraries and obtaining the latest software updates. Many of the most active pages are dedicated to providing end-user software support. The Internet is truly one of the best ways to obtain software assistance.

Figure 131: The Busy Microsoft Technical Support Web Page at www.microsoft.com/support/

Users of our products frequently upload support files and send email queries to our software and engineering support staff. They can even visit our Web support page to download product maintenance updates.

Figure 132: WaterCAD Update Page Via Dialog at http://www.haestad.com/Update/update.html

In fact, our newest products incorporate direct email connection to Haestad Methods technical support. These built-in functions let you do such things as automatically send a problematic WaterCAD project file along with related diagnostic files to our ftp server.

Haestad Methods, Inc. www.haestad.com

Putting a Web Server to Work for Your Company

You've seen how pointing a Web browser at the Internet can benefit your organization. However, you really can't achieve the greatest benefits until you stake out your own territory on the Web.

Here, we will share some ways that other civil engineering organizations are using the Internet for active communication. Afterward, you will be ready to carry your company's message of service and success to the Internet.

Sharing Your Vision

If you're already using the Web, you probably realize that it holds valuable potential for marketing and gaining broad international exposure of your services. A corporate Web page is more than a billboard located along the information highway because, unlike a highway sign, you're not relying solely on random drive-by exposure. Rather, you expect interested people to deliberately track you down on the Web, whether they know your specific Web address or simply search for you by keywords (your company name or products, for instance).

Surfers will frequently come across a Web site when it is mentioned on another site about related services. By simply clicking the mouse button, they can then jump to the new site. These "virtual endorsements" of one site by another are highly prized because they can substantially increase a company's exposure.

For example, you can get to the Haestad Methods Home Page from many other home pages owned and operated by consulting firms, university professors and agencies that use our products. One example of a cross-reference link is shown below.

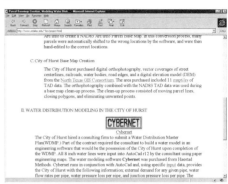

Figure 133: A Courtesy Link to the Haestad Methods Web Site at http://www.utdallas.edu/~lizs/project.html.

Source: Stolz, Elizabeth, "Parcel Basemap Creation, Modeling your Water System, and Utilizing GIS for Spatial Analysis", City of Hurst, Texas

Specialized industry sites that are operated by individuals or service organizations will add categorized links to your pages. A keyword search for "Haestad Methods" using AltaVista reveals that the company's Web site is referenced by hundreds of Web locations.

Communicate, Transact with Clients

You can leverage Internet technology to enhance or extend your ability to communicate with project owners, architects and subcontractors. The Web is a universal pipeline that is replete with opportunities to

> *"Virtual endorsements" of one site by another are highly prized. They can substantially increase a company's exposure.*

extend its basic page-serving function. You can integrate database, email or ftp server technology into your Web site and actually deliver project-specific drawings, specifications and reports to contractors or owners.

Both Netscape and Microsoft have advanced standard binary protocols for extending Web functionality – plug-ins and ActiveX, respectively. You can use Netscape compliant plug-ins, ActiveX client controls or serve up document files recognized by ActiveX-enabled applications. These approaches let you display files that exist in other formats besides those implemented using the universal HTML format (e.g. Microsoft Word .doc files).

Clearly, using the Web is faster and far less costly than using express mail, fax or long-distance phone service. Extended Web functionality enhances building a client communication framework that will streamline the way you do business.

One of Haestad Methods' clients, GZA GeoEnvironmental Inc., has put the Internet to work for its clients through creative utilization of Web technology. In fact, this firm's aggressive adoption of the technology could actually help it win customers and maintain a competitive edge over others in its field.

Figure 134: GZA CustomerLink ^{SM} Page at http://secure.gza.net

GZA has completed several projects where client-consultant communication and coordination were largely done over the Web. Their exclusive CustomerLink ^{SM} technology provides a password-protected entry into a Web facility that allows users to review progress reports, initiate task orders and track invoices. GZA provides a ProjectLink ^{SM} facility within CustomerLink that facilitates the exchange of actual detailed project deliverables – reports, schedules and drawings.

You can explore GZA's vision by visiting its corporate home page at http://www.gza.net. There, GZA has set up a sample project that demonstrates the CustomerLink technology.

Recruit New Employees

Many companies post employment opportunities on their Web sites. For professionals looking for a job, the Web is fertile ground.

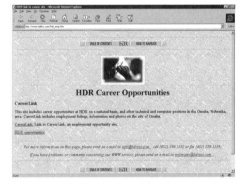

Figure 135: Career Opportunities at HDR Inc. are Browsed via www.hdrinc.com

One advantage of posting jobs on the Internet is that the prospect can often obtain a good feel for the company and its focus by browsing its full Web content. It also allows job prospects to prequalify themselves: If they don't like what they see on the Web, they're not likely to waste your time by applying for a job.

Success Stories

Many civil engineering consultants are carrying their message to the online community via their own customized Web pages. These civil engineering corporate Web sites provide an overview of the firm – its history, thumbnail descriptions of successful projects, related links, corporate contacts and a variety of other information of interest to current and potential clients.

Black and Veatch, based in Kansas City, Missouri, employs 6,100 people in 80 offices worldwide and boasts a strong Web presence. Launched in July 1995, the B&V Web server presents a wealth of information about the company and its project experience. The index page organizes the content into four key technical sections: power, infrastructure, process, and buildings. Visit a technical section to see the firm's capabilities and request printed technical brochures.

Figure 136: The Black and Veatch Corporate Page at http://www.bv.com/

The site features an online magazine where the firm can showcase high-profile projects and detailed technical accomplishments. Visitors navigating through the specialty pages can locate, identify and email the firm's principals and engineers who have contact responsibility in specific areas of interest.

The Black and Veatch page also features the WAIS freeware search engine, which lets a user automatically search the site's Web content.

Figure 137: The Malcolm Pirnie Corporate Page at http://www.pirnie.com/

This same Web gadget is used on the home page of Malcolm Pirnie, an environmental consulting firm that employs more than 1,000 people. The top page features an attractive engineering office lobby motif.

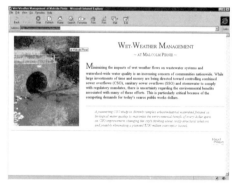

Figure 138: A Keyword Search on Malcolm Pirnie's Web Page of "Combined Sewers" Yields Detailed Project Information

The company also implements an effective navigation strategy for its visitors. Enter a key word in its text search field and the WAIS engine will provide a listing of all server links that contain the keyword – a junior edition of

AltaVista. Visitors can also navigate to specific content at a site index page organized around service areas – a sort of mini-Yahoo index.

The first page in a Web home site serves primarily as the information index. It's here that visitors will form their first impression of the organization, so a great deal of attention usually goes into organizing the composition, appearance and content of this "front door."

Both the Black and Veatch and Malcolm Pirnie pages are attractive. They feature professional-quality graphics, are simple to follow and allow easy user interaction.

Do you need media directors, journalists and professional graphics artists to construct and maintain a Web server? Emphatically no!

Wilbur Smith Associates, an international engineering and planning consulting firm with headquarters in Columbia, S.C., maintains a corporate home page that offers links highlighting its qualifications and experience in transportation, economic feasibility, engineering design and other specialized areas.

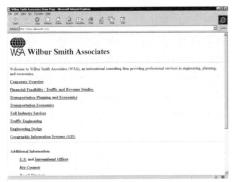

Figure 139: The Wilbur Smith Associates Corporate Page at www.wilbursmith.com

Instead of image maps, its index page employs simple text links that deliver visitors to more detailed information presenting the firm's specific project experience. For example, take

the jump to Geographic Information Systems and get a brief technical overview of GIS and a listing of recent and active projects. Additional links will propel you to detailed project descriptions.

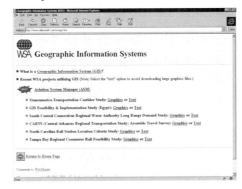

Figure 140: Visit Wilbur Smith Associates' GIS Project Showcase via www.wilbursmith.com/wsagis.htm

The WSA Web site serves up the same information that its marketing division would offer in a printed brochure. This site follows one of the tenets of Internet publishing – emphasize content over flash.

The WSA page has a clean, attractive and uncluttered appearance. It delivers a nice level of content and is not burdened with graphics that strain browser performance and increase Web development time. Consequently, it has a snappy response in a browser that enhances the overall effectiveness of the site.

Building Your Web Page

To establish an organizational presence on the Web, you simply need to make a Web page available. How you do that depends on various considerations, including your objectives, available technical knowledge, computer resources and budget.

For corporate Web sites, there are two hosting options available:

- **Virtual host.** Your Web page is hosted

remotely by a company that specializes in providing this service. This is the least expensive approach, but there are limitations governing how you operate your page.

- **Local host.** Your Web page is hosted on your own Internet network server. While more expensive, this option gives you unlimited control over the operation of the site.

Service Provider

A connection to the Internet is the first item required. An Internet service provider, or ISP, can provide you with the physical connection to the Internet.

The first ISP that you deal with will probably provide one very important service for your company – registering its second-level domain name into the domain name system (DNS) managed by the Internet Network Information Center (http://rs.internic.net). This name will serve as your unique Internet address. For example, Haestad Methods Inc. has reserved the name "haestad.com". No one else in the world can use that domain name for as long as the company continues to pay the annual $50 maintenance fee. The name you choose should be easy to remember and should be selected with care because it will serve as your Internet signpost for some time to come. A domain name is portable and can be carried from one ISP to another.

The Internet service provider business is quite competitive. Unlike cable or local telephone services, you might have a number of providers in your area offering a variety of billing and service packages.

Other services that your ISP can provide are email storing and forwarding and Usenet access. Many service providers offer virtual Web host services. Because this might be a valid option for your Web startup, you should be sure to discuss this with your potential service provider.

A list of Internet service providers can be found on the Web at http://thelist.iworld.com/. Of course, if you don't have Internet access, you'll have to take a look in the yellow pages. Or simply call Haestad Methods, and we'll be happy to give you a list of ISPs in your area.

Bandwidth

Bandwidth is Internet jargon for the size of the information pipe. The larger the pipe, the faster your Web page data will move onto the Internet. The bandwidth you ultimately achieve will depend on the bandwidth the ISP can provide. A low-cost – but barely adequate – Web host could be run on a 28.8k modem connection. The ISP would provide you with a dedicated modem and number for your connection. Higher bandwidth connections are possible through the use of ISDN (64k to 128k) or leased lines (56k to 45Mbps).

> *Bandwidth is Internet jargon for the size of the information pipe. The larger the pipe, the faster your Web page data will move onto the Internet.*

Find out how much bandwidth your ISP can offer. This will affect your ability to effectively handle the growing crowd of visitors who will flock to your Web site as you introduce new content or capabilities.

The question of available ISP bandwidth becomes even more crucial as you contemplate higher connection speeds. With a 28.8K connection, your server's modem is the bottleneck and ISP bandwidth is not an issue. This will not be the case if you run at 45Mbps. So connection speed might dictate whether to use a local provider or seek a large regional provider with many high-speed connection points to the Internet.

Virtual Hosting

For starters, especially if you go with a 28.8k modem connection, you might want to consider using your ISP's virtual host services. This way, visitors to your page will not be put off by slow server response time. Web surfers are becoming less tolerant of pages that load slowly, and if takes too long, they might "hang up" on you, much like a telephone customer who is left on hold too long.

Even on a virtual host, you will write the content and organize your Web page. The essential difference is that you will upload the Web page files to the virtual host. But from a Web visitor's point of view that's transparent.

The cost of virtual Web hosting varies from one provider to the next. In general, you can expect to pay about $75 a month, plus a one-time Web setup charge of perhaps $200. Make the ISP explain any limitations that may apply concerning access limits and allowable Web space – which could increase your fees or prevent you from expanding your Web site.

Web Content

Remember that the Web is about publishing. Most of the content that will find its way into the company's maiden page is very likely residing on a hard-drive somewhere in the organization right this minute. If you publish

If you publish corporate brochures, churn out Standard Form 254/255s or prepare formal proposals, you probably have a wealth of raw content at hand.

corporate brochures, churn out Standard Form 254/255s or prepare formal proposals, you probably have a wealth of raw content at hand. If it already exists in desktop publishing or word processing format, you are very close. Setting up your Web then becomes a process of reformatting the text and images into a hyper-media presentation using HTML.

A host of tools is available for creating HTML – Microsoft FrontPage and Netscape Navigator Gold are two in use at Haestad Methods. These tools provide a WYSIWYG editor, which allows page editing in an environment that graphically displays the content in the same format that it will appear in an actual Web browser – what you and your visitors will see. This is great for beginners since they are not forced to memorize HTML control tags.

As the Web authors gain more skill and knowledge, they frequently forego the WYSIWYG style editors and use native HMTL tags for formatting. This gives the Web author greater control over page appearance. In fact, the Haestad Methods Webmaster edits entirely with HTML tags in an ASCII text editor.

Local Server

If your organization chooses to run a local Web server, you will need server software. The two major players in the computer platform arena on the Internet are UNIX® and Windows NT®.

Haestad Methods runs a dedicated Windows NT server. Most of our clients will be taking the same approach, simply because the vast majority of our users are running Windows or DOS applications on PCs.

Many commercial and freeware (free) products are available for a variety of computer platforms. In the latest release of NT Server 4.0 Microsoft has bundled Internet Information Server, a Web server package. (Apache HTTP Server is a free Web server available for the UNIX platform.)

The cost to locally host a site depends on the choices you make for hardware, software and connection speed. Of course, most cost estimates don't include the cost of time and effort associated with maintaining a Web presence. Someone in the organization must act as Webmaster – the individual who has primary responsibility for maintaining and updating the site.

And In Conclusion

In this introductory article, a great deal of time was spent introducing technical concepts, reviewing case studies and examining costs associated with startup and operation. In a way, the transition to the Web is akin to the adoption of CAD by engineering organizations.

With CAD, initially a lot of energy was spent looking at startup costs, selecting and comparing alternatives and overcoming skepticism. Eventually, management came to the realization that the manpower costs of the technicians and engineers using the system (and their training) eclipsed the costs of these issues. These true costs are offset by the productivity gains realized by the organization.

As the World Wide Web becomes a standard component of your company's communication infrastructure, you will discover that the collection, authoring, organization and presentation of the content of your Web site are where the true costs are. You will also find that the more adept you get at producing this

content and exploiting Internet technology, the more productive your company will become.

And just like with CAD, there were early adopters and late adopters of the technology. All had different experiences and some achieved more reward than others. Will your organization be an early adopter or a late adopter of the Internet technology? It's almost too late to decide.

Get Started on the Web

What you'll need:

A computer with a modem (a decent Pentium can currently be purchased for about $1500), a phone line, and preferably Windows NT or Windows 95.

What you'll do:

• **This is the hardest part: find an Internet Service Provider. You have most likely seen or heard commercials on television or on the radio. Even if you haven't seen them (or haven't paid too much attention to them) Internet publications (like Internet World or NetGuide) always have service provider ads in the back.**

• **After signing up with the provider, just fill in the information for the Dial-up adapter in Windows 95, or the Dial-up networking in Windows NT. Your service provider can provide you with more detailed instructions.**

• **That's it! You will officially be a Netizen, and you will be able to browse the Internet for business, pleasure, or both.**

HAESTAD AND
THE GIANT MOLD

*Engineers put WaterCAD's versatility to the test
and help save a manufacturing project*

Engineers Arlen Work and Steve Starkel knew they had to scramble.

A manufacturing company was having trouble with one of the molds it was making, and if the problem persisted, its contract might be jeopardized and it could lose precious business. The problem needed to be resolved immediately.

The company didn't have its own engineer on staff – it normally doesn't need one, after all – and so it called in Work and Starkel, who are field design engineers at the Mid-America Manufacturing Technology Center (MAMTC), an extension program on the campus of Wichita State University in Wichita, Kansas, that assists small manufacturers in problem-solving.

The problem with the mold was obvious, but the solution wasn't – until they brought in a computer software modeling program from Haestad Methods, that is. In the end, the

> *If the problem persisted, the company could lose precious business*

project would prove not only the determination and skill of Work, Starkel and the manufacturing employees, but it would show beyond a shadow of a doubt just how versatile yet easy to use the software is.

The manufacturer is a small company that makes all sorts and sizes of aluminum molds that it supplies to plastic fabricators, who then create a variety of plastic products and parts.

One of the company's contracts required it to build a colossal mold – a 4-foot-high chunk of aluminum that tipped the scales at 4,000 pounds and would be used to make plastic picnic coolers.

The giant mold presented a new challenge for the employees: It was about twice the size of any mold they'd made before. But they were up to the task, and in the end, they could chalk it up as a good learning experience, too.

The process of making the mold was the same one the manufacturing company used for other molds; only the size was different.

The aluminum molds are made of two halves, with a cavity in the center shaped in the form of the plastic product that will later be manufactured. To make the plastic parts, a hot plastic sheet is placed into the mold, and the two halves are pushed together. The plastic is then cooled to set, and when the mold is opened, the product pops out – perfectly formed if everything goes right.

Before shipping finished aluminum molds to its customers, the manufacturing company puts them through a quality control test run to make sure they are working properly.

And it was no different for the giant mold. The employees added the hot plastic sheet, sealed the halves, waited until it cooled, and then opened the mold.

And out popped a misshapen cooler with a droopy top. Needless to say, Quality Control and the mold company's customer weren't pleased.

The problem quickly became apparent: The plastic wasn't being properly cooled in the mold.

The aluminum mold absorbs the heat energy from the plastic sheet and must be cooled by water. That's accomplished by creating a mini-water distribution system within the mold itself – a system of dozens of channels that directs water throughout the chunk of aluminum. The channels are created by drilling a series of holes into the mold and then plugging them in certain places. Cold water is then run through an entrance in the mold, and the flow is

The flow had to be redirected. But how? With 45 parallel water channels in one network, it would be a significant analytical challenge

channeled by the plugs until it exits through another hole – with the cooling cycle running continuously.

But somehow the water wasn't flowing properly through the 4,000-pound picnic cooler mold. Although the lower half of the mold was getting an adequate supply, flow to the upper half was insufficient. That meant the top half of the plastic wasn't getting cooled – and when the picnic cooler popped out, the top sagged because it wasn't fully set.

The company needed help, and fast. So it called in Work and Starkel. They, too, saw that the problem was obvious.

"When the mold halves come apart, the cooled plastic keeps it shape," Work noted. "But the hot plastic sags and doesn't keep its shape, so you get a deformed product."

The flow obviously had to be redirected. But how?

"With 45 parallel water channels in one network, it's a significant analytical challenge," Work acknowledged.

For two days after Work and Starkel were called in to help, they hunched over their paper and calculators, trying to understand the problem one channel at a time. Which channels were the culprit? But they quickly realized that their approach just wasn't practical.

"It would take at least two weeks on paper," Work noted. And they certainly didn't have that luxury; the customer was waiting – and growing nervous.

"For the plastics fabricator, the option was to find a new mold supplier that could cool their parts adequately," Work said. "But, of course, the company did not want to lose that business."

Work had heard about a couple of water distribution modeling programs that he thought might be able to help. After all, the channels in the mold were really just a scaled-down water system. So he called a university about a software program it designed, but he lost interest because the product did not have a responsive customer support staff.

And then he called Haestad Methods – and hit pay dirt.

He had heard of Haestad's WaterCAD program from a civil engineering professor, Dr. Paul Work (no direct relation) at Clemson University, who had recently reviewed other Haestad software. Work thought it might be the key to the cooling flow dilemma.

"WaterCAD seemed to be more user-friendly and had a dedicated support staff," Arlen Work said.

With the help of Haestad technicians, Work electronically downloaded a copy of WaterCAD; there was no time to wait for a mailed copy, even overnight shipment.

"I was very demanding when I ordered this because we had to get started right away," Work admitted, "and we downloaded it from the bulletin board and actually did not have to wait for next-day delivery."

Once it was installed on his computer, he and Starkel immediately began using the program, modeling the mold's internal network of channels using WaterCAD's sophisticated and comprehensive modeling features.

"If you were a water molecule, you wouldn't know if you were flowing in metal pipes or in drilled metal channels," Work pointed out. "We simply typed in pipe sizes that matched the drilled dimensions, with correct parameters for surface roughness and mitered corners, gave it an input flow stipulation, and the

solution from the software told us how much flow was going through each of the mold's channels in the cooling network."

WaterCAD also told them how much water was flowing to the top areas of the troubled mold.

"Once we simulated by computer how the existing configuration performed, we were able to alter those water channels," Work said. "We changed them in the computer model and were able to analyze dozens of possible fixes that restricted flow in the lower channels to force water to the upper channels."

The entire job took them one and a half days, including the time spent learning to use the software.

They compiled and presented the best solutions to the droopy picnic coolers. With this information the mold maker and plastics manufacturer quickly resolved the problem, saving the mold from the scrap heap. The company was back in business, the customer was happy, and the plastic picnic coolers popped out perfectly.

"The software helped us model what we feel were very close to real conditions," Work said. "If we had not had the computer simulations, we would have used guesswork – trial and error – and that would have taken us much longer to find a solution. In an extreme case, the contract may have gone to another mold maker."

Work and Starkel were so pleased with WaterCAD that they are now considering other ways – some also out of the ordinary – to put it to use for them again.

"We think we might be able to use WaterCAD for in-ground sprinkler systems in yards," Starkel said. "We could use it again in cooling metal molds. And maybe even the radiators of car engines or industrial heat exchangers."

YOUR $495 SUPERCOMPUTER IS ON ITS WAY

The next generation PC is just beyond the horizon, and when it arrives it promises to be cheaper to operate, easier to upgrade and environmentally friendly - and it will level the playing field among consumers and businesses alike.

Fifty years ago, ENIAC – the Electronic Numerical Integrator, Analyzer and Computer – weighed in at 50 tons, had a mean time between failure of 30 seconds, took a whopping one-fifth of a second just to count to 5,000, and cost millions of dollars.

Today, you can buy a complete Pentium PC for just over $1,000 that makes ENIAC look like an abacus.

And tomorrow, you'll be able to buy a small-appliance sized PC called a network computer for about $500 – bringing supercomputing power to any room in your home or office.

How can this be possible?

By coupling the awesome depth and breadth of the Internet with the software prowess of Microsoft Corp. and the better performance in smaller packages that has become Intel's

trademark. Welcome the Wintel NetPC – your next supercomputer.

Microsoft's NetPC initiative is the effort to open the Internet to everyone by relieving configuration woes and standardizing the desktop at a consumer-friendly cost: that magic $500 price point. Essentially a closed-box, Windows-based PC, the NetPC is also intended to fend off a host of Microsoft's hardware and software competitors. What do *we* think? Will the NetPC steal your heart and replace your favorite newspapers, TV shows, videos and magazines? No. But you better believe it will *deliver* them to you, and much sooner than you might expect.

Rise of the Internet

Before we plunge into the specifications for the network PC, let's review the rise of the incredible Internet – the information superhighway – and demystify as many buzzwords as possible in the process.

It all began more than a decade ago as PCs won the battle over centralized, time-sharing computers and dumb terminals. Thus was born the "fat-client" – the smart, peripheral and expansion board-laden PC whose growing user base soon supplied the incentive for new paradigms in software that far outstripped anything ever available on a mainframe in power and interactivity.

Yet something was missing – the ability to connect and communicate with other computers. Thus, PC networks were born and the shift from PC-centric to network-centric computing was on. Toward the end of this network-centric era we are now in, the Internet and, more importantly, its friendly, ubiquitous, graphical World Wide Web component have come to the foreground and made the stand-alone PC nearly obsolete.

As the breadth and depth of information on the Internet has increased, server administration and bandwidth have become top priorities. Concurrently, the mainstream productivity applications of word processing, spreadsheet and database have stagnated, and the creative efforts of the world's greatest software developers have shifted to a new breed of applications – for communicating. The presence of an untapped Internet market of people who don't yet own PCs, coupled with the ability to migrate PC functions to a communicating network that finally offers

> *Toward the end of this network-centric era we are now in, the Internet, and more importantly, its friendly, ubiquitous, graphical World Wide Web component have come to the foreground and made the stand-alone PC nearly obsolete*

compatibility and bandwidth, has brought us to the network PC.

The leading candidate for the network PC is the Microsoft Windows/Intel microprocessor architecture – known as Wintel. Microsoft's specification for this architecture is referred to as "NetPC." Simplicity is its guiding principle: Instead of monstrous shrink-wrapped applications that are delivered on CD-ROM, you run "applets" – small program fragments that provide just the functionality you need, integrating with other applets as required, then are gone from your network PC. Essentially, the network PC is just an Internet browsing device, though a very sophisticated one.

Competition for the Network PC

But Microsoft has plenty of competition in its vision of a network PC. The big spenders are Sun Microsystems, Oracle and IBM, which together have set a competing standard called the Network Computing Architecture, or NCA. Whereas Microsoft specs a 100 MHz, 16 meg RAM Pentium with hard drive (a machine whose cost we expect to approach $500 by the fourth quarter of 1997), the NCA seems to sidestep specific hardware requirements, deferring to a hodgepodge of proprietary microprocessors.

Some telephone, cable and even TV companies, like Zenith with its new Diba Internet appliance, or others with their set-top boxes and built-in keyboard operated by remote-control, are getting into the act. But the real battle is between NCA and the Wintel

NetPC. With NCA's server-centric vision of downloading your operating system, applications and browser to a machine with proprietary hardware at boot time, we expect sluggish performance. For our money, the Wintel NetPC standard is the one to watch.

Implications of the Network PC

There are a number of powerful reasons why we believe the network PC is destined to change your computing landscape forever:

Cheaper to Operate

Some people predict that total operating cost could be reduced from current figures of about $12,000 per PC annually to as low as $100 by 2000. Whatever the actual figures, almost nobody will argue that a simpler client PC with fewer local software and hardware options to configure will be far cheaper for organizations to support. In many businesses, the network PC will be easily justified simply by its ease of use and the ability to administer it from a central server. The network PC lets a company "load-balance" its computing resources, so that employees, customers and executives all get exactly the right level of computing power (and expense).

Easier to Upgrade

Because your network PC gets much of its intelligence by being connected to the Internet, it is far easier to upgrade and far less likely to become obsolete with each passing year. The machine is a flexible front-end to the world's most advanced servers, which will keep it routinely supplied with the latest and greatest software innovations. Rather than upgrading the network PC, organizations will put

Your network PC is far easier to upgrade and far less likely to become obsolete

resources into upgrading servers and Internet standards. With the state-of-the-art, object-oriented, Internet programming language Java embedded, the network PC can change and grow its behavior at the click of a download.

Environmentally Friendly

Just think of the environmental implications of receiving most of your information – software, video, audio, print – in electronic form over the Internet via a network PC. Less junk mail, less newsprint, fewer floppy disks and CD-ROMs in the trash can, no more late-night runs to the video store. In fact, we expect network PCs to complete the trend away from printed documentation – a trend that Haestad Methods has been an early contributor to with our extensive online help, interactive tutorials and easy-to-use Windows software.

Democratizing Force

Lastly, the Internet and network PC can't help but level the playing field for information distribution. If you have any doubt, just log onto the Internet this evening and browse some personal home pages. Anybody and everybody can publish on the Internet. And your information is as accessible as ours or CNN's or USA Today's. There are few barriers to entry in this wild new world of electronic publishing on the Web.

Of course, there are a few drawbacks to the network PC.

It can't run high-end Windows, such as some CAD-based numerical models; it doesn't interface to other computers (except through the Internet); anything less than 16 meg RAM will be inadequate for Java and other large Internet extensions; and – separated by a slim few hundred dollars from low-end PCs – it's hard to justify on a cost basis alone. But these are not fatal flaws. They simply guarantee that the fully loaded desktop PC will live on for many applications.

Desktop PC Lives On

Regardless of who wins the battle for the software soul and silicon heart of the network PC, the high-end desktop workstations we use for engineering applications won't be going away. True, the PC can be expensive and complex to operate. And it has been widely criticized for the total cost of ownership and administration in business settings. Yet there remain many crucial tasks that only a fully equipped PC can handle.

A fully loaded Pentium PC operating at over 200 MHz with at least 64 meg RAM and a 2 gigabyte hard drive will be standard equipment to access the latest multimedia features on the Web, to run sophisticated CAD applications on large software models, or any time you simply want to get your work done as quickly and efficiently as possible.

The Final Word

In the end, we believe that the network PC, rather than "freeing" the world from Intel and Microsoft as some industry pundits predict, will *reconfirm the superiority of the Wintel architecture.* And it will, for the first time, make that architecture available to everyone.

PC sales recently surpassed TV sales; soon, there will be more homes missing televisions than missing network PCs, which is to say *very* few. And network PCs will reinforce a new era of sensitivity to, awareness of and communication about environmental issues. Online documentation will become commonplace. Printed manuals – heavy, expensive, and wasteful – will become relics of the past.

Yet network computers will not disrupt the current computing environment so much as complete it. There is no sense in replacing

fully loaded PCs where they are effective: on the engineer's desktop doing design; in the home office doing desktop publishing; or working on the road in laptops. Yet more and more, the network PC will be seen as the machine of choice where stand-alone PCs have become expensive and irrelevant: on corporate desktops and in school classrooms, for example. In the words of Oracle CEO Larry Ellison, an early network PC visionary, "The idea is to offer a $500 device, not limit the world to $500 devices."

Author: Darrow Kirkpatrick

Computer Companies on the Web

Microsoft Corp.

http://www.microsoft.com
Redmond, Wash.
(206) 882-8080

Sun Microsystems

http://www.sun.coom
Mountain View, Calif.
(415) 960-1300

IBM

http://www.ibm.com
Armonk, N.Y.
(800) 426-3333

Oracle Corp.

http://www.oracle.com
Redwood Shores, Calif.
(415) 506-7000

$9,600,000,000
AVAILABLE
THROUGH SDWA

Are you getting your share?

Utilities and public health departments around the country are scrambling to get their share of billions of dollars in loan funds that will be distributed beginning this year to help improve the quality of the nation's drinking water.

Ray Jarema, PE, is one of the people feeling the pressure, and it's no wonder. This is one of the biggest funding packages ever to hit the drinking water industry, and he wants to make sure everything goes smoothly. Jarema, the engineering supervisor in the water supply section of the Connecticut Department of Public Health, will spend the next several months making sure the agency has developed a flawless strategy to obtain the federal funding to upgrade hundreds of community water systems in the state.

"After all, there's 21 million dollars here at stake," he noted.

And that's just for Connecticut. All told, the 50 states will get nearly $1.3 billion this year through the Safe Drinking Water Act (SDWA). By 2003, more than $9.6 billion will have been invested into the massive program to improve the safety of America's tap water.

This funding package is one of the biggest to ever hit the drinking water industry.

"It's a major undertaking – very significant," said Fred Pontius, a compliance engineer with the American Water Works Association. "Virtually every utility or water distribution agency will be affected one way or another."

President Clinton reauthorized SDWA in early August 1996 – the first time it has been revamped in 10 years and probably the last time it will be for another decade. Amendments to the act call for sweeping changes that are designed to protect and improve the quality of America's public drinking water supplies, from new approaches in prevention to a better regulatory program.

One of the greatest thrusts of the law is to ensure that drinking water is safe from the most dangerous contaminants, such as cryptosporidium, coliform bacteria, radon and metals.

Water Still Poses a Health Threat

Even today, water-borne illness is a hazard to public health, although not on the scale it was before the turn of the century. Millions of people still risk getting sick every time they drink their own tap water, according to the Environmental Protection Agency, which is administering the SDWA.

In a recent report, EPA Administrator Carol Browner warned that "we can no longer take safe drinking water for granted."

Although the SDWA met with some resistance, it was eventually hailed by environmentalists and water industry officials alike, who see it as a vast improvement over existing law because it combines tougher measures with greater flexibility for states.

"A new, stronger Safe Drinking Water Act will mean greater protection for every American family each time they drink a glass of water," Browner said after a congressional vote to reauthorize the legislation in early August.

> *Although the SDWA met with some resistance, it was eventually hailed ... as a vast improvement over existing law*

A few days later, on Aug. 6, President Clinton signed the act into law.

"It balances responsible regulatory improvements with common-sense measures to help states and water systems prevent drinking water contamination problems in the first place," Clinton said. "The act is in several respects a model for responsible reinvention of regulations. It replaces an inflexible approach with the authority to act on contaminants of greatest risk and to analyze costs and benefits, while retaining public health as the paramount value."

History of Drinking Water Protection

John Snow's Vision

The Safe Drinking Water Act itself dates back to 1974, when it became the first federal legislation for municipal water systems in the United States.

But modern policies were actually shaped by events that unfolded across the Atlantic in the 19th century.

One of the key incidents was a cholera epidemic that struck London in 1854. A visionary doctor named John Snow set out to prove that contaminated drinking water was the culprit.

Snow, an epidemiologist, visited the homes of the people who had died of cholera and found out which company supplied their drinking water – competing companies often supplied water to different houses on the same street. He was convinced that one of the water pipelines was contaminated. By charting the incidence of the disease, he showed that more than 500 cases occurred within 10 days over a radius of some 250 yards centered on the Broad Street area of London.

His data showed that a work house in the area that had its own private well had only seen five deaths among the 535 inmates. Similarly, a brewery on Broad Street that never used water from the Broad Street pump had no cholera cases among its 70 workers.

Snow discovered that the Southwark and Vauxhall Company drew its water from the river Thames downstream, where it was indeed polluted. The Lamberth Company, on the other hand, drew its water upstream from London, where it was free of pollution. Snow ordered that the pump supplying the contaminated water be shut off, effectively bringing the cholera epidemic to an end. It was the first real campaign to safeguard the public from their own drinking water supplies.

The expanding base of medical knowledge, led by people like Snow and Louis Pasteur, combined with pressure from social reformers and simple aesthetic concerns, paved the way for the installation of sewage systems and water purification processes during the Industrial Revolution – and became the foundation upon which modern practice was built.

U.S. Sets Standards

At the turn of the century, the U.S. government stepped in to actually establish drinking water standards.

The first standards were set in 1914 with the Interstate Quarantine Regulations, which were designed to protect the health of individuals on interstate conveyances, such as public transportation.

Those standards were revised periodically through the 1970s, when several federal laws were finally passed to protect water as a resource: the 1972 and 1974 amendments to the Federal Water Pollution Control Act – known as the Clean Water Act – followed by the Safe Drinking Water Act in 1974 and the Solid Waste Management Act of 1976.

Water on the Web

http://www.haestad.com

http://www.ewg.org

http://www.awwa.org

http://www.asce.org

http://www.hydroweb.com

http://www.nspe.org

http://www.cdc.gov

http://www.epa.gov

http://www.wateronline.com

http://www.wqa.org

http://www.uwin.siu.edu

It was the SDWA, however, that was specifically meant to protect drinking water from contamination.

The act allowed the EPA to restrict the level of contaminants permitted in drinking water, standardizing water quality regulations across the country. It also regulated other issues that could adversely affect water quality, including underground waste disposal, the protection of aquifers as a sole source of supply, and wellhead protection areas.

In the beginning, the SDWA's focus was on coliform bacteria. But in 1986, when the act was reauthorized, it was expanded to address more contaminants, including microbiological pollutants, radon and metals. In addition, it also required the EPA to develop a list by 1989 of 83 more contaminants that were to be regulated – and to expand that list by 25 contaminants every three years (the latest reauthorization alters that requirement).

SDWA Met with Criticism

But as with virtually any new regulation, the SDWA was the subject of great debate as it came up for renewal.

Congress and some private-interest groups were worried about the costs of meeting the new requirements. Environmentalists and citizens' groups, on the other hand, were more concerned about preserving the environment and protecting public health. Adding fuel to the debate, there was still some scientific uncertainty over the amount of contamination and the extent to which drinking water was meeting water quality standards.

The Safe Drinking Water Act fell victim to the disputes in 1991 and technically expired. But the issue was continually resurrected.

Finally, in the summer of 1996, the debate was put to rest and Congress reconciled different versions of the new legislation, paving the way for President Clinton to reauthorize the SDWA.

Protecting Water Supplies

The EPA is still hashing out many of the details of both the funding and the new requirements that water suppliers must meet. The SDWA contains dozens of provisions that outline new regulations on source water, ground water, contaminant selection, standards, disinfection byproducts, small water systems, public notification, and monitoring, to name just a few. (See sidebar for more details.)

"The EPA is just beginning to implement the law, and as they do they will set regulations, and the individual states and municipalities will have to begin complying," said Pontius, the AWWA compliance engineer.

Among other things, the new law will make more information available to the public than ever before. In many cases, Americans will now have direct access to information about the safety of their drinking water supplies, potential contaminants and local water quality.

Incidence of Water-borne illnesses in the United States, 1985-1994

Year	No. of Outbreaks	No. of Cases	States Affected
1985	7	1,240	MA, PR[1], VI[2], WI, WO, VT, NY
1986	10	659	AL, CA, CT, ME, MS, NY, OK, UT, VT
1987	8	16,922	CT, GA, ND, NH, PA, PR, VT, WI
1988	6	310	CO, PA, OK, WA
1989	6	1,345	AL, CO, MO, NY, VT
1990	5	319	CO, IL, MO, PA
1991	2	10,049	PR
1992	9	3,423	AK, ID, NV, OR, PA
1993	9	404,013[4]	HA, MO, MS, NV, NY, PA, SD, WI
1994	5	503	NH, NMI[3], TN, WA

[1] PR = Puerto Rico,
[2] VI = Virgin Islands
[3] NMI = Northern Mariana Islands (Saipan)
[4] In Milwaukee, WI, the deaths of more than 100 people were attributed to the outbreak.

Source: Data compiled from the Centers for Disease Control and Prevention

Haestad Methods, Inc. www.haestad.com

Thousands Getting Sick

Although vast improvements have been made in the nation's water system since the days of John Snow and the cholera epidemics, there's no question Americans are still susceptible to water-borne disease and illness. Few people, however, probably realize the extent to which outbreaks occur – most of the media attention is focused on food-related illnesses caused by E. coli and salmonella.

But data from Centers for Disease Control and Prevention show that thousands of people are still getting sick every year from drinking their own tap water.

In many cases, water-borne disease outbreaks simply go unnoticed or unreported, said Dr. Dennis Juranek, an associate director in the CDC's division of parasitic diseases, giving people a false sense of security. And when they do get sick, they don't connect it to their drinking water.

"Most of us don't feel that every time we take a drink of water we could get sick," Juranek said. "I think our water is among the safest in the world, but it's not totally risk-free."

Outbreaks Not Reported

That point was driven home in Milwaukee in 1993, showing just how dangerous public drinking water can be. In what is one of the worst outbreaks in recent history, more than 100 people died and a frightening 400,000 became ill after drinking water that was contaminated by cryptosporidium.

"That's the extreme," Juranek said. "In some cases, it's difficult for a community to even

Data from the Centers for Disease Control show that thousands of people are still getting sick every year from drinking their own tap water.

detect an outbreak. If you have a smaller community with only 100 or 500 ill out of 10,000, it could be missed."

Another problem: Reporting an outbreak is not required under federal law unless it's connected to a violation or water treatment failure. Otherwise, it is done strictly on a voluntary basis, Juranek noted.

"The bottom line," he said, "is that what gets reported to the CDC is definitely an underestimate."

Since 1993, 10 million Americans have been asked to boil their water to guard against possible illnesses caused by microbiological contaminants like cryptosporidium, the EPA said in a report it released in late January. In addition, more than 11 million people receive unfiltered surface water, even though states have determined that the water poses health risks from microbiological contaminants.

Focus on Prevention

The SDWA, as amended, sets clear schedules for developing standards for potentially deadly contaminants like cryptosporidium. It also requires that the needs of special populations be taken into consideration – the elderly, infants and children, pregnant women, and people with diseases such as AIDS and HIV, for instance – when setting standards to ensure even stronger protection.

As part of the consumer information provisions, the EPA has just started a campaign to educate the public about drinking water. The agency plans to publish a booklet in question-and-answer format and is soliciting input from the water industry. In addition, the agency is putting together various work groups to address SDWA issues.

Under the new law, potential pollution threats to sources of local water must also be identified and assessed – part of a stronger prevention program. The SDWA isn't entirely rigid, though; it provides states with a flexible, common-sense framework to develop and fund local projects to protect the rivers, streams, lakes and groundwater that provide our tap water. And it affords them the latitude to monitor the chemicals they need to monitor.

Software Programs Help Design Improvements

Complying with the stringent provisions in the SDWA will require water utilities to make

improvements right at the source – the water distribution systems themselves.

That means that water mains, laterals, storage tanks, injection stations, pumping systems and other system components must be upgraded. To make those kind of improvements, the water utilities will need sophisticated modeling studies that simulate the operation and hydraulic performance of actual distribution systems. At the same time, the modeling studies must also simulate the transportation, decay or growth of contaminants or disinfectant substances that migrate through the pressurized distribution network.

Software modeling programs, such as WaterCAD from Haestad Methods, can help consultants and engineers comply with the SDWA requirements. Some of WaterCAD's

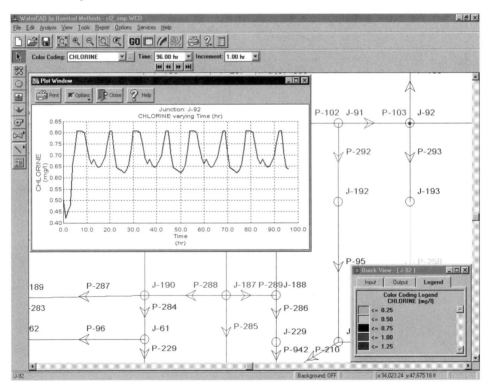

Figure 141 – Chlorine Analysis During an Extended Period Simulation

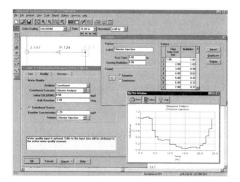

Figure 142: Water Quality Analysis

features include:

- Modeling the loss of disinfectant chlorine residuals that guard against bacterial growth as the potable water moves slowly from the treatment plant to household taps at the limits of the system.

- Planning for supplemental injection of disinfectants at locations other than the source.

- Identifying locations of seriously aged water that occurs in dead-end or underutilized areas of the network.

- Planning system improvements that affect optimal blending of water supplies from multiple sources that have distinctly different chemical constituent concentrations.

- Predicting tracks of contamination arising from cross-connections or leaks.

- Modeling the formation and transportation of suspected carcinogenic disinfection byproducts, such as trihalomethanes.

- Modeling the depletion of dissolved oxygen.

$9.6 Billion Available

While the intention of the Safe Drinking Water Act is a noble one – to protect the health of Americans consuming a basic commodity – it is generating some fear and anxiety in the water industry (questions and concerns posted in electronic newsgroups and bulletin boards on the Internet speak to this).

That's because the provisions will prove to be a financial burden to some water companies, particularly smaller ones, which have fewer consumers to share the costs. In the past, fewer regulations meant fewer costs to pass along to users. But the water companies unwittingly hurt themselves by keeping the rates low – too low in some cases. Lacking reserve funds, some municipalities haven't been able to make improvements in their water systems or haven't been able to meet the costs of monitoring and testing as federal requirements were implemented.

"They've been trying to meet the current rules, and people who haven't been able to meet the current rules will have to now," Pontius said. "It's been for lack of funding. The vast majority of water systems are meeting the EPA regulations. But now they're issuing stricter standards, newer standards, and some systems are old and need to be upgraded. But now they'll have the state revolving loan fund, and I don't think anyone will turn that money away."

Loan Fund Distribution

The loan fund – formally known as the Drinking Water State Revolving Fund – is perhaps one of the most important nonsafety provisions included in the Safe Drinking Water Act.

The state revolving fund has a whopping $9.6 billion available through 2003 to help water systems and municipalities finance the provisions they're required to meet under the SDWA. But there is always a catch, of course,

---

and the caveat here is that the money isn't a pure giveaway – for most communities, it will be made available in the form of low-interest loans.

The money will be distributed based on a formula that takes into consideration a state's population, its land area, and the number and types of water systems. (See related chart for a state-by-state list.) The formula, however, is set only for fiscal year 1997 and is expected to be revised after that.

Before the funding provision was added, previous versions of the Safe Drinking Water Act were criticized because, unlike the Clean Water Act, the SDWA had never provided any financing resources. Critics condemned it as just another unfunded state mandate passed along by the federal government. They also noted that many of the nation's roughly 60,000 community water systems – the vast majority of them small – lacked the funds to meet the costs of complying with the SDWA.

In fact, in a report in 1995, the EPA said that an outdated and deteriorated U.S. drinking water infrastructure "poses a fundamental long-term threat to drinking water safety."

Funding Offers Hope

But now, the state revolving fund is giving many communities the chance they'd been waiting for.

"If funding continues like it's supposed to, it'll make a big difference for the drinking water program," Pontius said. "It certainly won't cover all the needs, but it certainly will cover some of the needs and keep things moving for some communities. Financially pinched communities will now have resources available, and that'll make a difference over time."

Under the funding guidelines, 15 percent of the allocation must be used to help small systems – those that serve fewer than 10,000 people. In addition, before a loan is given to a small system, the system must prove that it can comply with the SDWA provisions.

While the funding is available generally in the form of loans, the new law does allow states to earmark up to 30 percent of their allocation for disadvantaged communities or to give grants to forgive the loans.

"That's both good and bad," Pontius said. "The argument is that at some point, the treatment plant, for instance, will wear out and will have to be rebuilt … and if the community can't pay back the loan, it probably doesn't have an adequate rate structure to support that."

Either way, consumers are likely to see their water rates increase as communities begin paying back the loans or beefing up their reserves for future needs.

'Straight Economics'

"There are still a lot of problems here," said Ray Jarema, the Connecticut Department of Public Health official. "It's not a rosy picture."

State Revolving Fund

The SDWA allows states two years to receive FY1997 capitalization grants. (Applications must be in to the EPA by July 1998.) States can then bank the set-aside for source water protection for up to 4 years. Funds can only be taken from FY 1997 funds for the assessments. Using SRF funds for source water protection assessments is a state option. States may use other funds for this purpose.

States with their SRF in place by mid-1998 should be able to receive their FY 1997 grant and exercise this set-aside option. States that are not ready by then will lose their entire FY 1997 allotment.

Juranek, the CDC official, said taxpayers are often put off by the expense of upgrading water systems.

"It's straight economics," he said. "We've gone into communities and investigated outbreaks – many of those with parasitic origins because they didn't filter the water and just disinfected with chlorine – and the public was outraged."

But that anger doesn't last long, he said.

"When they are presented with the costs, they quickly change their minds," Juranek noted, "and say, 'Oh, we've been drinking that water for years.' How much do people want to pay for better water quality?"

But the economics aren't all bad.

A Business Boom

The new funding provision is also expected to boost business in the drinking water industry.

For one thing, small community water systems that don't have the on-staff expertise will likely need consultants to help with the funding application process itself. In addition, all sorts of businesses will be called upon to help make improvements and upgrades in water systems once the funding starts being distributed on the local level.

"We've never had this kind of program before for drinking water," Pontius noted. "It'll mean more demand for services all around – contracting, construction, design, engineering."

Jarema agreed. "If utilities get money to do a project they normally couldn't or wouldn't do, that generates work activity on the local level," he said. "It produces additional jobs and spurs the economy."

States Gearing Up to Collect Money

Obtaining the state revolving funds will be complicated, but not impossible. Among other things, states must decide which agency will administer the program, secure legislative authority for it because of a local matching funds requirement, and develop a priority ranking list of projects to fund. Each allotment of money will be available for two years. For instance, to receive funding for fiscal 1997, states can submit applications up to July 1998, Pontius said.

However, a publication called Inside EPA, a weekly report from Inside Washington Publication, said in its Nov. 22, 1996, issue that few states seemed prepared to apply for the funds because they are overwhelmed by the application requirements. The report, which is not affiliated with the EPA, quoted unnamed agency officials as saying that "only a handful of states" will be ready to apply for funds by fiscal year 1997. It also quoted an unnamed state official as saying that "there is a turf battle" among the states over the funds.

The EPA disputed the report, saying most states are preparing to apply for the funding.

"Oh, they're working very actively on it," said Connie Bosma, chief of the agency's regulatory implementation branch. "They are very busily preparing. Many states already have their legislation passed."

The EPA, she said, expected an "onslaught" of applications to begin in February or March. And she said it's "not likely" that states would pass up such an opportunity.

Pontius, too, said states, for the most part, are diligently pursuing the loan funds.

"Some states that are ready to go can get their application in right away," he said. "Other states will have to get their program together, and for them the funding would become retroactive. It does look like some will go right up to the deadline."

Colorado Moves Fast

Colorado and Connecticut are among the states aggressively moving to secure their share of the loan funds.

The Colorado Department of Public Health and Environment had a list of priority projects ready when the legislature convened in January, for instance. It also has matching funds in place, said Jerry Biberstine, who is section chief of the department's drinking water program. As it is, he said, the money will not go far enough to meet the demands.

"Colorado gets more than $15 million the first year," he said. "By bonding that, we can actually lend close to $45 million, and that only touches the first 20 of the 128 systems we have identified as needing help, and that doesn't touch all the private systems on our list either."

Biberstine and other water officials were also trying to change state law so that the money can be used to help finance projects at private water systems, which is now prohibited.

"We hope to get that change because about 50 percent of the water systems are privately owned," he noted, "yet they still have to comply with the Safe Drinking Water Act."

Connecticut Nearly Ready

The Connecticut Department of Public Health is also putting together a priority funding list, Ray Jarema said.

"It's sort of an educational process," he said. "It's important that we get some kind of

EPA Survey:
Water Infrastructure Needs $12.1 Billion

The Environmental Protection Agency's first nationwide survey of drinking water utilities indicates that communities need $12.1 billion in the immediate future to help protect public drinking water supplies.

Of that, $10.2 billion – 84 percent – is needed to protect water supplies from microbiological contaminants. The remainder of the $12.1 billion is needed to protect against exposure to lead, nitrates and other regulated contaminants that may have adverse health effects.

The EPA estimates that $138.4 billion will be needed over the next 20 years to replace or upgrade the nation's drinking water infrastructure, including treatment, pipes to deliver water and storage tanks. Of that amount, large water systems serving more than 50,000 people account for the largest share of the reported need, $58.5 billion. Medium (serving between 3,301 and 50,000 people) and small systems (serving 3,300 or fewer people) also report substantial needs – $41.4 billion and $37.2 billion, respectively.

American Indian and Alaska Native systems report 20-year needs totaling $1.3 billion. Significantly, about $1.1 billion of this total is considered "current need" for drinking water system improvements. American Indians and Alaska Native water systems face special challenges in providing safe drinking water, including isolation, arid conditions and arctic climates.

information out to the utilities, and then in the latter part of 1997, we'll give them a better picture of where we stand. We'll give them an application form and then more details of the entire plan."

Connecticut is slated to receive $21.4 million in fiscal 1997 and expects a funding package to be in place by spring, Jarema said. The state has more than 605 community water systems that will be eligible, in addition to numerous nonprofit noncommunity systems.

"I'd like to think we're in position to do this in 1997," Jarema said. "The legislation is in place. We're not clear what issues the EPA may require down the road ... but barring any unforeseen circumstances, we should be ready."

He is helping formulate a project criteria list that will first be subjected to an internal review. Later, the department will sponsor meetings with consultants and private water utilities and issue a fact sheet.

"There are still a lot of unknowns, but we're a lot further along than some states," Jarema said. "You're talking about a lot of work, and on a legislative basis, a lot of selling if you haven't done any of this yet."

But in the end, he said, the tedious work will pay off – for both water utilities and the public.

"Looking at it from a public health perspective, a lot of local utilities can get funds at a reasonable rate and complete their projects," Jarema said. "We weren't waiting around to make improvements where they were needed, but this should help quite a few utilities, and that will help our consumers, too."

SDWA REQUIREMENTS

The Safe Drinking Water Act, reauthorized in August 1996, has dozens of new amendments that make demands of the Environmental Protection Agency, states and individual water systems around the country.

The provisions address a variety of issues, but some of the major changes include new prevention approaches, better consumer information, changes to improve the regulatory program, and funding for states and local water systems.

Many of the amendments don't take effect for several years. Here are just a few of them, as outlined by the EPA:

Consumer awareness

Consumers will have more access to information than ever before. By August 1998, the EPA must issue regulations that will spell out how community water systems must prepare and distribute an annual consumer confidence report. The report, written in easy-to-understand terms, must include information about the source of the drinking water, water quality and the levels of contaminants. Systems serving fewer than 10,000 people may be able to publish the reports in newspapers. Those with fewer than 500 may be able to simply notify customers that the report is available, in lieu of actually mailing it to them. The new regulations also clarify the requirements for public notification of violations.

In addition, the EPA must maintain a safe drinking water hotline for consumers: (800) 426-4791

Capacity development

By October 1999, each state must obtain the authority to ensure that new community water systems and nontransient noncommunity water systems have the technical, financial and managerial capacity to meet National Primary Drinking Water Regulations. Lacking such authority, the water system will receive only 80 percent of its allotment from the Drinking Water State Revolving Fund.

In addition, by August 1997 states must submit to the EPA a list of community water systems and nontransient noncommunity water systems that have a history of significant noncompliance, as well as the reasons.

The EPA is authorized to make grants to universities to establish and operate small public water system technology assistance centers. The centers would conduct training and technical assistance about the information, performance and technical needs of small water systems.

Operator certification

By February 1999, the EPA must publish guidelines specifying the minimum standards for certification and recertification of operators of community and nontransient noncommunity water systems – done in partnership with

states, public water systems and the public. Two years after that, 20 percent of a state's revolving fund allocation will be withheld if the state is not implementing an operator certification program. Through grants given to the states, the EPA must reimburse training and certification costs for operators of systems that serve fewer than 3,300 people.

Drinking water studies and research

The EPA must develop a strategic plan for drinking water research and present it to Congress and the public for review. Within five years of enactment of the SDWA, the EPA must provide a national estimate of water-borne disease occurrence. The EPA and the Centers for Disease Control must establish a national training and public education campaign to educate professional health care providers and the general public about water-borne disease and possible symptoms caused by contaminants, including microbial contaminants.

In addition, within four years of enactment – and periodically as new data become available – the EPA must conduct studies to identify subpopulations at greater risk (such as infants, children and pregnant women) than the general public for adverse health effects from exposure to contaminants in drinking water. The results must be reported to Congress.

The EPA also may conduct screening for estrogenic substances.

Contaminant selection and standard-setting authority

The EPA's authority to set a maximum contaminant level goal (MCLG) and regulate contaminants is expanded to include contaminants that may adversely affect human health; are known or likely to occur at a frequency and level of public health concern in public water systems; and that if regulated present a meaningful opportunity to reduce the health risk of people served by public water systems.

By early 1998 and then every five years after that, the EPA must publish a list of contaminants that are not subject to any proposed or final national primary drinking water regulation (NPDWR) and that are known or expected to occur in public water systems and may require regulation.

Health risks, risk reduction and costs can now be considered under the EPA's standard-setting authority. When it proposes an NPDWR, the EPA must publish a cost-benefit analysis.

The EPA will no longer be required to regulate an additional 25 contaminants every three years. Instead, starting in 2001 and then every five years after that it will have to determine whether to regulate at least five of the contaminants listed as potential contaminants for regulation. In addition, if a contaminant poses an urgent health risk, the EPA can issue interim regulations, but within three years it must make a regulatory determination on the contaminant.

Disinfectants and Disinfection Byproducts

The EPA must promulgate an interim Enhanced Surface Water Treatment Rule (ESWTR), a final ESWTR, a Stage I Disinfectants and Disinfection Byproducts Rule, and a Stage II Disinfection Byproducts Rule in accordance with the schedule published in the proposed Information Collection Rule. If there is a delay in any rule, all subsequent rules must be completed by a revised date that reflects the intervals for the delay.

The EPA can consider risk trade-offs in setting the Stage I and II standards. The considerations used in proposing the DBP rule in 1994 will be treated as being consistent with the risk-risk authority for the standards.

The standard-setting flexibility does not carry over to establishing a maximum contaminant level in Stage I or Stage II standards for cryptosporidium or for contaminants that are DBPs.

DWSRF CAPITALIZATION GRANTS FOR FY 1997

Based on FY 1997 appropriation of $1,275,000,000
Interprets "available funds" to mean amount after set-asides

State	Population	Area	Community Water System	Non-Transient Non-Community Water System	Transient Non-Community Water System	Estimated Final Allocation	Percent of Available Funding
	20%	10%	66%		14%		
CT	3,276.80	5,544	607	1,029	2,947	21,408,200	1.70%
ME	1,235.70	35,387	418	411	1,830	12,653,200	1.01%
MA	6,011.40	10,555	516	290	810	14,344,600	1.14%
NH	1,125.00	9,351	755	468	1,060	13,754,800	1.10%
RI	997.9	1,545	88	70	312	12,558,800	1.00%
VT	576	9,615	460	220	644	12,558,800	1.00%
NJ	7,879.00	8,722	628	1,314	3,033	27,947,300	2.23%
NY	18,181.50	54,475	3,128	824	6,763	59,167,700	4.71%
PR	3,599.30	3,515	446	43	4	12,558,800	1.00%

DWSRF CAPITALIZATION GRANTS FOR FY 1997 (Continued)

State	Population	Area	Community Water System	Non-Transient Non-Community Water System	Transient Non-Community Water System	Estimated Final Allocation	Percent of Available Funding
	20%	**10%**	**66%**		**14%**		
DC	578	68	2	0	0	12,558,800	1.00%
DE	700	2,489	243	107	298	12,558,800	1.00%
MD	4,965	12,407	509	510	2,534	17,640,900	1.40%
PA	12,048.00	46,058	2,328	1,538	6,947	53,270,700	4.24%
VA	6,491.00	42,769	1,556	808	1,888	29,442,400	2.34%
WV	1,820.00	24,231	668	253	884	12,558,800	1.00%
AL	4,185.50	52,423	607	86	185	12,558,800	1.00%
FL	13,673.50	65,517	2,198	957	3,767	45,132,600	3.59%
GA	6,917.00	59,441	1,652	352	689	25,775,000	2.05%
KY	3,789.00	40,411	537	164	131	12,558,800	1.00%
MS	2,638.20	48,406	1,287	128	191	16,474,200	1.31%
NC	6,934.90	53,733	2,611	877	6,900	46,114,100	3.67%
SC	3,643.00	32,007	779	312	550	14,821,600	1.18%
TN	5,099.00	42,146	542	83	585	12,776,200	1.02%
IL	11,697.00	57,918	1,868	644	3,986	38,502,400	3.07%
IN	5,713.00	36,420	937	772	3,455	25,712,100	2.05%
MI	9,465.10	96,776	1,516	2,436	11,431	59,681,100	4.75%
MN	4,494.60	85,747	963	1,694	9,407	42,086,000	3.35%
OH	11,091.00	44,828	1,523	1,198	6,672	43,073,000	3.43%
WI	5,016.40	64,851	1,253	1,111	10,756	41,546,400	3.31%
AR	2,424.00	53,182	718	74	657	12,558,800	1.00%
LA	4,294.10	51,842	1,379	277	572	20,420,300	1.63%
NM	1,502.30	109,069	625	148	508	12,759,800	1.02%
OK	2,973.60	68,164	1,235	162	435	17,561,900	1.40%
TX	18,028.50	268,601	4,641	854	1,619	70,153,800	5.59%
IA	2,813.20	56,270	1,170	163	637	16,857,300	1.34%
KS	2,528.30	82,235	921	85	119	14,095,000	1.12%
MO	5,234.00	69,708	1,363	230	985	21,857,600	1.74%
NE	1,601.80	77,257	630	256	543	12,824,000	1.02%
CO	3,563.50	102,869	810	160	1,144	16,784,100	1.34%
MT	800.8	138,904	694	219	980	14,826,200	1.18%
ND	610.9	69,372	324	46	256	12,558,800	1.00%
SD	655.5	69,180	486	33	317	12,558,800	1.00%
UT	1,850.00	81,279	407	64	437	12,558,800	1.00%
WY	465.1	94,867	314	106	358	12,558,800	1.00%
AZ	3,766.20	82,584	851	282	666	16,938,300	1.35%
CA	31,172.30	162,818	3,795	869	4,396	75,682,600	6.03%
HI	1,172.00	10,932	127	16	7	12,558,800	1.00%
NV	1,379.60	108,647	299	76	298	12,558,800	1.00%
AK	597.7	656,288	517	0	954	27,039,000	2.15%
ID	1,089.20	82,287	750	242	1,096	14,157,800	1.13%
OR	3,019.70	97,185	928	330	1,507	18,920,500	1.51%
WA	5,203.40	67,308	2,381	304	1,579	31,145,900	2.48%

Haestad Methods, Inc. www.haestad.com

WHITE HOUSE UTILITY DISTRICT USES TECHNOLOGY TO MANAGE GROWTH

CYBERNET and billing functions to improve operations, optimize capital expenditures and increase responsiveness to water customers

In the last 8 years the White House Utility District, under the leadership of General Manager Bill Thompson, has:

- Reduced its overhead by $250,000 per year while increasing responsiveness to its water customers

- Reduced system leakage by 40% of its previous rate

- And grown by more than 50%

all at the same time. How did they do this? Read on.

WHUD

The White House Utility District (WHUD) serves Sumner, Robertson and Davidson from its sole office located in White House, Tennessee. This utility district is the largest in Tennessee and one of the five largest in the United States (based on area), currently serving 20,000 customers located throughout 600 square miles of north central Tennessee and south central Kentucky.

About five years ago Bill Thompson started development of a then-new Geographic Information System (referred to as GIS). In the most simple terms, Geographic Information Systems are large databases of information connected to maps. A computer operator can look at a map on-screen, move a cursor to certain objects on the map, select the object and have a database of information "pop-up" on-screen about the selected object. These systems have grown in popularity and utility in recent years, as the constantly declining price and increasing power of computers have made them accessible to a wider variety of applications.

To accomplish the initial development, Bill hired Tom Settle (a GIS consultant now with MapSouth) to set up the system. Tom selected Atlas software and began the process of collecting the data, building the databases and developing the maps.

Shortly after this, WHUD retained White Taylor Walker/GM (partner company of WTW+Garver, a GarverPlus Company) to assist with this project. The task was to analyze the entire water distribution system, recommend improvements, and develop a process in conjunction with the GIS that would help streamline utility operations.

System Modeling

GarverPlus engineer Barry Cloyd, CADD technician Tom Guss and Tom Settle worked together to develop a method to import the GIS model of the utility system directly into another computer program called CYBERNET (a water distribution system modeling program). While the data still had to be completed and verified, this step saved having to recreate the entire distribution system in the water modeling software. Thus pipe sizes, types, lengths, elevations, directions, and numerous other system data that were collected and keyed into the GIS system came directly into the CYBERNET program to be analyzed.

White House Utility District

1996 Customer Base:	20,000
Total Area:	600 square miles
Projected Growth:	1,000 customers/year
Treatment Capacity:	13 MGD
Total Pipes:	2,000 miles
Pumps:	20
Tanks:	14
Max. Elevation Change:	600 feet
Current Employees:	41

Once there, the engineering analysis began. Problem areas and potential problem areas were identified. Long-term capital improvement plans have been developed that will optimize the financial investment of the utility and maximize the service to the customer. Line upgrades, water treatment plant additions, location and sizing for new tanks and other necessary appurtenances – totaling over $16 million – have all been planned.

Integrated Billing

In addition to the CYBERNET model, Bill Thompson wanted the GIS software integrated with their billing system. The primary reason for doing this was to aid in responding to customer requests and to help manage leakage.

For leak control WHUD compares actual billing data to flows projected by the CYBERNET model and work orders for known leak repairs. They can adjust meter reader's routes to fit any pressure zone, street or other configuration at any time to verify their data and check for leakage. Doing this has reduced their system leakage by over 40% of their previous rate in the past few years. This is a significant improvement.

For customer service, WHUD now also maintains (through GIS) a computerized history of work orders for system repairs. They can easily synopsize work performed for pressure problems, taste and odor problems, and line replacement. As they detect identifiable trends they can then budget accordingly for the optimum course of action for each part of their system.

Daily Operations

Integrated billing and the CYBERNET model have both helped the daily operation of the utility in many ways. For example, Pat Harrell, WHUD engineer, receives information requests from an average of 3 developers per week. They want to know such things as what kind of normal pressure they can expect to receive, any necessary improvements that would be required to provide fire flows at various locations, the required geometry of new systems they might install and various other items. Using the CYBERNET model has cut his response time by well over half of that required by more traditional methods, and it has given him greater confidence in the accuracy of the predicted result. The examples of the usefulness of this system are many, but recently in one particular area of the 600-square-mile system he detected a problem with water pressure being lower than predicted by the model. To verify the condition of the lines and accuracy of the model, work crews conducted field investigations. These investigations revealed a large valve that was unmarked on the district's Record Drawings. Not only did they locate the valve, they discovered it to be partially closed. Pat notes they immediately raised water pressure by as much as 25 psi by fully opening this old, unrecorded valve.

Bill Thompson also notes that managing daily work orders has greatly improved since they began using the integrated system. Managing new taps, leak repairs and the other myriad of items that must be attended to daily is now much better. These items are entered into GIS and managed through the billing system. After each task has been entered, work supervisors can actually print maps of the system that identify the locations of work to be performed.

> *Using the CYBERNET model has cut his response time by well over half of that required by traditional methods, and it has given him greater confidence in the accuracy of the predicted result.*

Route planning and scheduling are then optimized in the office, thus making better use of the utility personnel.

Regarding overhead reduction, Bill notes that this increased efficiency has allowed them to reduce staff, mainly through normal attrition and retirement. This has reduced their overhead by more than $250,000 per year – while still adding over 1,000 new customers annually for the past few years.

Future Directions

The entire WHUD staff is excited about the future and is investigating plans to continue their system integration. For example, they plan to merge their SCADA (Supervisory Control and Data Acquisition) system into GIS. This will enable them to automatically record system conditions at any given site when any customer calls noting difficulties. Again, this will aid work crews in effecting repairs. WHUD also plans to install Global Positioning System (GPS) units in every field vehicle, with a direct radio link back to the GIS system in the office. Thus whenever an emergency situation arises they can immediately re-route the nearest repair crew to the area affected.

We are pleased to be associated with the White House Utility District, people who are genuinely "Committed to Excellence" in every area.

Reprinted with permission from GarverPlus Engineers, Volume 9 Number 3 (Nov., 1996)

PLANNING IS EVERYTHING

In the world of software, as in medicine, an ounce of prevention is worth a pound of cure. Find out how well-designed software can help you avoid pitfalls.

Many Haestad Methods' programs share a common codebase, and as a result many of the features are available in more than one program. You have seen how rapidly program enhancements can be incorporated between versions 1.0 and 1.5 of our programs, and now you can see the same forward progress leading into version 2.0.

Why should you care what's "under the hood" of a software program?

The City Street Parallel

In many ways, software development parallels the development of city streets. In a small town, street layout is not crucial – there are usually not enough streets for a traveler to become confused and lost.

But when the small town grows into a large city, the amount of planning that went into the original street layout becomes crucial, and poorly laid out streets become confusing, intimidating, and dangerous. Anyone who has visited a city like Boston can attest to this – the small towns have grown together into a system that even lifelong Bostonians have trouble navigating.

When a city is well thought-out and planned from the start, the result is a street system that is simple to understand and navigate. Software has the same characteristics. For small software programs, such as a simple pipe flow calculator, the underlying software code is probably not of concern. The program doesn't have enough features to become confusing.

As the program grows and adds features, the importance of a good foundation becomes apparent. If the program was designed from the beginning to accommodate growth and change, the process is smooth and the result is beautiful. If not, the process is tedious and error-prone, and the result is a hodge-podge of pieces that don't quite fit together.

So why should the internal "street map" of a software program influence your purchasing decisions? Some of the most compelling reasons are summarized below.

Stability

All software has bugs when it is initially coded. It's not a pleasant thought from the point of view of a programmer (or the user), but it is the truth. There are bound to be typographical errors, syntax errors and, unfortunately, logic errors. After all, programmers aren't superhuman, they're just a little (well, maybe a lot) different from the rest of us.

When the software has a sturdy, well-planned architectural base, it's easy for programmers to debug the code (follow the street map). This helps coders catch and repair problems – and to avoid problems (wrong-turns) in the first place.

Scalability

When the city has a good arterial and collection system, development and growth can occur more rapidly without adversely affecting the existing traffic.

Well-planned software also allows for rapid development, adding features and making use of the existing foundation. This kind of architecture also provides more growth capabilities for the future, so the practical life of the code base is drastically increased.

Flexibility

Through interviews and beta testing with engineers from around the country, we try to create software that will meet the needs of the majority of our users. Once the program is released, there are undoubtedly going to be suggestions from our users for how certain features can be improved or how the format can be rearranged to make the software more intuitive – and we certainly welcome these constructive criticisms and suggestions.

Our object-oriented architecture allows these changes to happen seamlessly and with little or no effect on the rest of the program. The next version of the product can then have the suggested improvements and enhancements, without risking damage to code that was previously working correctly.

The Future

What is the combined effect of all of these benefits? For the user, the results are incredible.

- Trustworthy software means that you can focus on the engineering judgments, input parameters, and interpreting results – the areas that an engineer is supposed to concentrate on.

- Common tools and interface provide product familiarity, even the first time you use a new program. This allows you to operate more efficiently, so you can finish your modeling in less time.

- Scalability and flexibility help ensure that the products will be updated and maintained in the future. While programs like HEC-2 may become obsolete and be replaced by software like HEC-RAS, you can bet that programs like FlowMaster, StormCAD, CulvertMaster, WaterCAD, and CYBERNET will continue to lead the field for decades to come.

For Haestad Methods, the results are pretty good, too.

- Bug-free software means we spend less time on support and patches, and therefore we can devote even more time to research and development, which helps continue the cycle.

- We have pride and confidence in our models, knowing that we have created the best software in the world. When our software has passed all of our quality checks and usability tests, we know that there's nothing out there that even comes close.

Author: John Powell

CYBERNET OR WaterCAD?

The answer is in the project requirements.

It's a question we've heard from hundreds of engineers over the past year – "Should I buy CYBERNET or WaterCAD?" With the release of WaterCAD 2.0 and CYBERNET 3.0, it's a question that's very easy to answer: whichever one you prefer.

Both programs have the exact same numerical engine, the same features and even many of the same dialogs. The only real difference between the two is that CYBERNET runs directly inside AutoCAD (just like it always has) and WaterCAD uses a stand-alone graphical editor that we've developed.

So the question really should be: "Which graphical environment do *you* prefer – AutoCAD or stand-alone?"

A Common Foundation

We've worked hard during the past few years to make a programming foundation that allows us to share many of the tools we develop across graphical platforms in Windows. This cross-GUI ability is an accomplishment that we are very proud of, and the result is that someone experienced with either CYBERNET or WaterCAD can sit down in front of the other program and immediately work

efficiently and comfortably. And being familiar with both of the most popular water distribution models in the world is certainly a benefit for any hydraulic modeler.

Stand-Alone

Someone in a recent newsgroup asked who developed the drafting program called "Stand-Alone" because it seemed to be a very popular program. While that question struck us all as rather amusing at the time, it did bring to light the fact that many of our clients don't know what stand-alone functionality offers and what the benefits of stand-alone technology are.

Flexibility

Stand-alone programs, by definition, have all the tools you need to functionally use the software within the specified operating environment (Windows, in most cases). For our software, this means that all the tools you need to drag and drop elements into a graphical network, analyze the model, and generate reports are included when the program is installed.

There are no requirements that you have AutoCAD, MicroStation or some other

---

drafting engine in order to use your system graphically. Even if the only other software you have installed is the Windows operating environment, you can use WaterCAD and all of its features.

Through the use of common file formats, such as the DXF format, you can even maintain compatibility with drafting programs without becoming hostage to them.

Future Expenses (Non-Expenses)

When a new version of your favorite drafting program is released, there is no need to purchase an updated version of the hydraulic model. The links are all done through common file formats and Windows.

This offers a great benefit for budgeting and future upgrades, as anyone with plug-in software can attest to. One of the biggest hurdles to upgrading AutoCAD, for instance, doesn't even involve AutoCAD itself – the problem is often that there are several add-in packages for engineering calculations that also need to be updated at the same time.

Inside AutoCAD

If stand-alone technology offers so much, why would anyone want or need a program that runs directly inside AutoCAD?

The truth is, they probably don't need a program to run inside AutoCAD, but they may certainly find that it is easier and more comfortable for them to work in that environment.

A Single Roof

Many people prefer working under "a single roof," where all of the needed engineering programs can be directly tied to the same AutoCAD drawing. This gives them the ability to make modifications to the drawing itself while they are working on various modeling tasks, changing back and forth between

revising drawing figures and working with the model.

Drafting Power

Obviously, our software is intended to offer intuitive solutions to the toughest hydraulics problems – not to rival the drafting capabilities of AutoCAD.

Working in AutoCAD gives the modeler direct access to the thousands of available AutoCAD commands. This offers an almost endless variety of possibilities for annotation, including leaders, text, and miscellaneous drafting commands that are simply not present in our stand-alone GUI.

Some of these tools might be incorporated into future versions of our stand-alone programs, but developing those tools takes time and resources away from other tasks that we would rather work on, such as improving the hydraulic models and reporting capabilities.

The Choice is Simple

Which model should you go with?

It really is just a matter of personal (or company) preference. It makes no difference to us; you'll get the same level of quality, the same features and a similar interface for both programs.

You can't lose.

Author: Robert Mankowski

THE METRIC PAYOFF

Conversion to the metric system will help companies reap perpetual savings, gain business and improve access to the global marketplace

What is the "payoff" for metric conversion? The answer is different for each organization or industry, but it can be estimated by calculating metrication costs and benefits. Costs include all the "up-front" costs of conversion, including administrative and technical time, paperwork, supplies, and training. Some industries may have substantial sales and capital equipment costs as well.

Benefits include the dollar value of the long-term gains from metric conversion. These gains come from two principal sources: (1) increases in productivity and quality brought about by the use of a decimal-based measurement system, and (2) the ability to more effectively compete in world markets. Some estimate that for measurement-based activities such as construction, savings from productivity and quality alone can amount to 1 percent of construction costs; others believe the percentage is even higher. Regardless of the amount, the savings are *perpetual*.

> *Benefits include increases in productivity and the ability to more effectively compete in world markets.*

For example, total metric conversion costs for the 50 state highway departments are estimated to lie between $50 and $100 million. The states spend about $20 billion on highway construction every year, so a 1 percent reduction in construction costs due to improved productivity and quality amounts to an annual savings of $200 million. At the 1 percent rate, the payoff for highway conversion takes 3 to 6 months with a savings of $100 to $150 million the first year and $200 million each succeeding year. Even at a tenth of this rate, the payback period is only 30 to 60 months with savings in each following year amounting to $20 million, in perpetuity.

For industry, the benefits of metrication as a passport to the global marketplace can far exceed productivity and quality gains, but each firm must assess its prospects based on the mix of products and services it provides. Some have been amazed at how metrication has increased sales; others have had to metricate just to retain market share. As Representative

Vernon Ehlers of Michigan noted in Congressional testimony this year: It is not just how much we will gain by metrication; it is how much we have been losing by not switching to the world's standard of measurement.

A parallel issue is the simultaneous retention of the inch-pound system in construction activities. The federal government soon will have about $25 billion in metric facilities entering the inventory each year, and it will become increasingly expensive to retain two measurement systems. We must, therefore, move completely to the metric system for all phases of the facility life cycle (i.e., design, construction, operations, and maintenance). The longer we delay in doing so, the fewer the benefits we will receive from metrication.

1996 Year End Report

- Virtually all major federal construction programs have been converted to the metric system.

- Billions of dollars in metric projects are under construction.

- Costs are in line with those for nonmetric construction.

- Problems have been minimal.

So reported federal agency representatives at the November 1996 meeting of the Construction Metrication Council. The table following this article is an agency-by-agency update.

Reprinted with permission from Metric in Construction, Nov.-Dec., 1996
(by the Construction Metrication Council of the National Institute of Building Sciences)

AGENCY	METRIC CONVERSION DATE FOR NEW CONSTRUCTION PROJECTS
General Services Administration	**January 1994** GSA's Public Buildings Service, the "federal landlord," builds for numerous federal agencies. Over $4 billion in metric projects are currently in design or under construction and several major metric projects have been completed.
Federal Highway Administration	**October 1996/2000** Last year, Congress pushed back the FHWA's 1996 deadline to 2000 but, of the 52 "states" (including the District of Columbia and Puerto Rico), 44 have adhered to the 1996 date, 4 are delaying for 1 year, and 4 (Hawaii, the Dakotas, and Rhode Island) are delaying until 2000. Metric projects totaling almost $3 billion are now under construction. In 1997, about $10 billion in metric projects will be awarded, increasing to about $15 billion in 1998 and reaching the $20+ billion FHWA total by 2000.
Army Corps of Engineers	**October 1996** $400 million in metric military projects are under construction or awaiting award and $730 million are in design. $550 million in metric civil works projects are under construction. Overseas, over $1 billion in metric projects are planned or are under construction.

AGENCY	METRIC CONVERSION DATE FOR NEW CONSTRUCTION PROJECTS
Naval Facilities Engineering Command	**October 1996** The Navy's FY 1997 construction program is metric and totals about $400 million.
Air Force	**October 1996** The Air Force's FY 1997 construction program, built largely by the Army and Navy, is metric.
Coast Guard	**In phases, beginning January 1996** Approximately $11 million in metric projects are under construction. All work ($50-100 million annually) will be built in metric after 2000.
State Department	**State Department has virtually always built in metric**
National Aeronautics and Space Administration	**October 1995** Each NASA field activity has designed and constructed at least one metric project to date. All future NASA projects will be built in metric.
Federal Bureau of Prisons	**Beginning October 1996** Four metric projects totaling $374 million are in the design stage, including federal detention centers in Houston and Honolulu and federal correctional centers in Victorville and Castle AFB, California.
Department of Veterans Affairs	**No date set at this time** Five metric projects are planned but only one has been funded to date. The recently occupied $70 million VA data center in Philadelphia, built by GSA, is the largest metric building constructed in the United States.
Smithsonian Institution	**January 1994** Virtually all work, including maintenance and repair, has been performed in metric for the past three years. The $30 million National Museum for the American Indian Cultural Resources Center was recently awarded under budget. Another $300 million in metric projects are in the planning or design stages.
Department of Energy	**January 1994 for major projects** Many DOE labs and sites have ongoing metric construction programs.
Environmental Protection Agency	**No metric policy on construction grants** EPA provides water and sewer grants to states and municipalities but is not involved in their construction.

Haestad Methods, Inc. www.haestad.com

AGENCY	METRIC CONVERSION DATE FOR NEW CONSTRUCTION PROJECTS
USDA Forest Service	**Beginning October 1996** The Forest Service's metrication schedule depends in large part on state highway metrication activities. Most projects are small and in remote locations and will be converted to metric as it is practical to do so.
Department of Agriculture	**January 1995** Major DOA projects are built by GSA in metric units. A $40 million office facility in Beltsville, Maryland, is under construction and the DOA's South Building will be renovated over 10 years for a total cost of approximately $160 million. Ten smaller projects are currently under construction or have been completed.
Indian Health Service	**January 1994** All projects are being designed and constructed in metric.
National Institute of Standards and Technology	**January 1994** All projects are being designed in metric. The $75 million Advanced Chemical Sciences Laboratory in Gaithersburg, Maryland, is under construction and will be completed in 1998. Five smaller projects have been completed.
U.S. Postal Service (USPS is not a federal agency)	**No date set at this time** But several metric pilot projects are under way.
Administrative Office of the U.S. Courts	**January 1994** All new federal courthouses have been built in metric by GSA since 1994. The total value of these facilities is well over $1 billion.
Internal Revenue Service	**January 1994** All major IRS buildings are built in metric by GSA. Smaller projects are designed in-house in metric. Four major renovation projects in Cincinnati, Kansas City, Ogden, and Austin total $100 million and will be completed by the end of 1996. Designs are nearly complete for a $100 million computing center in Martinsburg, West Virginia, and a $30 million IRS complex in Beckley, West Virginia.
Naval Sea Systems Command	**No formal date** The metric design of the LPD 17 amphibious assault ship is complete. Two other ships, the SC 21 and the ADC(X), are being designed in metric. NAVSEA's conversion is proceeding on a program-by-program basis.

SOFTWARE MARKETPLACE

Appendix Contents

Haestad Methods, Inc. www.haestad.com

FEATURE SHOWCASE

You've heard a lot about these features and you've even seen some of them in previous versions – but if you haven't been in touch with Haestad Methods in a few months, you're probably missing more than you think!

For years, Haestad Methods has been dedicated to developing an object oriented programming foundation. An amazing amount of time, effort, and thought has been involved in developing this architecture, but the end result proves what the Haestad Methods civil and software engineers have believed in all along – there is no amount of "hacking" that can make up for a good design process.

The object-oriented design concept is a simple one: every part of a program has its own duties and behaviors, and it can perform certain tasks when prompted. This means that it doesn't matter if WaterCAD is creating a pump curve, StormCAD is generating a profile, or CulvertMaster is making a culvert performance curve – the graph object behaves in the same manner and with the same options. Feature enhancements can then be made to the graphing behavior, and every product that uses those graphs will automatically have those enhancements.

The architecture allows the programs to go even further than that, though. Through objects, there is a separation between the underlying model and the user interface. This allows programs like WaterCAD and CYBERNET to share a common numerical engine, common database connectivity, common table functionality, and an unlimited number of other features – even though the graphical user interface component is completely different for the two programs.

This commonality offers the modeler a more familiar, comfortable modeling environment for the different programs, as well as the promise of constantly improving features and options.

The best part is, the benefits of these features are already apparent in FlowMaster, StormCAD, CulvertMaster, and WaterCAD.

And this is just the tip of the iceberg.

Stand-alone Graphical User Interface (GUI)

If you prefer to work outside of AutoCAD, but you still want a graphical model, use the stand-alone interface. Although you can still share information with drafting programs, it certainly isn't required – all the tools you need are built-in.

- Define your entire system using our exclusive CAD-style drag and drop interface. Other drafting programs, such as AutoCAD or MicroStation, are not required.

- Import DXF files from your favorite drafting program if you want to work with background graphics. With a DXF background, you can actually work to scale and have the same coordinate system as your original drawing.

- Work schematically if you prefer – use the model to define the system connectivity and enter pipe lengths yourself.

- Mix and match scaled and schematic sections if you want, overriding specific pipe lengths with user-defined values. This is especially handy in tight areas of a drawing that is primarily to-scale.

- Insert new junctions, valves and pumps into existing pipes with a click of the mouse. The pipe will be automatically split in two.

- Morph existing elements by simply dropping the new type of element on top of it. It's never been easier to change an inlet into a junction or a reservoir into a tank.

- Double-click on any element to open a tabbed dialog editor. The tabs make it quick and easy to locate and change the information you're looking for.

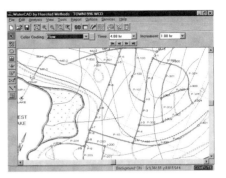

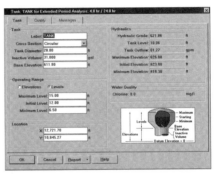

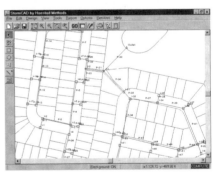

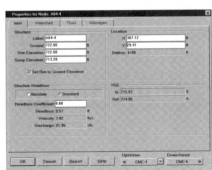

AutoCAD-Based Graphical User Interface (GUI)

If you prefer working directly inside your drafting environment, there's a solution for you, too. The programs still share the functionality and features of the stand-alone products, but provide the drafting environment you're looking for.

- Define your entire system within AutoCAD using standard AutoCAD-style toolbars and layout techniques.

- Perform all of the same AutoCAD functions you would otherwise.

- Use AutoCAD to digitize your system, and convert existing polylines (plines) into pipes.

- Work schematically if you prefer – use the model to define the system connectivity and enter pipe lengths yourself.

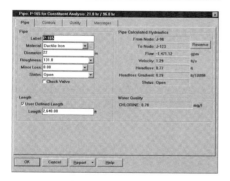

- Mix and match scaled and schematic sections if you want, overriding specific pipe lengths with user-defined values. This is especially handy in tight areas of a drawing that is primarily to-scale.

- Insert new junctions, valves and pumps into existing pipes with a click of the mouse. The pipe will be automatically split in two.

- Morph existing elements by simply dropping the new type of element on top of it.

- Select a pipe or node and open a tabbed-dialog editor to change input data or view the analysis results.

Database Connectivity

- Link directly to databases and spreadsheets, such as Jet (Microsoft Access), dBASE, Paradox, Btrieve, FoxPro, Excel, Lotus and ODBC.

- Tie into existing GIS systems and other databases to get model input – cut your data input time from a few hours or days to just a few minutes.

- Import or export data (synchronize data) to and from multiple databases at once or update a single link at a time.

- Add and remove objects from the database, based on their presence or absence in the model.

- Store data directly inside the model, so there is no chance of accidentally ruining your hydraulic data by editing a database or spreadsheet.

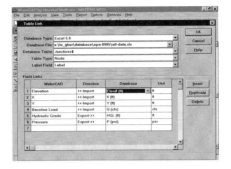

Engineering Libraries

- Use the built-in engineering libraries to control which elements are available for design purposes. For example, during a storm-sewer pipe design, StormCAD won't tell you that you need a 14.657" pipe – it will tell you that you need a 15" pipe (or, if you've chosen not to use 15" pipes in your design, it will suggest an 18" pipe).

- Change default values for roughness, minor loss values, chemical constituents and other commonly referenced values. If you want concrete pipes to default to a Manning's roughness of 0.012 instead of 0.013, just change it in the library and that will be the default every time you create another concrete pipe.

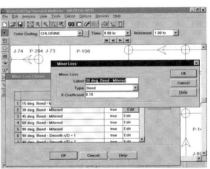

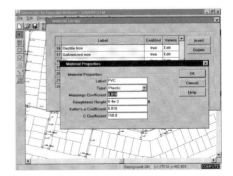

   Haestad Methods, Inc. www.haestad.com

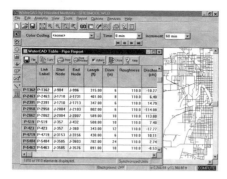

Built-in Tables

- Completely customize tables and create your own – you decide what variables are displayed and the order in which they appear.

- Drag and drop columns and rows to rearrange them.

- Drag and drop column heading borders to change the column width.

- Change column headers to be any label that you enter.

- FlexUnits allow you to change the units for any characteristic.

- View the same data side-by-side in different units for easy conversion and comparison.

- Filter the table to include only those elements that match your criteria.

- Sort the table in ascending or descending order according to any variable.

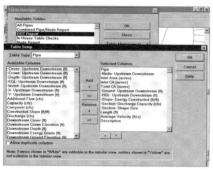

- Perform global edits to the elements in a table (the entire network or a filtered subset). Set all the elements to a fixed value or apply a multiplication, division, addition or subtraction factor.

- Update element coordinates in tabular format and watch the drawing update when you exit the table.

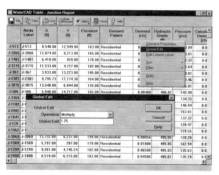

- Copy tables to the Windows clipboard, where the data can be pasted into spreadsheets, word processors and other Windows programs.

- Write a table to an ASCII tab-delimited or comma-delimited file, where it can then be imported into almost any data management or reporting program.

Output

- Generate summaries of the system behavior.

- Create detailed reports for an element or a group of elements with a click of the mouse. All data is presented in a logical, report-ready format.

- Use customizable tables to present the data in the order you choose. Manipulate the tables to suit your needs. Customization features include filtering, sorting, and selecting the variables you want to display in an order you control.

- Preview your reports, graphs, and tables before you print, in true WYSIWYG (What-You-See-Is-What-You-Get) format.

- Use the Windows clipboard to copy data into any spreadsheet, database or word-processor.

- Color code according to any variable – pipe size, flow rate, velocity, elevation, constraint violations, etc.

- Profile along a pipeline. You control the path of the profile, and the variables you want to show on the profile.

- Share graphics with AutoCAD, Microstation and other popular drafting programs through DXF files.

- Create accurate, beautiful contours based on elevation, hydraulic grade line, pressure, and other variables.

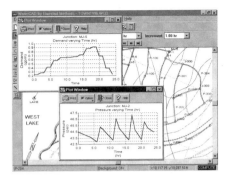

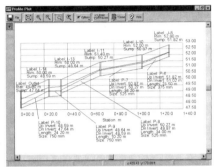

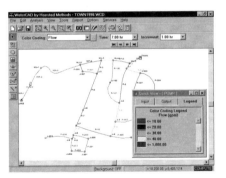

Haestad Methods, Inc. www.haestad.com

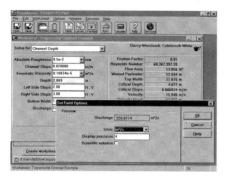

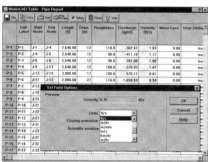

FlexUnits

Haestad Methods first introduced FlexUnits with the FlowMaster for Windows program, and the metrication process has been easy ever since.

- Change the units of any field just by right-clicking with the mouse button. For example, display flowrates in cubic feet per second (cfs), gallons per minute (gpm), cubic meters per second (cms), liters per second (l/s), million gallons per day (mgd), etc.

- Choose the display precision for any field. This will control not only how the number is displayed on-screen, but also how it is printed out in reports.

- Mix and match English and S.I. (metric) units freely – even compare the same value in different units side-by-side in tabular form.

- Change the entire project back and forth between English and S.I. units or just change the units for a few characteristics at a time.

On-line Tutorials and Help System

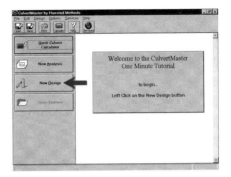

- The tutorials allow you to follow the arrows and click your way through the program – and it's not a video clip or a series of bitmap slides, it's the actual program.

- Get familiar with the program and the interface the first time you use it, just by running through the one-minute tutorial.

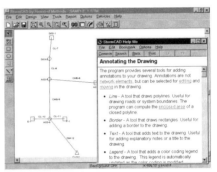

- Run the more detailed tutorials for a more in-depth look at some of the features.

- The comprehensive on-line help system offers context-sensitive help on every topic, from anywhere in the program.

- Click on the "Help" button from any screen, press the <F1> key at any time, or right click with the mouse to open the help system. If the answer you're looking for doesn't appear immediately, just type a keyword into the index and let the help system find the answers.

Haestad Methods, Inc. www.haestad.com

SOFTWARE SHOWCASE

*Detailed feature information for the best
hydrology and hydraulics software available.*

Showcase Contents

CYBERNET 3.0 & WATERCAD 2.0
Pressure Network Analysis ($195 - $15,000)

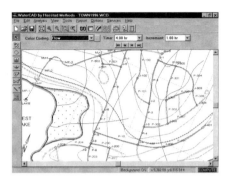

Feature Showcase Items

The following features have more detailed descriptions in the Feature Showcase:

- **Graphical User Interface (GUI)**

- **Built-in Tables**

- **Database Connectivity**

- **FlexUnits**

- **Engineering Libraries**

- **On-line Tutorials and Help**

Hydraulic Analysis

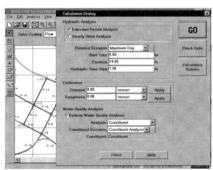

- Perform both steady-state and extended period simulations.

- Automatically determine available fire flow, based on pressure and flow constraints. View in an instant the areas of your system that are acceptable, and those areas that need improvement.

- Watch as state-of-the-art matrix techniques provide unprecedented solution speed.

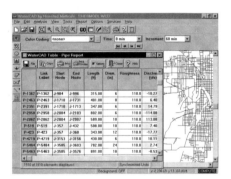

- Use various pipe materials: cast iron, ductile iron, PVC, etc.

- Calculate using any common friction method: Hazen-Williams, Manning's and Darcy-Weisbach.

- Calculate the network under different supply-and-demand scenarios and easily compare results.

- Control pressure and flow completely by using flexible valve configurations.

CYBERNET 3.0 & WATERCAD 2.0

(Continued) Pressure Network Analysis

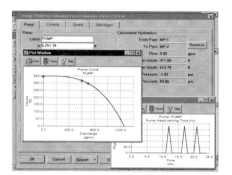

Pump Analysis

• Experiment with different pump behaviors using automated pressure and timer controls.

• Specify multiple point pump curves or constant horsepower pumps – even variable speed pumps.

• Automatically adjust pump status and speed due to changes in system pressure.

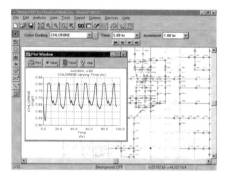

Water Quality Analysis (Optional)

• Superset of algorithms developed by the Environmental Protection Agency.

• Determine the age of water anywhere within the network.

• Identify source trends throughout the system.

• Track the growth or decay of substances such as chlorine and fluoride as they travel through the distribution network.

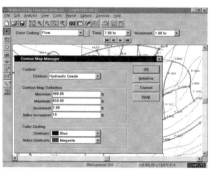

Output

See information in the Feature Showcase.

• Create graphs of time variable data (tank levels, pump operation, pipe flowrates, etc.).

• Produce contours of elevation, HGL, pressure, chemical concentration and more.

STORMCAD 2.0

Storm Sewer Design and Analysis ($295 - $1,495)

Feature Showcase Items

The following features have more detailed descriptions in the Feature Showcase:

- **Graphical User Interface (GUI)**

- **Built-in Tables**

- **Database Connectivity**

- **FlexUnits**

- **Engineering Libraries**

- **On-line Tutorials and Help**

Hydraulic Analysis

- Analyze pressure or partial (free surface) flow conditions automatically, including transitions.

- Calculate hydraulic grade lines using standard-step gradually varied flow algorithms. Solve for subcritical, critical and supercritical conditions based on drawdown and backwater.

- Choose different section materials and shapes for individual pipes: circular, box, arch and even elliptical.

- Calculate using any common friction method: Manning's, Kutter's, Hazen-Williams and Darcy-Weisbach.

- Compute structure headlosses with a standard coefficient or compute AASHTO junction losses.

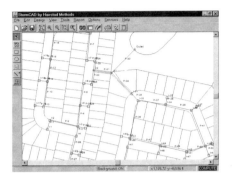

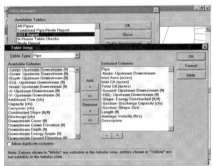

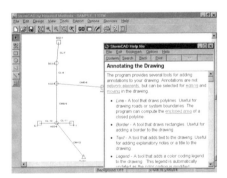

Haestad Methods, Inc. www.haestad.com

STORMCAD 2.0
(Continued) Storm Sewer Design and Analysis

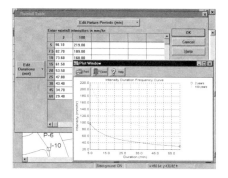

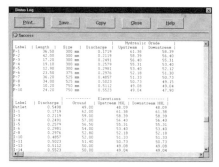

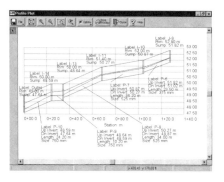

Rainfall and Watershed Analysis

• Use the widely accepted Rational Method or specify your own method by directly entering peak flows.

• Specify equations, tables or Hydro-35 for I-D-F data and then plot out the curves. Reuse your rainfall data for all projects in that region.

• Work with an unlimited number of sub-watershed areas and C-coefficients for each inlet.

• Enter external contributing areas and additional flows.

• Automatically compute carryover flows based on HEC-12 style inlet calculations.

Automatic Design

• Analyze existing systems or create a new design automatically.

• Set minimum and maximum constraints for cover, slope and velocity, and let StormCAD size the pipes and set the inverts for you.

Output

See information in the Feature Showcase.

• Create profiles from any structure in the network.

• Choose whether or not to display the HGL, ground elevations and annotations.

• Output profiles to the DXF format and import them into your drafting program, too.

CULVERTMASTER
Culvert Design and Analysis ($495)

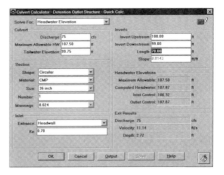

Feature Showcase Items

The following features have more detailed descriptions in the Feature Showcase:

- **FlexUnits**

- **On-line Tutorials and Help**

Hydraulic Analysis

- Use an integrated design/analysis interface for your culvert locations.

- Quickly calculate simple cases with Quick Culvert Calculator.

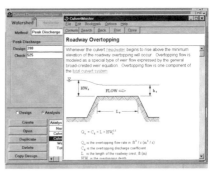

- Quickly navigate your design and analysis models using tab dialogs to edit the model's watershed, tailwater and profile information.

- Analyze pressure or partial (free surface) flow conditions automatically, including transitions.

- Calculate hydraulic grade lines using standard-step gradually varied flow algorithms, solving for subcritical, critical and supercritical conditions based on drawdown and backwater.

- Check roadway or weir overtopping.

- HDS-5 inlet control computations.

- Handle multiple mixed section types and shapes at the same embankment crossing.

Haestad Methods, Inc. www.haestad.com

CULVERTMASTER

(Continued) Culvert Design and Analysis

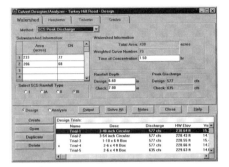

Rainfall and Watershed Analysis

- Use the widely accepted Rational Method, SCS Graphical Peak method, or directly specify a peak flow.

- Enter equations, tables or Hydro-35 for I-D-F data (for rational storms).

- Plot I-D-F curves from rainfall data and reuse your data for all projects in that region.

- Choose a type I, IA, II, or III storm for SCS peaking.

- Work with an unlimited number of sub-watershed areas and C-coefficients or CN values.

- Specify different events for a design storm and check storm.

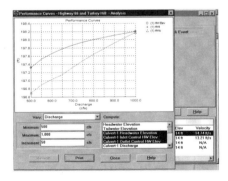

Automatic Design

- Analyze existing systems or create a new design automatically.

- Solve for headwater, discharge or culvert size.

- Use various pipe materials and choose different section shapes for the design trials – circular, box, arch and even elliptical.

- Quickly choose a modeling alternative with a simple click of the mouse.

- Organize your design trials with CulvertMaster's scenario management.

- Compare design trials using graphical and tabular views.

FLOWMASTER PE
Pipe and Ditch Sizing ($95)

Feature Showcase Items

The following features have more detailed descriptions in the Feature Showcase:

- **FlexUnits**
- **On-line Tutorials and Help**

Worksheet Management

- Create an unlimited number of worksheets to manage the data for your entire project.

- Solve for any unknown – flow, slope, channel width, pipe diameter, section roughness, etc.

- Review calculated values such as flow area, wetted perimeter, hydraulic radius, velocity, energy grade and more.

Pressure Pipes

- Perform a quick check or design on a pressure pipe faster and easier than doing it by hand or even using a spreadsheet. Just enter the information you know and let the program automatically update the solution.

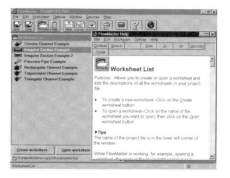

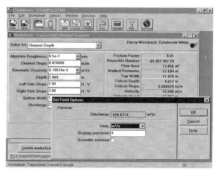

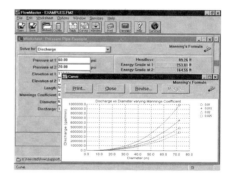

Haestad Methods, Inc. www.haestad.com

FlowMaster PE

(Continued) Pipe and Ditch Sizing

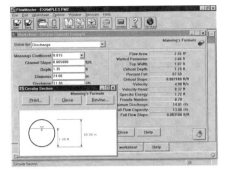

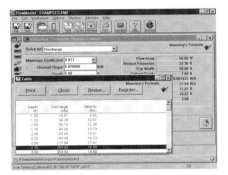

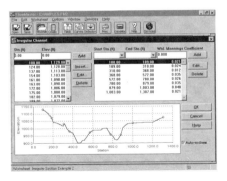

Geometric Open Channels

Geometric shapes include:

* Circular

* Rectangular (including square)

* Trapezoidal

* Triangular

* Model your ditches and swales in FlowMaster, regardless of their shapes. Find out how high the water will be or determine how steep you need to make it. This program has the flexibility to give you the answers you're looking for.

Irregular (Natural) Channels

* Enter the geometry and variable roughness for your irregular sections (open or enclosed) and let FlowMaster do the hard work.

* Model irregular open and closed cross sections effortlessly.

* Determines weighted roughness based on Horton's and Lotter's equations.

* Get results in seconds with a click of the mouse. Don't waste hours trying to calculate this type of section by hand.

VISUAL HEC-PACK

Flood Hydrographs and Water Surface Profiling ($295 - $495)

Flood Hydrographs with Visual HEC-1

• Layout the system graphically. Schematics make it much easier to keep track of your watershed basins and interconnections. Laying out the project is as simple as clicking with the mouse and entering your data – there's no need to worry about card sequences and numeric input formatting.

• View hydrographs at any point in the network, in tabular format or graphically.

• View hydrographs on-screen, print them out, or export them to other software programs (spreadsheets, word processors, etc.) via the Windows clipboard.

• Import existing HEC-1 datasets and let Visual HEC-1 show you the system schematic automatically. You can start using Visual HEC-1 immediately and – best of all – it uses the standard HEC-1 numerical engine, so you know it will be approved.

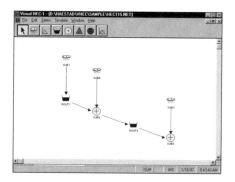

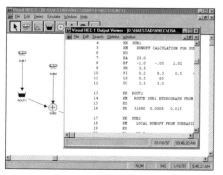

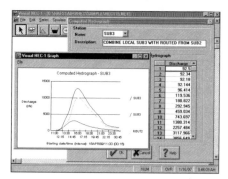

Haestad Methods, Inc. www.haestad.com

VISUAL HEC-PACK
(Continued) Flood Hydrographs and Water Surface Profiling

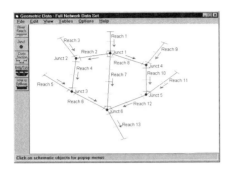

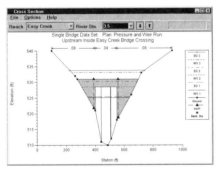

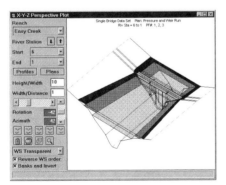

Water Surface Profiling with HEC-RAS

- Schematically lay out your river system, to make it much easier to keep track of your river reaches and interconnections. Laying out the project is as simple as clicking with the mouse and entering your data. There's no need to rearrange card data for different analyses.

- See your cross-sections as you work, right on screen. Enter data for bridges and culverts, and you can immediately view the graphical representation. Not only is that great for output, but it also makes error checking much faster.

- Generate tables with the numbers you need to back up your results. Tables can be used "as-is" or customize them for your own purposes.

- View the results from a bird's-eye-view with X-Y-Z perspective plots. These show not only your cross sections and structures, but also the water surfaces for several flood events.

PONDPACK 6.0
Watershed Modeling and Pond Design ($1,995 - $2,995)

Watershed Networks and Interconnected Pond Routing

- Model fully networked watershed scenarios with multiple areas, reaches and ponds, including interconnected network diversions.

- Model multiple connected ponds.

- Calculate reverse flow (or prevent reverse flow by using flap gates).

- Model tidal outfalls.

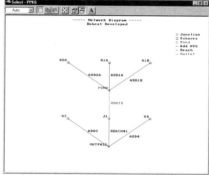

Rainfall and Runoff

- Model any duration or distribution, including synthetic or real events. Compute SCS graphical peak discharge or use rational I-D-F data. You can even create distributions from I-D-F curves.

- Import rainfall tables from TR-20 or Pond Pack version 5.

- Model multiple return events within a single calculation run.

- Calculate adjusted CNs or weighted rational C-coefficients.

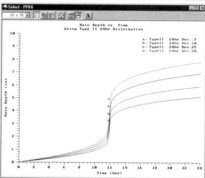

Time of Concentration

- Use built-in Tc Calculators for Carter, Eagleson, Espey/Winslow, FAA, Kerby/Hathaway, Kirpich, Length/velocity, SCS Lag, TR-55 Tc, Sheet, Shallow Concentrated, Channel, and User defined flows.

- Model multiple in-line Tc paths.

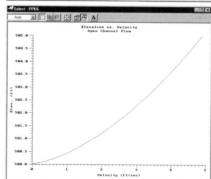

Haestad Methods, Inc. www.haestad.com

PONDPACK 6.0
(Continued) Watershed Modeling and Pond Design

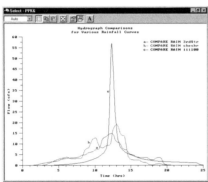

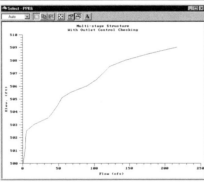

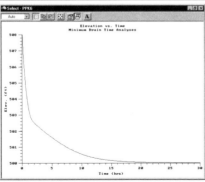

Hydrographs

• Use the SCS unit hydrograph procedure (both triangular and curvilinear methods).

• Allow for adjustment of the unit hydrograph shape factor.

• Model using the Santa Barbara Urban Hydrograph procedures.

• Calculate SCS TR-55 hydrographs.

• Generate Rational Method Hydrographs (including the Modified Rational Method).

Outlet Structures

• Model orifices, broad crested weirs, V-notch weirs, irregular weirs, culverts, stand pipes, perforations, inlet boxes and user defined structures.

• Check for tailwater effects.

• Model reverse flow.

• Model flap gates (either flow direction).

• Create multiple rating curves for interconnected pond routing.

Water Quality

• Determine first flush volume.

• Find minimum drain time as well as detention times.

• Compute pond infiltration and reach infiltration.

PONDPACK 6.0
Watershed Modeling and Pond Design (Continued)

Routing

- Route through pipes (including underground storage).

- Perform channel routing through natural, parabolic, rectangular, triangular and trapezoidal channels.

- Split (divert) hydrographs for ponds with multiple outfalls.

- Removes pond and reach infiltration hydrographs from system.

- Performs interconnected pond routing.

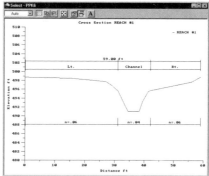

Reports

- Organize output automatically by category, then create a table of contents and index for full drainage report.

- Customize reports (print a summary or only a portion of the report items) and fully customize units (English and/or metric).

- Compare dozens of curves on a single graph.

- Display network diagrams graphically: rainfall curves, I-D-F curves, hydrographs, infiltration hydrographs, time-elevation, time-volume, channel cross sections, flow rating curves, volume rating curves, coefficient curves, and interconnected pond results.

- Export AutoCAD DXF capabilities for all graphics, including scaled watershed diagrams.

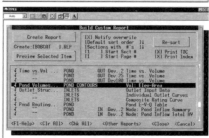

SOFTWARE PRODUCT LISTING

Haestad Methods products, Spring 1997

Software Categories

Windows programs are ready to run in Windows NT and Windows 95

Prices are subject to change without notice

OPEN CHANNEL FLOW & CULVERT ANALYSIS

CulvertMaster for Windows

Culvert Design and Analysis

CulvertMaster is an intuitive program that helps civil engineers solve culvert hydraulics problems. The program allows the user to quickly move between Quick Culvert Calculator, Culvert Designer and Culvert Analyzer. It allows the engineer to quickly build a set of design trials, compare them with tabular and graphical views, and then copy the selected design trial into a site analysis model where additional drainage components can be considered, such as weir overtopping. Each model component (tailwater, watershed, etc.) allows the engineer to choose from several alternative methods.

For more detailed information, see the Software Showcase.
Single User License: $495
5-User License: $1,495
10-User License: $2,495

FlowMaster PE for Windows

Open Channel Flow and Pressure Pipes

This is the next generation of Haestad Methods' popular FlowMaster program, used by over 10,000 engineers and technicians worldwide. We've preserved FlowMaster's fundamental mission – to provide instant and easy access to the important hydraulic working formulas with no learning curve. FlowMaster has an advanced graphical interface, WYSIWYG reporting, and superior on-line documentation.

FlowMaster can solve for any variable, and it completes the computations in a fraction of the time it takes to perform the calculations by hand. There are several section types available for analysis, including:

- Pressure Pipes

- Circular Channels

- Trapezoidal Channels, including Triangular and Rectangular Channels

- Natural (Irregular) Shapes – Including Closed Shapes

For more detailed information, see the Software Showcase
Single User License: $95
5-User License: $295
10-User License: $495

HEC-RAS for Windows

River Analysis System

 HEC-RAS was developed as the eventual replacement to the HEC-2 software program. It computes water surface profiles throughout a river system for subcritical, supercritical, or mixed flow regime. HEC-RAS can be used for analyzing natural or manmade channel systems, culverts, bridges, and floodway encroachments.

River network layout is graphical, and cross-sections and 3-dimensional perspective plots can also be generated. Tables are customizable, and data can be viewed on-screen, sent directly to a printer, or copied to the Windows clipboard.

For more detailed information, see the Software Showcase
Upgrade from HEC-2: $295
New user: $495

HEC-2 or HEC-2e

Water Surface Profiles (DOS)

The HEC-2 program computes water surface profiles for steady, gradually varied flow in natural or man-made channels. It handles subcritical and supercritical flows and can model obstructions such as bridges, culverts, weirs and floodplain structures. HEC-2 has applications in managing flood plains, evaluating floodway encroachments, identifying flood hazard zones and designing channel improvements. It is used extensively for developing FEMA flood plain studies.

HEC-2 computes over 80 different output variables, such as discharge, flow depth, flow area, velocity, energy gradient, computed water surface elevation, critical water surface elevation, energy losses, width of submerged area, and volume of excavation for channel improvements.

* Please note that HEC-2 is becoming an outdated program. We recommend using HEC-RAS (see above) instead, if possible.
Price: $495

WSPRO (HY-7)

Bridge Waterways Analysis Model (DOS)

WSPRO was designed to satisfy FHWA policy that requires a thorough evaluation of design alternatives for the hydraulics of bridge waterways. It is a comprehensive model that is well-suited for analyzing alternative designs for bridge openings and associated approach embankments. The program implements a sophisticated method for distributing conveyance through the bridge opening in the main channel as well as adjacent relief openings. Bridge openings are automatically superimposed on the existing channel cross-section to greatly simplify the data entry for bridge geometry.
Price: $495

WSP-2

SCS Water Surface Profiles (DOS)

WSP-2 uses the Standard-Step Method to determine flow characteristics and water surface profiles in open channels. It includes the effects of such obstructions as bridges, culverts and roadway restrictions. It can model normal or skewed bridge openings with or without piers, restricted channel flow through a bridge, orifice flow under a submerged bridge, and weir flow over a submerged bridge. It can model road restrictions by computing the head loss through rectangular, circular or arch culverts, and it can compute the amount of weir flow over the roadway for a given discharge. (Haestad Methods' WSP-2 also supports the LISLE modification for Illinois users.)
Price: $495

DWOPER/Network

Dynamic Wave Model (DOS)

DWOPER is a hydrodynamic model for dynamic wave reach routing and water surface profile analysis. It is based on unsteady flow equations and is useful in situations where mild bottom slopes or unsteady backwater effects from tides or large tributaries preclude using standard routing models. DWOPER is a general-purpose unsteady flow model that has wide applicability to rivers of varying physical features, such as irregular geometry, roughness, lateral inflows, flow diversions, off-channel storage, bridge shock losses, lock and dam operations, and wind effects. The Network option of DWOPER allows for the analysis of closed conduit systems. It will also compute the losses at manholes and outlets.
Price: $795

Haestad Methods, Inc. www.haestad.com

DAMS AND RESERVOIRS

DAMS2

Structure Site Analysis (DOS)

DAMS2 can develop inflow hydrographs from historical data as well as SCS or other standard design rainfall distributions. The program will generate, add, reach-route and reservoir-route hydrographs using the methodologies outlined in the SCS National Engineering Handbook. The program automatically computes tables for principal outlet structures, such as circular or box conduits, combination risers and a variety of emergency spillway configurations. The program can also account for the effects of reservoir sedimentation.
Price: $495

DAMBRK

Dam Breach Flood Forecasting (DOS)

DAMBRK uses state-of-the-art theory on dam failures and hydrodynamics to predict dam-break wave formation and downstream progression through successive dam failures. DAMBRK analyzes dam breach effects using:

- Definition of the geometric breach properties

- Computation of the outflow hydrograph using breach description, reservoir inflow, reservoir storage characteristics, spillway outflows, and downstream tail water elevations

- Dynamic routing of the hydrograph through the downstream valley to find the resulting water surface elevations and flood wave travel time

Price: $990

BREACH

Dam Breach Erosion Model (DOS)

BREACH models the breaching of an earthen dam because of overtopping or piping failure. It uses dam material properties and geometry to predict the discharge hydrograph and breach characteristics, such as size, shape and time to form. The dam can be man-made or naturally formed by a landslide, and its core material can differ from the outer material. Output for BREACH includes time to fail, time to peak, peak outflow, final breach properties (depth, bottom width, top width and side slopes), and final water surface elevation in the reservoir.
Price: $495

PRESSURE PIPE NETWORKS

CYBERNET 3.0 for AutoCAD Windows

AutoCAD Pipe Network Flow Analysis

WaterCAD 2.0 for Windows

Stand-alone Pipe Network Flow Analysis

 CYBERNET 3.0 and WaterCAD 2.0 have identical features and options. The only significant difference is that the CYBERNET 3.0 program runs directly inside AutoCAD (Releases 13 and 14, Windows only). CYBERNET 2.0 operates inside AutoCAD Releases 11, 12 and 13 DOS, and will only be available for a short time as earlier versions of AutoCAD are upgraded to Release 14.

Both CYBERNET and WaterCAD are graphical network models that allow you to visually construct a pressure system on-screen. Lay out the network, adding tanks, pumps, regulating valves, and other system components to build a precisely scaled system map or a simple network schematic.

The embedded hydraulic algorithms then solve the network, automatically computing hydraulic grades, pressures and flows throughout the system. Other calculations are also available, such as advanced water quality (constituent tracking, source identification, and age) and automated fire flow analysis. The results of these analyses can then be displayed graphically, through contouring, color-coding, and time variable graphs.

This graphical modeling technology has proven to substantially reduce the amount of time required to produce a finished analysis, as well as greatly enhance the presentation and interpretation of model results.

For more detailed information, see the Software Showcase.

Pricing	Number of Pipes								
	25	50	100	250	1,000	2,000	5,000	10,000	> 10,000
Hydraulic Analysis Only	$195	$295	$495	$995	$1,995	$2,995	$4,995	$9,995	Please Call
With Advanced Water Quality	Included			$995	$1,495	$2,995	$4,995	$7,995	$14,995	Please Call

Haestad Methods, Inc. www.haestad.com

SEDIMENTATION

HEC-6

Scour and Deposition (DOS)

For the evaluation of long-term river and reservoir sedimentation behavior, HEC-6 simulates the transportation of sediment in a stream and can determine both the volume and location of sediment deposits. It uses any one of twelve different sediment transport functions in its calculations. It can analyze dredging operations, shallow reservoirs, and scour and deposition effects for rivers. HEC-6 can also model the fall and rise of movable bed material during several flow cycles.
Price: $495

SEDIMOT-II

Hydrology and Sedimentology (DOS)

An ideal tool for obtaining construction phase stormwater regulatory compliance, SEDIMOT II generates, adds and routes hydrographs and sediment load through multiple subareas, reaches and reservoirs. It also estimates efficiency of sediment removal by detention ponds and grass filters. Output from the program includes peak sediment concentration, sediment basin trap efficiency, sediment load discharge, peak effluent sediment concentration and peak effluent settleable concentration.
Price: $495

STORM AND SANITARY
SEWER NETWORKS

StormCAD 2.0 for Windows

Storm Sewer Design and Analysis

 StormCAD for Windows uses a state-of-the-art graphical interface to allow you to construct storm sewer systems. Just drag and drop pipes, bends, inlets and junctions directly into your system; right click on the item to enter values; and hit the calculate button to perform all system calculations. StormCAD allows you to use rainfall tables, equations or Hydro-35 data to predict rainfall volumes. Circular pipes, boxes, ellipses, and pipe arches are supported for conveyance of system flows. Flow calculations handle all pressure and varied flow situations, including hydraulic jumps, backwater and drawdown curves. It even performs HEC-12 style inlet and carryover computations.

For more detailed information, see the Software Showcase.

Single User License			5 User License			10 User License		
10 Inlets	25 Inlets	Unlimited	10 Inlets	25 Inlets	Unlimited	10 Inlets	25 Inlets	Unlimited
$295	$795	$1,495	$795	$1,995	$2,995	$995	$2,995	$4,995

SewerCAD for Windows (Call)

Sanitary Sewer Design and Analysis

SewerCAD for Windows uses a state-of-the-art graphical CAD-like interface (including AutoCAD and Microstation DXF support) to allow you to construct sanitary sewer systems. Just drag and drop pipes, bends, inlets, junctions and pumps directly into your system; right click on the item to enter values; and press the calculate button to perform all system calculations.

WATERSHED HYDROLOGY

POND PACK 6.0

Detention Pond Design Made Easy

 Pond Pack is ideal for modeling general hydrology and runoff from site development. In addition to SCS unit hydrograph methods, the program can compute hydrographs using the Rational Method, Modified Rational, Santa Barbara, SCS TR-55, and DeKalb procedures. PondPack computes time of concentration, weights CN values and Rational "C" coefficients, computes peak discharges, generates and plots hydrographs, and performs pre- and postdeveloped analyses. You can use standard SCS rainfall distributions or use customized rainfall distribution tables and I-D-F curves for your design area. All equations, assumptions and procedures are included in the report-ready output, so engineers and reviewers can easily identify them.

PondPack also performs analysis for interconnected pond routing, including time variable outfalls (such as tidal influences) and reverse flows.

Built-in time of concentration calculators are available for numerous popular methods, including Carter, Eagleson, Espey/Winslow, FAA, Kerby/Hathaway, Kirpich, Length/velocity, SCS Lag, TR-55 Tc, Sheet, Shallow Concentrated, Channel, and User defined flows.

Routing capabilities include pipes, natural channels, parabolic channels, rectangular channels, triangular channels, and trapezoidal channels.

The customized report builder allows you to organize output automatically by category, and then create a table of contents and index for the full drainage report. Reports are fully customizable.

For more detailed information, see the Software Showcase.
Upgrade from PondPack 5.0: $1,995
New User: $2,995

Visual HEC-1 for Windows

Floodplain Hydrology and Watershed Modeling

 Visual HEC-1 allows you to graphically create, modify, display, and run HEC-1 data. Just draw your network on the screen using the tool palette, double-click on any element to enter data, and click to calculate the network. Network schematics make it much easier to keep track of your watershed basins and interconnections. Laying out the project is as simple as clicking with the mouse and entering in your data. There is no need to worry about card sequences and numeric input formatting with Visual HEC-1.

Import existing HEC-1 datasets and start using Visual HEC-1 immediately. Best of all - it uses the standard HEC-1 numerical engine, so you know it will be approved! View hydrographs at any point in the network, in tabular format or graphically. As with all output, the hydrographs can be viewed on-screen, printed out, or exported to other software (spreadsheets, word processors, etc.) via the Windows clipboard.

For more detailed information, see the Software Showcase.
Upgrade from HEC-1: $295
New user: $495

HEC-1 or HEC-1e

Flood Hydrograph Package (DOS)

HEC-1 generates hydrographs from rainfall or snow melt, adds or diverts them, then routes through reaches, reservoirs and detention ponds. HEC-1 models multiple streams and reservoir networks and has dam failure simulation capabilities. It handles level-pool routing for reservoirs and detention ponds, and routes through stream reaches using Kinematic Wave, Muskingum, Muskingum-Cunge, Modified Puls, and other methods. HEC-1 supports five methods for computing infiltration and abstraction losses and computes unit hydrographs using the Clark, Snyder and SCS dimensionless hydrograph methods.

*Please note that Visual HEC-1 (see above) offers a much friendlier graphical interface, and we recommend Visual HEC-1 over the standard DOS based HEC-1 program.
Price: $495

TR-20

Project Formulation Hydrology (DOS)

TR-20 is an excellent tool for watershed models that require hydrograph generation, addition or diversion, reach routing or multiple pond network analyses. The program uses SCS methods to generate runoff hydrographs based on precipitation amounts specified for any storm duration. TR-20 computes hydrographs using standard SCS rainfall distributions and also allows you to enter your own rainfall distribution, time increments and duration.
Price: $495

HMR52

Probable Maximum Storm (DOS)

HMR52 computes basin-average precipitation for probable maximum storms (PMS) and finds the spatially averaged probable maximum precipitation (PMP) for a watershed. It uses the methods specified in the NWS Hydrometeorological Report No. 52 and is applicable to areas east of the 105th Meridian (near the eastern border of Wyoming). PMP data computed with HMR52 can be used directly with HEC-1 to compute hydrographs for the probable maximum flood (PMF). The PMF is typically the basis for dam spillway design and failure analysis.
Price: $495

HECWRC

Flood Flow Frequency (DOS)

HECWRC performs a statistical analysis of historical stream flow data and plots the resulting flow/frequency curve. The program places both the observed and computed probability curves on the same plot. HECWRC uses the Log-Pearson Type III distribution to compute the frequency curve. The curve ordinates are computed both with and without the expected probability adjustment.
Price: $495

HEC-4

Monthly Stream Flow Simulation (DOS)

HEC-4 will analyze monthly stream flows at interrelated stations. It statistically analyzes the stream flow data and generates a sequence of hypothetical flows for watersheds with similar characteristics – for any desired time period. The program will also reconstitute missing stream flow data on the basis of concurrent flows observed at other locations.
Price: $495

SERVICES AND ORDERING

Haestad Methods' technical support staff consists of civil engineers and computer experts who will answer your questions about any of our 30-plus products. Our comprehensive support covers everything from basic program operation to complex modeling techniques.

Our free support hotline is applicable to every Haestad product, regardless of the date of purchase. There are no maintenance fees or support contracts – we support each product for as long as you use it. For answers to your questions about any of our programs, general hydrology and hydraulics, and computer-related topics, call Haestad Methods technical support today.

Ordering Information

Please contact Haestad Methods with any questions or for the most recent pricing.

- Voice: (203) 755-1666 or Toll-free: (800) 727-6555

- Fax: (203) 597-1488

- Internet: Email: info@haestad.com or visit: http://www.haestad.com

- BBS: (203) 756-1921

- Snail Mail   Haestad Methods, Inc.
                  37 Brookside Road
                  Waterbury, CT, USA 06708

Purchase and download programs and updates
for immediate use from our internet web site, at

http://www.haestad.com

CONTINUING

EDUCATION

The Continuing

Education Unit ®

Appendix Contents

All workshops listed are fully accredited by the
International Association for Continuing Education and Training and the
Professional Development Registry for Engineers and Surveyors.

WORKSHOPS AT A GLANCE

Water Surface Profiles ($795, 2.4 CEU's)

In this three-day seminar, you will enjoy a great atmosphere where you will focus on new HEC-RAS software modeling, results interpretation and graphical presentation options for water surface profiles.

Floodplain Hydrology ($795, 2.4 CEU's)

In this extensive three-day course, you will learn how to select the appropriate Visual HEC-1 option for your studies, how to estimate model parameters, how to organize program output and how to interpret VHEC-1 results. It is a hands-on seminar, with workshops that let you develop experience in every topic covered, using real catchment data.

Urban Stormwater Management ($795, 1.6 CEU's)

In this course you will learn the newest, practical hydrology and stormwater management techniques, from urban hydrology through open channel hydraulics, pond design, and much more. Theory is reinforced through "hands-on" design exercises using the extremely powerful and most popular hydrology software in use today: Haestad Methods' PondPack.

Storm Sewer Design ($795, 1.6 CEU's)

In this extensive two-day workshop, you will learn how to design, analyze and optimize storm sewer systems with hands-on, real-world problems.

Water Distribution Modeling ($795, 1.6 CEU's)

In this two-day water distribution network modeling course, you will learn the latest techniques to identify flow and pressure problems, regulate valves, pumping, calibration, and other simulation strategies. The latest state-of-the-art software, the WaterCAD computer model is used as the learning vehicle for this hands-on workshop.

Water Quality Analysis ($295, 0.8 CEU's)

This one-day water quality analysis course teaches fundamental techniques for modeling the water quality processes of multiple source network systems. You'll learn how to simulate the transport, reactions and blending of source constituents, calibrate a water quality model, and design and size tanks with consideration to the water quality aspects of the system.

1997 SCHEDULE OF WORKSHOPS

January
Phoenix, AZ

Embassy Suites, Airport West
6-7	Urban Stormwater Management
8-9	Water Distribution Modeling
10	Water Quality
13-14	Storm Sewer Design
15-17	Floodplain Hydrology

February
Boston, MA

Harborside Hyatt
5-7	Floodplain Hydrology
10-12	Water Surface Profiles
13-14	Urban Stormwater Management

March
Atlanta, GA

Wyndham Gardens Midtown
5-6	Water Distribution Modeling
7	Water Quality Analysis
10-11	Urban Stormwater Management
12-14	Floodplain Hydrology
17-19	Water Surface Profiles
20-21	Storm Sewer Design

April
Austin, TX

Embassy Suites Austin Airport North
7-8	Urban Stormwater Management
9-11	Floodplain Hydrology
14-15	Storm Sewer Design
16-17	Water Distribution Modeling
18	Water Quality Analysis

May
Cincinnati, OH

Crowne Plaza
12-13	Urban Stormwater Management
14-15	Water Distribution Modeling
16	Water Quality Analysis
19-20	Storm Sewer Design
21-23	Water Surface Profiles

June
San Francisco, CA

Embassy Suites Airport South
9-10	Urban Stormwater Management
11-12	Water Distribution Modeling
13	Water Quality Analysis
16-17	Storm Sewer Design
18-20	Water Surface Profiles

Haestad Methods, Inc. www.haestad.com

July
Toronto, ON (Canada)

Holiday Inn on King
7-9   Water Surface Profiles
10-11   Storm Sewer Design
14-15   Urban Stormwater Management
16-17   Water Distribution Modeling
18   Water Quality Analysis

August
Salt Lake City, UT

Best Western Olympus
6-7   Water Distribution Modeling
8   Water Quality Analysis
11-12   Storm Sewer Design
13-15   Floodplain Hydrology
18-20   Water Surface Profiles
21-22   Urban Stormwater Management

September
Philadelphia, PA

Adams Mark's Hotel
3-4   Water Distribution Modeling
5   Water Quality Analysis
8-9   Urban Stormwater Management
11-12   Storm Sewer Design

October
Orlando, FL

Delta Orlando Resort
13-14   Urban Stormwater Management
15-16   Water Distribution Modeling
17   Water Quality Analysis
20-21   Storm Sewer Design
22-24   Water Surface Profiles

November
Nashville, TN

Union Station Hotel
10-11   Storm Sewer Design
12-13   Water Distribution Modeling
14   Water Quality Analysis
17-18   Urban Stormwater Management
19-21   Floodplain Hydrology

WATER SURFACE PROFILES

Featuring HEC-RAS ($795, 2.4 CEU's)

Donald V. Chase, Ph.D., PE, an assistant professor of civil and environmental engineering at the University of Dayton, is a recognized authority in numerical modeling and computer simulation. Participants of Haestad Methods workshops have broadly commended his expertise.

He conducts funded research and teaches both graduate and undergraduate courses in environmental engineering, focusing on water resource systems. Some of the projects he has received grants and contracts to study:

- "Improved Methodologies to Generate Pumping Schedules for Fixed and Variable Speed Pumps"

- "Enhancing ADDAMS Application Through Use of an Integrated Environment"

- "Evaluation of Transient Analyses Performed on the DWSD Water Transmission System"

- "Hydraulic Characteristics of CON/SPAN Bridge Systems"

Before receiving his Ph.D. from the University of Kentucky, Dr. Chase helped conduct and manage research on water distribution systems for the U.S. Army Corps of Engineers at its Waterways Experiment Station. As a researcher and consultant, he has performed numerous water surface profile analyses using the Army Corps' HEC-2 computer model.

Dr. Chase has several journal papers to his credit and has also served as a paper reviewer for ASCE journals. In addition, he has participated in numerous proceedings and given many technical reports and presentations. He was named "Best Lecturer" by the University of Dayton Panhellenic Council in the fall of 1996.

His professional memberships include the American Society of Civil Engineers, the American Water Works Association, and Water for People. He served on the board of directors of the Dayton section of the National Society of Professional Engineers. He is chairman of the ASCE Environmental Engineering Task Committee and has served on several other ASCE and AWWA committees.

Water Surface Profiles
Agenda – Day 1

Open Channel Hydraulics Review

- Channel Properties
- Flow Regime/Froude Number
- Continuity
- Energy Concepts
- Momentum Concepts
- Uniform Flow - Normal/Critical Depth
- Gradually Varied Flow

Water Surface Profile Computation

- Gradually Varied Flow Function
- Methods of Solution
- Energy Equation
- Momentum Equation
- Hand Computation Example
- Significance of Results

Introduction to HEC-RAS

- Next-Generation Engineering Software
- HEC-RAS Capabilities
- Water Surface Profile Computations
- Mixed Flow Regime Modeling
- Junction Analysis
- Improved Bridge Hydraulics
- Improved Culvert Modeling
- Multiple Opening Feature
- Graphical Data Entry and Results Presentation

- What the Future Holds
- Unsteady Flow Model
- Sediment Transport Model
- Integrated River Analysis System Environment
- Frequent Uses of Program
- Water Surface Profiles
- Floodway Delineation
- Encroachment Options
- Bridge Analysis
- Culvert Analysis
- Differences Between HEC-RAS and HEC-2

HEC-RAS: Basic Data Requirements

- Channel Geometry
- Location of X-Sections
- Field Surveys
- Topographic Maps
- Manning's Roughness Values
- Field Surveys
- Literature Reported Values
- Variation with Depth/Distance
- Composite Manning's Roughness
- Model Calibration

Q & A Session

Water Surface Profiles
Agenda – Day 2

HEC-RAS: Basic Data Requirements

- Channel Discharge
- Flood Insurance Studies
- Hydrologic Analysis
- Rating Curve
- Historical Values
- Starting Water Surface Elevation
- Observed High Water Marks
- Flood Insurance Studies
- Critical Depth
- Slope-Area Method

Constructing a HEC-RAS Project

- Entering Geometric Data
- Entering Steady-Flow Data
- Importing Existing HEC-2 Data Files
- Performing Profile Computations
- Defining a Plan
- Conducting the Simulation
- Viewing Output
- Tabular Output
- Graphical Output
- Generating Reports
- Copying and Pasting Graphics
- Printing Output

Workshop 1: Subcritical Flow Profiles

- Data Requirements
- Performing a Simulation
- Interpreting the Results

Workshop 2: Supercritical Flow Profiles

- Data Requirements
- Performing a Simulation
- Interpreting the Results

Encroachment Analysis

- Corps of Engineers 404 Permits
- State Permits/Local/Floodplain Coordinators
- Encroachment Options
- Floodway Analysis

Workshop 3: Determining Floodway Limits

- Data Requirements
- Performing a Simulation
- Interpreting the Results

Q & A Session

Water Surface Profiles
Agenda – Day 3

Bridge Analysis

- Bridge Data
- Roadway/Deck Data
- Pier Data
- Abutment Data
- Low Flow Methods
- Energy Equation (Normal Bridge)
- Yarnell Equation (Special Bridge)
- Momentum Equation
- High Flow Methods
- Energy Equation
- Pressure/Weir Flow
- Bridge Modeling Options

Workshop 4:
Evaluating Bridge Hydraulics

Culvert Analysis

- Culvert Hydraulics
- FHWA's HDS 5 Method
- Culvert Data
- Roadway/Deck Data
- Culvert Characteristics
- Culvert Modeling Options

Workshop 5:
Designing a Culvert
Using HEC-RAS

Multiple Opening Analysis

- Examples of Multiple Openings
- Solution Methodology
- Multiple Opening Modeling Options

Workshop 6:
Multiple Opening Analysis

Additional HEC-RAS Features

- Multiple Profile Run
- Tributary Profiles
- Varying Channel Discharge
- Optional Friction Loss Equations
- Others

Q & A Session

FLOODPLAIN HYDROLOGY

Featuring Visual HEC-1 ($795, 2.4 CEU's)

David T. Ford, Ph.D., PE, is a world-renowned authority in hydrologic engineering, water-resources planning and system analysis. He is president of David Ford Consulting Engineer and has gained wide respect as a lecturer and instructor for workshops sponsored by Haestad Methods and other groups. He has taught more than 50 post-graduate courses in hydrologic engineering for U.S. universities, government agencies, and numerous international organizations.

Dr. Ford's vast technical expertise includes:

- Hydrologic engineering. Rainfall-runoff analysis, flood forecasting, urban drainage, hydrologic statistics, risk analysis, and reservoir system analysis.

- Decision-support systems. Large-scale system optimization, database management, geographic information systems, system integration.

- Natural resource policy analysis.

- Technology transfer training.

Dr. Ford has served as project manager and chief engineer for projects ranging from application of an off-the-shelf rainfall-runoff model for sizing a detention pond in California, to designing and developing from scratch a complete decision-support system for real-time runoff forecasting and flood-control reservoir operation in India.

He has written and co-authored numerous journal articles and contributed to several books. He has also given dozens of presentations around the world, including such topics as "Impact of Reservoir Flood-Control Operation on Interior-Drainage Facilities," "Computer Models for Water Excess Management," and "Reinventing Water Resources System Engineering."

He is a member of the American Society of Civil Engineers and is vice chairman of the Water Resources Systems Committee of the Water Resources Planning and Management Division. His honors include being named a Fulbright Fellow, Portugal, and a Hawley Fellow for the Texas section of ASCE. In addition, he is a member of the Chi Epsilon, Tau Beta Pi, and Phi Theta Kappa honorary fraternities.

Floodplain Hydrology
Agenda – Day 1

Introduction to Floodplain Hydrology

- Information Needs for Floodplain Management Planning

- How the X-YR Discharge Can Be Estimated

- Role of HEC-1 in Estimating the X-YR Discharge

Rainfall Specification

- Rainfall Requirements for Runoff Computation with HEC-1

- Computation of EUD of Rainfall

- Temporal Distribution of Rainfall

Runoff Volume Computation

- Determination of Excess Rainfall

- Treatment of Impervious Area

- The Initial and Uniform-Rate Loss Model

- Loss Rates as a Function of Land Use and Soil Type

Surface Runoff, Routing, Storage

- How HEC-1 Models the Runoff Process

- Unit Response Function Theory and Application

- HEC-1's Baseflow Model

How the HEC-1 Package Works

- Details of the Software

- Description of the HEC-1 User's Manual

- Example of Input

- Mechanics of Data Entry and Program Execution on PC

- What's in the Output

WORKSHOP 1: Simple Rainfall Runoff Calculation

Parametric (Synthetic) UH

- Overview of Parametric UH

- Snyder's UH

- HEC-1 Input/Output for Snyder's UH

- Clark's UH

Q & A Session

Floodplain Hydrology
Agenda – Day 2

Calibration of HEC-1

- Objective of Calibration
- Calibration Techniques
- Criteria for Comparing Simulated and Observed Hydrographs
- Optimization Procedures
- HEC-1 Input/Output for Calibration

WORKSHOP 2: Calibration of Program HEC-1

Parameter Estimation for Ungauged Catchments

- Definition of the Problem
- Solutions
- Development of Parameter-Predictive Relationships
- Examples of Relationships

SCS Models

- Overview of SCS CN Loss Model
- CN Estimation for Ungauged Catchments
- Composite CN
- Pitfalls in Estimating CN
- SCS UH
- UH Parameter Estimation for Ungauged Catchments
- HEC-1 Input/Output for SCS Loss Model and UH

WORKSHOP 3: Ungauged Catchment Analysis with SCS Technique

Design Storms

- Need for Design Storm
- Definition of Design Storm
- Sources of Depth-Duration-Frequency Information
- SCS Temporal Distribution
- Corp's Balanced Distribution
- What's the Proper Duration of a Design Storm
- HEC-1 Input/Output for Design Storms

WORKSHOP 4: Design-Storm Runoff Computation

Q & A Session

Floodplain Hydrology
Agenda – Day 3

Complex Catchment Modeling

- How to Model Complex Catchments

- Overview of Flood Routing

- 1-D Equations of Motion in Open Channel

- How Can We Solve These

Streamflow Routing

- Storage Routing

- HEC-1 Input/Output for Storage Routing Muskingum Routing

- HEC-1 Input/Output for Muskingum Routing

- Muskingum-Cunge Routing

- HEC-1 Input/Output for Muskingum-Cunge Routing

- How to Select the Proper Routing Model

WORKSHOP 5: Multi-Subcatchment Runoff Calculation with HEC-1

Modeling Catchment Changes

- HEC-1 Input/Output for Modeling Alternative Development

- HEC-1 Input/Output for Modeling Detention Ponds

- HEC-1 Input/Output for Modeling Diversions and Flood Bypasses

- HEC-1 Input/Output for Modeling Off-Stream Storage

WORKSHOP 6: Analysis of Catchment Changes

Q & A Session

URBAN STORMWATER MANAGEMENT

Featuring Pond Pack ($795, 1.6 CEU's)

Michael K. Glazner is chief architect of the Pond Pack. Since joining Haestad Methods in 1987, he continues to focus much of his skill on technical writing, training and support, and writing articles about stormwater issues.

Mr. Glazner's past engineering experience includes flood plain delineation and designing regional and on-site detention facilities, drop structures, open channels, energy dissipation structures, inverted siphons, streets, storm sewer systems, and erosion control structures.

He has given a wide range of presentations in the fields of hydrology and hydraulics and computer applications. He has served as a speaker at the ASCE National Conference on Hydraulic Engineering, Annual Conference for the Association of State Dam Safety Officials, Computational Hydrology Institute's International Symposium, American Public Works Association Seminar, Southwest Stormwater Management Symposium, and a variety of other civil engineering courses and workshops.

As a frequent instructor for Haestad's workshops, Mr. Glazner consistently gets high ratings from participants.

During the last six years, more than 1,200 engineers have participated in his classes – testament to his popularity and skill. When you meet him, you'll quickly realize why this course has become the standard by which all others are judged. Mr. Glazner's technical expertise and his down-to-earth style, sprinkled with tidbits of humor, are sure to capture and hold your interest.

He received his BS in civil engineering from Texas A&M University in 1983, graduating summa cum laude. In 1983, he was also honored with the Engineering Achievement Award and the Outstanding Civil Engineering Student Award. He earned his Master's degree in civil engineering from Texas A&M in 1985.

Urban Stormwater Management
Agenda – Day 1

General Hydrology

- Rainfall
- Rainfall Measurements
- Rainfall Distributions
- Infiltration
- Runoff Depth & Volume
- Time of Concentration Equations
- Factors Affecting Hydrograph Shape

Open Channels

- Reach Routing
- Mannings Equation
- Circular, Trapezoidal, Parabolic
- Natural Channels
- Backwater Effects
- Channel Exercises

Hydrology Exercises

- Estimating Return Frequency for an Actual Storm
- Adjusting Runoff CN's to Reflect Development
- Antecedent Moisture
- Runoff Depth & Volume
- Time of Concentration
- Rainfall Curves
- Runoff Hydrographs
- Adding Hydrographs

Rational Method

- Runoff C Coefficients
- I-D-F Curves
- Storm Duration

Comparison of Rational Method with Other Methods

- Rational C vs. SCS CN
- Storm Duration
- Hydrographs
- Runoff Volumes

Hydrograph Methods

- Overview of HEC-1 & TR-20
- SCS Unit Hydrograph Method
- Santa Barbara Urban Hydrograph
- Modified Rational Method

Q & A Session

Urban Stormwater Management
Agenda – Day 2

Detention Pond Overview

- Pond Routing Concept
- Impacts of Detention
- Regional vs. On-Site Detention
- Maintenance
- Water Quality
- Steps for Designing Detention

Pond Sizing

- Estimating Required Storage
- Grading Plan Volumes

Outlet Structures

- Performance Rating Curves
- Weirs, Orifices, Stand Pipes, Inlet Boxes
- Tailwater Effects
- Culverts
- Inlet Control
- Outlet Control
- Single Stage Outlets
- Multistage Outlets
- Structures in Series

Pond Routing

- General Theory
- Routing Exercise

Watershed Exercises

- Predeveloped Conditions
- Postdeveloped Conditions (without detention)
- Pond Storage Estimate
- Pond Grading Plan Volumes
- Outlet Structure Design
- Post Developed Conditions (with detention)
- Comparison of Pre vs. Post

Interconnected Ponds

- Overview of Interconnected Pond Modeling (ICPM)
- Tidal Outfalls
- Interconnected Example

Additional Topics

- Culvert Routing
- Retention Ponds
- Pond Infiltration
- Detention Time

Q & A Session

STORM SEWER DESIGN

Featuring StormCAD ($795, 1.6 CEU's)

Michael E. Meadows, Ph.D., PE, is an associate professor in the Department of Civil and Environmental Engineering at the University of South Carolina, where he teaches the senior design course as well as undergraduate and graduate courses on hydraulics and hydrology – his specialties.

Since receiving his Ph.D. in civil engineering from the University of Tennessee in 1976, Dr. Meadows has given numerous presentations as an invited lecturer, been a frequent contributor to technical and engineering reports, and served as a consultant on such projects as:

- Urban drainage system design and performance

- Building flooding from subsurface drainage

- Impact of urban development on off-site drainage systems

- Software upgrade for wastewater pump station and network analysis

Dr. Meadows is the co-author of two textbooks on stormwater runoff, "Stormwater Modeling" and "Kinematic Hydrology and Modeling." He has also written numerous papers on improved methods for estimating stormwater runoff and evaluating drainage system performance.

In addition, Dr. Meadows has designed software for urban stormwater drainage system simulation, culvert hydraulics, sediment pond performance, and wastewater pump station performance.

Some of his honors and awards include a Research Achievement Award, College of Engineering, South Carolina; the Samuel Litman Distinguished Professor Award in Engineering, University of South Carolina; and the R.E. Shaver Award for Excellence in Teaching, Department of Civil Engineering, University of Kentucky.

His professional affiliations include the American Society of Civil Engineers, the American Water Resources Association, the American Society of Agricultural Engineers, and the Society of Primitive Technology.

Storm Sewer Design
Agenda – Day 1

Overview of Storm Sewer Design

- Elements of a Storm Sewer System
- Terminology
- Design Philosophy

Hydraulics Review

- Types of Flow
- Conservation Principles
- Hydraulic and Energy Grade Lines
- Friction Loss Equations
- Specific Energy
- Critical Depth
- Froude Number
- Classification of Flows
- Uniform Flow
- Manning's Equation
- Normal Depth

Workshop 1: Travel Time in Sewers

Hydrology Review

- Watershed Delineation and Measurements
- Return Period and Risk
- Rainfall Data/IDF Curves
- Time of Concentration
- Rational Method
- TR-55 Graphical Peak Discharge Method

Workshop 2: Calculating Time of Concentration and Design Flows

Planning a Storm Sewer

- Layout
- Manhole Types and Spacing
- Pipe Material

Design Considerations

- Maximum and Minimum Velocities
- Pipe Slopes
- Cover and Elevation Requirements
- Surcharge
- Design Drawings

Workshop 3: Storm Sewer System Design

- Determine Design Flows and Design a Multiple-Pipe System by Hand and Using StormCAD.

Q&A Session

Haestad Methods, Inc. www.haestad.com

Storm Sewer Design
Agenda – Day 2

Nonuniform Flow and Controls

- Channel Classification
- Flow Profiles
- Flow Profile Analysis
- Theory
- Direct Step Method
- Standard Step Method
- Inlet and Outlet Controls
- Energy Loss through Manholes
- Hydraulic Jumps

Workshop 4: Hydraulic Grade Line Calculation

- Calculate Hydraulic Grade Line for Hydraulically Mild and Steep Sewers under Nonsubmerged and Submerged Tailwater Conditions.

Workshop 5: Optimization of Storm Sewer Systems

- Apply StormCAD Constraint-Based Design Features to Automatically Design a Sewer System to Meet Velocity, Slope and Cover Constraints.

Structural Requirements

- Vertical Load
- Live Load
- Pipe Strength
- Bedding

Construction Methods

- Open Trench
- Rock Excavation
- Cohesive and Noncohesive Soils

Permit Requirements

- Documents
- Drawings
- Permit Application

Q&A Session

WATER DISTRIBUTION
& WATER QUALITY

Featuring WaterCAD ($795, 1.6 CEU's)
Water Quality Workshop ($295, 0.8 CEU's)

Thomas M. Walski, Ph.D., PE, is one of the premier instructors of water distribution modeling in the world. He has vast experience in such areas as:

- Water distribution hydraulics, water and wastewater system management; and operation, design and cost-estimating

- Economics of water resources systems

- Water and sewer system rehabilitation

- Computer applications in environmental engineering

He has written more than 40 peer review papers and three authoritative books on the issue – "Analysis of Water Distribution Systems," "Water Supply System Rehabilitation," and "Water Distribution Systems: Simulation and Sizing." In addition, Dr. Walski has presented numerous conference papers and has written dozens of technical papers, reports, manuals and letters on such issues as water quality, water conservation,

and the economics of water distribution. He has also served as a reviewer, produced videotapes and been called on as an expert witness.

Dr. Walski is also active in a variety of professional organizations and committees, including the American Society of Civil Engineers, the American Water Works Association, the Water Pollution Control Federation, and the Northeastern Pennsylvania Chapter of the World Future Society. He also serves on the boards of Ecologia and the Anthracite Scenic Trail Association and is a past editor of the Journal of Environmental Engineering.

Some of his awards and honors include Best Paper Award for the AWWA Distribution and Plant Operations Division; Best Practice Oriented Paper for the ASCE Water Resources Planning and Management Division; and Honorable Mention for Outstanding Federal Environmental Engineer.

Haestad Methods, Inc. www.haestad.com

Water Distribution Modeling
Agenda – Day 1

Hydraulic Review

- Basic Working Equations
- Units of Pressure and Flow
- Solution Methods

How to Apply Models

- What Data do you Need?
- Assessing Level of Detail
- Defining Modeling Objectives

Defining Network Models

- Basic AutoCAD Commands
- Basic Network Components
- Pipes / Junctions / Boundary Conditions

Workshop 1: Network Building

- Formulate, Construct and Solve a Basic Network Model

Other Pressure Network Components

- Pumps
- Representation in Model
- Generating System Head Curves
- Regulating Valves
  Pressure-Reducing Valves
  Flow-Control Valves
  Pressure-Sustaining Valves
  Pressure-Breaker Valves
  Throttle-Control Valves

Workshop 2: Pumping Systems

- Pumps, RVs, Check Valves and Minor Losses in the Model

Q & A Session

Open Lab

Water Distribution Modeling
Agenda – Day 2

Model Calibration

- Where Do You Go for Data?
- What Do You Adjust and When?
- Identifying Bad Data
- Selling the Model to O&M

Workshop 3: Calibration

- Applying Calibration Techniques Using WaterCAD

Planning System Improvements

- Establishing Pressure Zones
- Pipe Sizing
- Pump Selection and Sizing
- Storage

Workshop 4: System Improvements

- Plan, Develop and Implement a System-Improvement Strategy Using WaterCAD

Extended Period Simulations

- Demand Schedules and Patterns
- Special Network Elements
- Storage Tanks
- Altitude Valves and Pressure Switches

Workshop 5: Extended Period Simulations

- Analyze the Network System's Response under Time Variable Conditions

Fire Protection

- Needed Fire Flow
- Insurance Ratings
- Fire Flow Analysis

Q & A Session

Open Lab

Water Quality Analysis
Agenda – Day 1

Review of WaterCAD

Water Quality Principles

- Why Model Water Quality?
- Use of Models
- Transport
- Kinetics
- Tanks
- Initial Conditions

Water Quality Modeling

- Input Required
- Setting up Runs
- Viewing Results

Workshop 1: Multisource Mixing Problem

Water Quality Calibration

- Tracers
- Water Analysis
- Adjustments

Workshop 2: Quality Calibration

Design and Operation for Water Quality

- Tank Sizing
- System Operation
- Main Flushing
- Booster Disinfectant

Workshop 3: Tank Design

SDWA Rules and Regulations

Q & A Session

ABOUT THE WORKSHOPS

Course Coordination and General Information

Under the leadership of **Houjung Rhee,** PE, the Continuing Education Department at Haestad Methods has blossomed into an internationally respected department.

Haestad is fully accredited by the International Association for Continuing Education and Training (IACET), allowing it to offer Continuing Education Units for its workshops.

As of December 1996, all of the hydrology and hydraulics courses offered by the department have also received full accreditation from the prestigious Professional Development Registry for Engineers and Surveyors, a continuing education registry sponsored by the National Society of Professional Engineers (NSPE) and the National Society of Professional Surveyors.

Thousands of people from around the world have taken the workshops, confident that Haestad Methods will keep them abreast of the latest trends in the industry and allow them to rub shoulders with some of the industry's leading experts.

Miss Rhee also has been instrumental in the design, development and support of hydrology and hydraulics software at Haestad Methods since she joined the company in 1990. She writes and evaluates software documentation to ensure clarity and develops online help and tutorials for new programs. In addition, she conducts software testing to verify conformity to design specifications.

She holds a BS in civil engineering from the University of Alaska at Anchorage and an MS in civil engineering from the University of South Carolina.

She also co-authored a paper called "Coastal Watershed Unit Hydrographs and Methods" for the ASCE National Conference on Hydraulic Engineering in 1991.

Miss Rhee is a member of the American Society of Civil Engineers, the American Institute of Hydrology, the American Public Works Association, the American Water Works Association, the Association of State Floodplain Managers, the New England Floodplain and Stormwater Managers Association, and Chi Epsilon, the Civil Engineering Honor Society.

INDEX

D

E

F

G

H

I

J

L

M

N

O

T

U

V

W